The Carnivalesque Defunto

This series of publications on Africa, Latin America, Southeast Asia, and Global and Comparative Studies is designed to present significant research, translation, and opinion to area specialists and to a wide community of persons interested in world affairs. The editor seeks manuscripts of quality on any subject and can usually make a decision regarding publication within three months of receipt of the original work. Production methods generally permit a work to appear within one year of acceptance. The editor works closely with authors to produce a high-quality book. The series appears in a paperback format and is distributed worldwide. For more information, contact the executive editor at Ohio University Press, 19 Circle Drive, The Ridges, Athens, Ohio 45701.

The Carnivalesque Defunto

Death and the Dead in Modern Brazilian Literature

Robert H. Moser

Ohio University Research in International Studies
Latin America Series No. 46
Ohio University Press
Athens

www.ohioswallow.com

Printed in the United States of America

16 15 14 13 12 11 10 09 08 5 4 3 2 1

The books in the Ohio University Research in International Studies Series
are printed on acid-free paper ∞ ™

Permission has been granted by The University of Wisconsin Press to reprint those portions of the text that have appeared in earlier form in their publications:

"Rosalina's Ghostly Seed: The Story of Miscarried Patriarchal Legacies in Autran Dourado's *Ópera dos Mortos,*" *Luso-Brazilian Review* 42, no. 1 (2005): 199–212.

"The Carnivalesque Defunto: Death and the Dead in Modern Brazilian Literature," in *Images of the Corpse: From the Renaissance to Cyberspace,* ed. Elizabeth Klaver (Madison: University of Wisconsin Press, 2004), 88–112.

Library of Congress Cataloging-in-Publication Data

Moser, Robert H.

The carnivalesque defunto : death and the dead in modern Brazilian literature / Robert H. Moser.

p. cm. — (Ohio University Research in International Studies. Latin America series ; no. 46)

Includes bibliographical references and index.

ISBN-13: 978-0-89680-258-2 (pbk. : alk. paper)

ISBN-10: 0-89680-258-2 (pbk. : alk. paper)

1. Brazilian literature—20th century—History and criticism. 2. Death in literature. 3. Dead in literature. I. Title. II. Series: Research in international studies. Latin America series ; no. 46.

PQ9555.M67 2007

869.09'35480981—dc22

2007042354

To Anne, Evelyn, and Charlotte

Contents

Acknowledgments

I wish to acknowledge friends, colleagues, and family members whose guidance and inspiration have enabled me to bring this book to fruition. I am truly fortunate to have so many engaging and supportive colleagues at the Department of Romance Languages at the University of Georgia. I am especially indebted to Luis Correa-Díaz, Lesley Feracho, Susan Quinlan, and Nicolás Lucero for their valuable insights and the advice they provided as I worked to expand my study of the *defunto* beyond the realm of Brazilian literature. Similarly, this book would not have been possible without the initial support of the faculty at the Department of Portuguese and Brazilian Studies at Brown University and, in particular, Nelson Vieira, whose sage advice and steady mentorship have been instrumental since the beginning of this project. I would also like to acknowledge the generous support provided by the Willson Center for Humanities and Arts at the University of Georgia, during the final stages of revising the manuscript. I am sincerely indebted to the editors at Ohio University Press—Gillian Berchowitz, Nancy Basmajian, and Thomas Walker—and to Beth Pratt, Jean Cunningham, copyeditor Bob Furnish, and the rest of the staff for their enthusiastic support of, and professional attention to, this book.

I am truly blessed to have parents whose love and encouragement are unwavering. I am deeply grateful to my father, Harry Moser, and my stepmother, Mary Jo, for their enduring support. My heartfelt appreciation goes to my mother, Barbara Racy, and stepfather, Ali Jihad Racy, who both read this study from start to finish and offered invaluable suggestions and guidance along the way. My stepsister, Millar Kelley, has enriched my life in countless ways. Finally, I would like to thank my wife, Anne, my two daughters, Evelyn and Charlotte, and our four-legged companion Popham, for being the source of so much joy in my life.

The Carnivalesque Defunto

Introduction

> Eu sei que o perna-de-pau era apenas um perna-de-pau. . . . Ainda assim. Qualquer morto é um césar. [I know that the peg-legged player was just a peg leg. . . . Even so, in death each of us becomes a caesar.]
>
> —Nelson Rodrigues, *Crônicas de futebol*

MY INTEREST IN the figure of the dead in Brazilian literature was sparked while reading the memoirs of Nelson Rodrigues, Brazil's greatest modern playwright. As admirers of Rodrigues's innovative and frequently lurid plays might expect, the topic of death forms a leitmotif throughout his *Memórias* [Memoirs] (1967). For example, death left an indelible mark on Rodrigues's childhood when, in October of 1918, an influenza epidemic ravaged the city of Rio de Janeiro, killing approximately fifteen thousand people in a two-week period. Rodrigues, six years old at the time, later described the funeral processions, wakes, and profound grieving that became daily spectacles in the Zona Norte neighborhood, where his family lived. It was also at this early age that he discovered that people actually die. (He and his family, of course, would never die, but others could.) Reflecting on this discovery, Rodrigues writes: "Às vezes, tento fazer uma antologia de mortos, dos meus mortos" [Sometimes I try to write an anthology of the dead, of my dead] (33). In fact, that is precisely what his memoirs are.

In Rodrigues's "anthology of the dead," one event eclipses the rest, however. At approximately two o'clock in the afternoon on December 26, 1929, a young woman named Sylvia Seraphim walked into the press office of the Rodrigues family newspaper, *Crítica,* and asked to speak with its editor in chief, Mário Rodrigues. Mário was unavailable, so she asked if one of his sons could attend to her. It was Roberto, Nelson's charismatic younger brother, who politely answered her request. In his *Memórias* Nelson recalls hearing, just moments later, the sound of a revolver being fired and his brother's instantaneous scream. Offended by a story that the newspaper had covered involving her supposed adulterous affair with a local doctor, Ms. Seraphim sought revenge, and when she was unable to find the owner, she settled for his son. Roberto died in a hospital two days later. Nelson would be scarred forever by the experience: "Roberto estava morto, mas ficara comigo seu grito, para sempre" [Robert was dead, but his scream would stay with me forever] (139).

What interested me initially, while reading Rodrigues's memoirs, was not so much the playwright's obsession with death per se, but rather the attitudes he expressed with respect to how the dead (in Portuguese, the *defunto* or *morto)* should be mourned and remembered. Specifically, Rodrigues laments the disappearance of those traditional mourning rituals that were so common during his youth and that, he felt, endowed the dead, as well as mourners, with true pathos and sanctity. Gone were the days, for example, when Brazilians regardless of their social class would tip their hats in the streets when a funeral procession passed by. Rodrigues places most of the blame for this loss on the introduction of the *capelinha,* or chapel, as the primary site for holding a wake, in place of the traditional home setting, with its familiar faces, smells, furniture, portraits, and so on (32). In the cold, impersonal walls of the chapel, those who come to pay their last respects act and feel like strangers, while the deceased are equally estranged.

Rodrigues's despair over the loss of traditional mourning rituals in Brazilian society is crystallized in his sentiments regarding *luto,* the custom of wearing black while grieving:

> Hoje, a dor não justifica nem uma gravata preta. Ninguém põe luto. Ainda outro dia, eu ouvia uma mocinha:—"O sentimento não está na

> côr." Está. O sentimento está, sim, no terno chegado da tinturaria. E no vestido negro. Em 1929, minha família vestiu-se pesadamente de luto. Meu pai, minha mãe, todos os meus irmãos. Cheguei a pensar em nunca mais tirar o luto, nunca mais.
>
> [Today the pain of losing a loved one doesn't even merit a black tie. No one puts on mourning clothes anymore. Just the other day, I heard a young woman say, "The feeling is not in the color." But it is. Yes, the feeling is in the dye of the black suit. And in the black dress. In 1929 my family always dressed in mourning. My father, my mother, all my siblings. I began to think that I would never again wear clothing that wasn't black.] (143–44)

The Rodrigues family's strong affirmation here of the luto tradition, in contrast to the comment of the young woman—"the feeling is not in the color"—exposes a widening gulf in Brazilian society between traditional and modern value systems, especially as they relate to death. The woman's comment reflects a quintessentially modern sentiment, that one's response to death is best expressed individually and internally. However, for Nelson the feeling resides precisely in the black tones of the mourner's jacket or dress, that is, in those external manifestations of grief that are part of the elaborate rituals designed to observe the death of a loved one. When divorced of such rituals, according to Rodrigues, both the deceased and death lose the serene dignity that is so intrinsic to them.

Rodrigues's preoccupation with the loss of traditional modes of relating to the dead in Brazilian society is encompassed within a larger discussion concerning the highly conflicted and largely unresolved interrelation between premodern and modern values systems concurrent in Brazil throughout the twentieth century. Rodrigues's sentiments are a microcosm of this dissidence because they articulate the position of both systems so succinctly. Written in the 1960s, his memoirs also express the power and persistence of cultural anachronisms in Brazilian society. By *cultural anachronism* I mean any cultural expression, value, custom, institution, object, and so forth that continues to reinsert itself in contemporary society, long after its form and function are determined to be, at least from a modern perspective, not only regressive but historically erroneous.

Of course, in any given society, on any given day, cultural anachronisms appear. Indeed, we are constantly confronted by reminders of our personal and collective histories, without which the present would be meaningless. Rather, it is the frequency and tenacity with which certain cultural anachronisms have invaded modern Brazilian society that is of primary interest in this study, particularly as they relate to the evolving relationship of the living to the dead. It may be said that ghosts, the dead who return, are anachronistic figures par excellence. As Jacques Derrida reminds us in *Specters of Marx,* the revenant breaks down rigid spatial and temporal boundaries when it makes its ethereal and untimely apparitions (10–11). Indeed, since classical times, ghosts have appeared in religious and secular literature as emblems of social unrest and unresolved pasts. Generally, they speak to the figurative or literal need for properly burying someone or something.

Upon reading Nelson Rodrigues's *Memórias,* however, I was primarily interested in his curiously intense *saudade* [longing, nostalgia] for traditional wakes and other mourning customs, and what that sentiment might tell us about Brazilian attitudes toward death and the dead. It was not until after rereading Machado de Assis's *Memórias póstumas de Brás Cubas* [The Posthumous Memoirs of Brás Cubas] (1880) that I began to gather evidence for the image of the dead as a recurring motif in modern Brazilian literature. Though *Memórias póstumas* was published forty-two years before the cultural watershed of Brazil's Modern Art Week in 1922, I subscribe to Enylton de Sá Rego's acknowledgment —shared by many other Machadian critics—that "these posthumous memoirs are a remarkably modern book" ("Warning," xiv), and it is in this spirit that I am including it in my study of "modern" Brazilian fiction.

While Brás Cubas undoubtedly lacks the quiet dignity of Rodrigues's idealized and august mortos (instead he is a rather noisy, vain, and indecorous defunto), he does possess, as a deceased narrator, a uniquely privileged position from which to view the world and reminisce about his life. Numerous critics, since the publication of *Memórias póstumas* in 1880, have offered explanations for the significance of deceased narration in Machado's peculiar dead man's tale. Yet, to my knowledge, none have begun their inquiry by first asking: What role did the dead actually play in the lives of the living in late-nineteenth-century Brazil? How would a dead man's voice resonate with the average Brazilian reader during this historical period? These questions, rooted in a sociohistorical analysis of mourning rituals and attitudes toward death and the dead in Brazil, allowed me to envision a broader scope of research, one that traced the image of the defunto over a longer period of Brazilian literary history.

The respective merits and limitations of diverse critical interpretations on deceased narration in *Memórias póstumas* will be considered in depth in chapter 3. The undeniable significance of Roberto Schwarz's work on Machado de Assis, and in particular that of his study *Um mestre na periferia do capitalismo* [*A Master on the Periphery of Capitalism*] as a reference for understanding *Memórias póstumas,* warrants a few preliminary words, however. According to Schwarz, Brás Cubas's posthumous claim to personal unaccountability and utter frankness in the afterlife is a mere reflection of the sociopolitical unaccountability he enjoyed in life as a member of the ruling class in mid-nineteenth-century Brazil. The novel's humor is manifested precisely in the "earthly passions" of its *defunto autor* [a writer who happens to be dead] who, to all intents and purposes, remains "vivíssimo" (*Mestre,* 58) ["very much alive" (*Master,* 38)]. For Schwarz there is no relevant distinction between Brás Cubas's terrestrial and posthumous positions.

Nevertheless, by insisting that Brás Cubas's posthumous, and therefore unrealistic, status is nothing more than a "finta do espírito" (24) ["witty fraud" (12)] Schwarz glosses over the very real connotations and expectations embedded in discourses with the spirit world in nineteenth-century Brazil (12). The precise nature of these discourses will be discussed in chapter 1. It is worth noting here that, even within the Brazilian intelligentsia of Machado's time, the dead were routinely summoned, and their messages seen to possess considerable credibility. For the lower classes, dialogue with the supernatural was a given. I am not proposing that *Memórias póstumas* be read as an elaborate literary séance in which the dead are conjured up, nor do I believe Machado de Assis intended that, or his contemporaries perceived it as such. Rather, I am suggesting that both the author and nineteenth-century reader of *Memórias póstumas* brought with them a deeply rooted and complex assemblage of expectations, experiences, beliefs, and disbeliefs concerning the role of spirits in everyday life. I contend that essentially the same holds true, with varying degrees and manifestations, for the twentieth-century works explored in this study. Indeed, as voices of a modern, secular age these nineteenth- and twentieth-century writers employ the defunto both as a rhetorical strategy and a device for sociopolitical commentary. By the same token, each author shares an appreciation for the profound, enduring resonance of this figure in Brazilian culture and, through narrative that perpetuates the symbolic force of the defunto, establishes their own particular, metaphorical dialogue with the dead.

That this dialogue might occur, in a modified and constantly evolving sense, during later historical periods was confirmed for me by the recurring motif of the resurrected defunto in twentieth-century Brazilian literature. As with the return of Brás Cubas from beyond the grave, the resurgence of otherworldly figures created by Jorge Amado and Érico Veríssimo, for example, are similarly riotous affairs, sharing very little in common with the chain-rattling, somber hauntings of the gothic literary tradition. The novels discussed in the following chapters are ghost stories of a different sort, whose revenants are more carnivalesque than phantasmal, more carnal than discarnate. This study will attempt to identify what is uniquely Brazilian about these carnivalesque defuntos by examining both the artistic and sociohistorical significance of this posthumous literary figure.

I argue that these otherwise chronologically and aesthetically disparate works are ultimately linked by the irrepressible force of the carnivalesque defunto as a living cultural anachronism in modern Brazilian society. Beyond this basic premise, and following the Bakhtinian tradition of viewing carnival as a ritual inversion of the prevailing social order, I am interested in how these carnivalesque defuntos manage to wreak havoc on the status quo and, in so doing, expose certain fissures, or points of tension, within Brazilian society. Complementary to my first premise is a second one, which argues that these subversive defuntos would be incapable of performing the functions I have outlined here, if they did not already enjoy an unusual degree of prestige and leverage within Brazilian society. For this reason, I have gone to considerable length in the first two chapters to provide both a sociohistorical and a literary justification for the presence of these figures in Brazilian literature.

Given that one of the primary roles of the dead in Brazil has been to intervene on behalf of the living, particularly in times of crisis, we can then ask the following basic questions as springboards into understanding the unique function of this topos in the context of each novel: In what way are these figures intervening in worldly affairs? And why are they intervening? In response to these questions I will be focusing on three primary objectives in this study: (1) to propose a rereading of those novels in which this topos emerges and, subsequently, to explore rhetorical strategies and sociohistorical problems linking these different works; (2) to consider how, in these works, coming to terms with the dead constitutes a metaphor for reconciling the past with the present and future; (3) to outline the historical development of a Brazilian relationship with death, and particularly the dead, and to explore the links between this relationship and the treatment that the topos receives in the literature.

In the following chapters I examine the evolving historical relationship between the living and the dead in Brazilian society, and establish a justification for the persistence of an underlying "spirit idiom," borrowing David Hess's term, even in modern times (*Spirits and Scientists,* 210). Special focus is given to the growth of Kardecian Spiritism in Brazil during the latter half of the nineteenth century. I also trace the image of the dead, and particularly the renascent dead, briefly within a Western literary tradition, then more specifically as a recurrent and salient figure within Brazilian literary history, and finally within the broader comparative context of the literature of the Americas. The relative significance of carnival and its ethos of *malandragem* [roguery] in Brazilian culture and literature will also be explored in this section.

I focus on the question of deceased narration in *Memórias póstumas de Brás Cubas* and the implications of Brás Cubas's intrinsically "bad death" and "wandering soul" within the context of Brazil's problematic transition from a slavocratic monarchy to a modern republic. Furthermore, I explore the relationship of Spiritism to Machado de Assis's novel, as well as the reemergence of posthumous narratives and figures in Machado's subsequent novels and short stories. Brás Cubas's "bad death" is juxtaposed to the relatively "good deaths" imagined by Jorge Amado for Quincas in *A morte e a morte de Quincas Berro Dágua* [The Two Deaths of Quincas Wateryell] (1961) and Vadinho in *Dona Flor e seus dois maridos* [Dona Flor and Her Two Husbands] (1966). Carnivalesque undercurrents and the role of popular culture in the author's critique of modern life are considered in the context of each novel. Finally, I examine the reappearance of the defunto topos in Érico Veríssimo's *Incidente em Antares* [Incident in Antares] (1971) and Autran Dourado's *Ópera dos mortos* [The Voices of the Dead] (1967), a novel which, while it does not share the carnivalesque features of the aforementioned works, does evoke a particularly intransigent veneration of the dead in Brazilian, and particularly *mineiro,* culture. Special attention is given to how both Veríssimo and Dourado make use of the unburied dead as a metaphor for Brazil's problematic relationship with both its past and the outdated sociopolitical institutions that continue to haunt it.

One literary critic who has explored ghostly figures comparatively in magical realist fiction of the Americas is Lois Parkinson Zamora. In *The Usable Past: The Imagination of History in Recent Fiction of the Americas,* she devotes a chapter to the subject, arguing that magical realist ghosts form part of what she calls an "ancestral impulse," whereby the "necrogeographies" of indigenous cultures are traced by the activities of these counterrealist apparitions (79). Zamora's comparative discussion of literary ghosts and historical imagination is brought into focus through a dialogue with some of the most influential writers of the Western Hemisphere—Octavio Paz, Jorge Luis Borges, Carlos Fuentes, Nathaniel Hawthorne, Gabriel García Márquez, Flannery O'Connor, William Faulkner, Juan Rulfo, among other American writers and intellectuals whose work is infused with the supernatural on one level or another. While the forms that ghosts assume, within the parameters of counterrealist fiction, and the messages they embody, are certainly multifarious, they are also linked by their ability to "make absence present" and, in so doing, to question Western modernity's basis for reality (77). As Zamora points out, "Ghosts embody the fundamental magical realist sense that reality always exceeds our capacities to describe or understand or prove, and that the function of literature is to engage this excessive reality, to honor that which we may grasp intuitively but never fully or finally define. Magical realist texts ask us to look beyond the limits of the knowable, and ghosts are often our guides" (77).

While the Brazilian literary ghosts discussed in this book do fulfill this oppositional role of looking "beyond the knowable" and engaging "this excessive reality," they do so in a way, as we shall see, that defies easy categorization within either a gothic mode or a Latin American "ancestral impulse." This raises a larger, related question. Despite the comparative breadth of Zamora's study, no mention is made of Brazil's own fantastic/counterrealist tradition, nor of its own literary ghosts, despite ample opportunity to do so in both instances. Brazil's omission from the comparative framework established by Zamora is by no means exclusive to her study but, rather, is symptomatic of a consistent tendency in literary criticism and historiography purporting to encompass "Latin American" reality. The following chapters aim to fill this lacuna by bringing to light the cultural, aesthetic, and sociohistorical complexities of Brazil's literary revenant.

Chapter 1

Death Is a Festa

The Historical Development of a Spirit Idiom in Brazilian Society

Desde que estou retirando
só a morte vejo ativa,
só a morte deparei
e às vezes até festiva.

[Since I have been migrating
the only lively thing I see is death,
only death have I come across
and at times it seems even festive.]

—João Cabral de Melo Neto, *Morte e vida severina*

Dirigir-se ao morto pelo designativo de defunto, o finado, o falecido, é tradicional no Brasil, provindo de Portugal. É uma reminiscência viva do poder mágico e evocador do nome, susceptível de fazer retornar ao convívio humano o desaparecido.

[To address the dead using the words *defunto, finado* (the departed), or *falecido* (the deceased) is traditional in Brazil and harks back to Portugal. It is a living reminder of the magic and evocative power of the defunto's name, which, if uttered, is capable of causing the deceased's return among the living.]

—Luis da Câmara Cascudo, *Dicionário do folclore brasileiro*

THE FINALITY OF death, argues anthropologist Robert Hertz in his seminal work *Death and the Right Hand,* is offset by society's desire to view it as a period of momentary separation: "For the collective consciousness death is in normal circumstances a temporary exclusion of the individual from human society. This exclusion effects his passage from the visible society of the living into the invisible society of the dead" (86). A basic premise of the present study is that the invisible society of the dead has historically played a key role in the construction of both social relations and collective identities in Brazilian society. The cultural currency and sustaining popularity of Spiritism in Brazil today, alongside popular Catholicism and the syncretic Afro-Brazilian religious traditions of Candomblé and Umbanda, is one facet of what American anthropologist David Hess calls Brazil's underlying "spirit idiom."[1] The term *idiom* aptly describes Brazilian society's profound connection with the spirit world, because it reiterates both the structural and communicative nature of that relationship. Similarly, focus is placed on the particular dialogue that interlinks this world with the afterworld.

Moreover, the epistemology of a spirit idiom in Brazil makes sense only in light of the country's own sociohistorical origins and development. The profound and enduring impact of Portugal's social model on its former colony is well documented.[2] Long before Pedro Álvares Cabral encountered the Brazilian coastline in 1500, popular Catholicism in Portugal had established a tradition of revering both saints and the dead. The cult of the dead forged a degree of intimacy between the living and the dead in Iberian popular Catholicism, creating a proximity that was officially discouraged by church authorities and Catholic dogma.[3]

The capacity of popular Catholicism to take hold in colonial Brazil was enhanced by the prominence and relative autonomy of the plantation system, emblematized by the *casa-grande* [slave master's house]. Far removed from official bureaucratic and ecclesiastical control, each plantation constituted a self-sustaining socioeconomic and spiritual unit. Gilberto Freyre, in *Casa-grande e senzala* (which appeared in English as *The Masters and the Slaves*) provides ample testimony to this spiritual autonomy, where, in addition to the master's house and the *senzala* [slave quarters], there usually existed a small chapel, overseen by a resident priest who remained subordinate to the plantation master (*Masters,* xxxiv). As in Portugal, the dead in colonial Brazil were buried in close proximity to the living, generally underneath the chapel, itself an annex of the casa-grande.[4] Orthodox Catholicism was, in the insular context of the plantation, distilled and modified into what Freyre describes as a "domestic" Christianity that was, in turn, pervious to the religious practices of African slaves in the senzala. A constant flux of social and religious customs between the casa-grande and the senzala provoked popular Catholicism's divinization of the dead to intersect with the Yoruba-based belief systems of Africans, for whom spirit mediumship and ancestral worship were central components of their religious life. Moreover, the fusion of Catholicism and Afro-Brazilian religions with indigenous culture is exemplified by the presence of *caboclos* [Amerindians] in Umbanda's pantheon of spirits.[5]

Roger Bastide argues that, while slavery was effective in severing the family network of Africans brought to Brazil, it did not succeed in destroying certain elements of ancestral worship nor the establishment of an Afro-Brazilian cult of the dead:

> this religion was so deeply rooted in the moral code and the civilization of all the peoples of black Africa that it could not fail to leave in the slaves and Creole Negroes certain mental attitudes at least, certain modes of behavior and emotional patterns concerning such things as the importance of burial, separation rituals between the living and the dead, or the idea that the souls of the dead rejoin the great spiritual family of ancestors beyond the ocean. This obligation to render due respect to the dead, lest they avenge themselves by returning to disrupt the lives of their children with illness or nightmares, explains why burial rituals remained so important to all Afro-Americans, even those who, like the Negroes of the United States, were most thoroughly assimilated into Western civilization. (*African Religions,* 128–29)

The perpetuation, however, of African religious and cultural practices distinguishes Afro-Brazilian society from many other former slave communities in the Americas, with the exception perhaps of certain

Caribbean nations such as Haiti, Cuba, and the Dominican Republic. The existence today of houses of the dead, such as the Bahian Casa dos Espíritos dos Mortos [House of the Spirits of the Dead] on the island of Itaparica, and the belief in *eguns* [anonymous spirits of the dead] within the Candomblé pantheon, is an indication of the prominent role the dead continue to play in Afro-Brazilian religious systems. The appearance of eguns and *feiticeiros* [shaman, conjurer], who specialize in exorcising the often malevolent influence of the dead on the living (in the works of Jorge Amado, for example), demonstrates how Afro-Brazilian conceptualizations of the dead have continued to intersect with Catholicism, mysticism, and other spiritual expressions in modern mainstream Brazilian society.

Although urban areas in colonial Brazil enjoyed relatively less autonomy from Portugal's administrative and ecclesiastical control than the surrounding plantations, certain institutions that contributed to the development of a spirit idiom did emerge within the sociopolitical and religious order of the cities. To begin with, the large concentration of African slaves in cities such as Salvador, Recife, and Rio de Janeiro ensured the constant presence of religious syncretism. The most important advocates in the transition between life and death, in an urban context, were the religious brotherhoods, or *irmandades.* Representing the interests of diverse sectors of colonial Brazilian society, from the aristocracy to the slaves, and attentive to many aspects of social welfare, the most important function of the brotherhoods was the safeguarding of a dignified death for their members. By ensuring that their deceased members were given a proper burial and funeral procession, and then conducting masses for their souls thereafter, the brotherhoods acted as the guardians of those rituals that, if observed, led to salvation. Similarly, direct appeal to the deceased, in the form of masses or alms, was very often conducted with the assistance of the brotherhoods. Gatekeepers between the world of the living and the world of the dead, they helped shape the particular grammar and nuance of Brazil's spirit idiom.

Salient Traits of the Brazilian Spirit Idiom

The confluence of the multiple historical forces described above endowed Brazil's spirit idiom with five essential characteristics:

(1) *Historically, interaction between the living and the dead has been one in which a relationship of close proximity is highly valued.* According to Gilberto Freyre, the dead occupied an intermediary and extremely familiar space within the family dynamic of the casa-grande during colonial times:

> Beneath the saints and above the living in the patriarchal hierarchy were the dead, who in so far as possible ruled and kept watch over the lives of their children, grandchildren, and great-grandchildren. In many a Big House [casa-grande] their portraits were preserved in the sanctuary among the images of the saints, with a right to the same votive lamp and the same flowers. Sometimes also women's braids and the curls of infants were kept. It was, in short, a cult of the dead that puts one in mind of that of the ancient Greeks and Romans. (*Masters,* xxxvii)

By linking together consecutive generations, the dead were critical protagonists in the creation and maintenance of what Freyre describes as "the patriarchal spirit of family cohesiveness" so prevalent in colonial Brazilian society (xxxvi). Even before the moment of death, this proximity was expressed at the bedside of the dying individual, or *moribundo,* around whom family members, religious figures, friends, acquaintances, and even strangers circled in a constant flow of prayers and condolences. A multitude of people was viewed as socially advantageous at the dying bed and in the funeral procession, for it signaled both communal support and greater social prestige for the dead. Indeed, the posthumous presence of the departed, the finados within the casa-grande extended beyond portraits and devotional flowers. The folkloric tradition of the colonial plantation house is rich with stories in which relatives witness apparitions of deceased patriarchs and matriarchs returning, for example, to settle an old score, or to point out the location of money buried long ago under the house. Either as haunting specter, or venerated ancestor, the dead "commonly embody all the joys, sorrows, and most characteristic actions of the life of the manor house" (*Masters,* xl). Throughout his introduction to *Masters and the Slaves,* Gilberto Freyre repeatedly calls attention to the burial of slaves and family members within the confines of the manor and its adjacent chapel. His preoccupation with this theme may be explained by what he considered to be the central role of the dead in forging a sense of continuity between the past, present, and future in a patriarchal society.

(2) Inherent in Freyre's observation is the idea that *the relationship between the living and the dead was not only close but active.* The dead not only "watched over" the living, they "governed" their lives to a certain degree. João José Reis, in *Morte é uma Festa: Ritos Fúnebres e Revolta Popular no Brasil do Século XIX* (1991), translated as *Death Is a Festival: Funeral Rites and Rebellion in Nineteenth-Century Brazil* (2003), describes the numerous nineteenth-century Brazilian contexts in which the dead were expected to intervene on behalf of the living (and vice versa), both during this life and in the afterlife:

> According to the brotherhoods' faith, which the doctors and now the bishops considered steeped in superstition, the living, the dead, and the saints were part of a ritual family that should be kept together. This more organic view of sacred space was part of a perception of this world and the next that saw the dead as somewhat divine. In the confraternities' chapels, people prayed *for* the dead as much as *to* the dead. Along with God and the saints, the departed helped to solve the problems of the living, although to a different extent. And just as in relations with the saints, the living should care for their dead to strengthen them. This meant, among other things, ensuring them a place that was ritually close to the divine beings. Caring for the dead also meant caring for the fates of the living. If not a guarantee, ecclesiastical burial was at least a prerequisite for salvation, and Bahian mortals therefore took a lively interest. (*Death,* 289–90; emphasis in original)

Intrinsically related to the reciprocity between the living and the dead was the common belief in purgatory, that place of temporary suffering where sins are paid for before salvation. In order to facilitate the soul's passage through purgatory the dead relied heavily on the intercession of the living, in the form of observed masses and promises to saints in exchange for the salvation of the soul of a loved one (Reis, "Cotidiano," 97). One fundamental difference between Catholic and Protestant doctrine lies in the latter's affirmation that the individual is wholly responsible for his or her own salvation, while the former views the soul's salvation as a collective effort. The Reformation doctrine of predestination effectively sounded the death knell in Protestant cultures for the concept of purgatory, thus eliminating the imperative for ritual gestures aimed at influencing the destiny of the deceased's soul.

Most often these gestures of arbitration were intended for close family members and friends. One of the primary functions of a will, for example, was to specify the number and nature of masses to be said for the deceased (102). At the same time, it was not uncommon for the living to intercede on behalf of those unfortunate anonymous souls who had died without a proper network of social ties. Reis points to the long-held custom of erecting a roadside cross entreating travelers to pray for the anonymous souls of those who had perished in a tragic accident (99). Often visitors left stones at the foot of these crosses as a means of tabulating the number of invocations made on behalf of the deceased. These ritual gestures were made with a common goal in mind: to aid those wayward souls in their journey toward salvation and complete integration with the realm of the dead.

The finados routinely returned the favor, by providing the living with moral and practical guidance in the resolution of worldly problems, and finally by advocating for the souls of these same loved ones at their own hour of judgment. As we shall see, the capacity of the dead to act as celestial advocates in both the life and death of the living is an important concept because it points to one possible justification for the recurrent presence of the revenant in Brazilian literature.

(3) Both Freyre and Reis suggest that *historically there has existed an ongoing dialogue between the living and the dead,* through religious rituals such as masses and funeral processions, as well as in the course of daily activities. This dialogue not only contributed to the unity of the ritual family made up of the living, the dead, and the saints, but also provided a sense of continuity and coherence among the living. Indeed, it may be said that the well-being of the community was linked to, and depended on, the preservation of good relations with the dead. It is, therefore, no coincidence that the dead were called on to intervene particularly in moments of either personal or social crisis.

The presence of *carpideiras* [keeners], with their incessant wailing, at wakes and funerals contributed to the intensity and public spectacle of death in nineteenth-century Brazil. Even in the absence of these paid mourners, it was generally the responsibility of the female family members to produce intense crying and lamentations. The degree of mourning was inevitably viewed as a reflection of the social status of both the deceased and the surviving family. As one priest described, "the louder the weeping the more illustrious the burial" (Reis, "Cotidiano," 109).

The observance of additional rituals and rites of passage was essential to any successful burial. Before it was transported from the home, for example, the body had to be bathed, perfumed, and dressed in the proper attire, which generally consisted of a hearse cloth modeled after those of the saints. Africans customarily wore simple white shrouds made of cotton. The choice of white by Africans was, in many cases, related to the color's association with the *orixá* [orisha] Oxalá, the creator. Within Catholicism, shrouding the dead in saintly dress prepared them for their passage into the celestial court, and the anticipated reward of God's grace. The preparation of the corpse for burial was a task that could only be performed by specialists. Reis quotes Brazilian folklorist Câmara Cascudo (from his article "Anúbis") with respect to the handling of the corpse: "'Not everyone had the privilege of being able to touch the corpse.' It was necessary, for example, to know how to communicate with the dead, so that he or she would cooperate with the operation: 'bend your knee, lift your leg, let me see your foot!' Or, 'Close your eyes to this world and open them to God'" ("Cotidiano," 113).

As soon as the corpse was properly dressed, the wake could begin. Generally the body was placed in one of the living spaces of the house, which was decorated with numerous candles and lavishly embroidered clothes and ribbons. Food and drinks were served in abundance until it was time for the deceased to be carried in a funeral procession to the burial site in a church or nearby cemetery. The processions, or *cortejos,* of nineteenth-century Brazilians, particularly of the urban aristocracy, were characterized by their dramatic display of wealth and pomp and, as such, were modeled after the religious festivals observing the burial of divine figures, such as O Enterro de Cristo [The Burial of Christ] on Good Friday and A Nossa Senhora da Boa Morte [Our Lady of Good Death] in August (116).

(4) Anthropologists and historians studying the culture of death have observed that in Brazil, as in most societies, *there exists an important distinction between a good death and a bad death.*[6] The religious currency enjoyed by O Nosso Senhor do Bom Fim [Our Father of Good Death] and A Nossa Senhora da Boa Morte in Portugal and Brazil, in the form of prayers, promises, and even churches named after these rituals, is a testimony to the significance of a good death in these cultures. As in Portuguese society, a good death in Brazil has traditionally been, above all, a matter of timing. Physical death should arrive no sooner nor later than the proper moment, as determined by both destiny and social customs. To die unexpectedly, away from loved ones, and without the opportunity to bring closure to one's affairs in this world epitomizes a bad death. Thus, dying well in Brazil traditionally involved the assistance of family and friends to perform those rituals meant to insure both a proper send-off to the next world and the maintenance of ties to this world. The consequences of a bad death, for both the individual and the community were highly undesirable, for they generally resulted in the deceased becoming a "wandering soul"

that haunted the community until some resolution was found.[7] The tormented figure of the wandering soul is closely affiliated with the condition of the unburied dead.

(5) The burials and funeral processions of colonial and imperial Brazil were undoubtedly solemn occasions; however, historical documents indicate that these events were anything but sober. *Rather they acquired many of the forms normally associated with carnivalesque festivities.* By all accounts, the funerals of the urban aristocracy, wealthy merchants, and upper clergy were sumptuous affairs involving a vast procession of lamenters from diverse segments of Brazilian society. Funerary pomp was added by musical accompaniment, the clanging of church bells, ornamental carriages, fireworks, banquets, and the lighting of countless candles. The participation of a large multitude of people, even strangers, in the funeral procession served many functions. According to Reis, "The capacity to mobilize many people, for example, was a sign of prestige for the deceased and the family, a symbol of secular power, and at the same time, extra protection for the soul of the deceased, which could benefit from the prayers of the crowd" ("Cotidiano," 117).

The funerals of infants, in particular, were celebrated occasions, in which the baptized child's purity and immediate transformation into an angel, were understood to be a given. Northern European visitors to Brazil in the nineteenth century who witnessed these festas for an *anjinho* were invariably shocked by the music, food, drink, gunshots, fireworks, and overall jovial attitude of the participants that characterized infant funerals (Reis, *Death,* 119–20). The Englishman John Luccock reported that the deceased child was "gaily dressed" for the funeral. In 1817, the Frenchman M. J. Arago "searched in vain for tears" at an infant funeral in Rio de Janeiro, while his countryman Ferdinand Denis noted that in both Rio and Bahia the *enterros de anjinho* possessed "a pomp that among us French was completely foreign and anything but funereal" ("Cotidiano," 112–13). Before 1900, 30 percent of newborns died within a year, and only a half of those who survived lived to be twenty (Martins, 71–72). The psychological wound caused by such high rates of infant mortality in the nineteenth century was partly offset by the celebratory function of the enterro de anjinho. According to Freyre, "The truth is that losing a young child was never for a patriarchal family the profound sorrow that it is for a family of today. There would be another one. The 'angel' had gone to heaven, that was all" (*Masters,* 388).

A crucial point here is that Brazilian funerals, throughout colonial times as well as in the nineteenth century, were based on a ritual model introduced by Catholic processions and religious festivities, such as O Senhor dos Passos, observed on the first Sunday of Lent, A Nossa Senhora da Boa Morte in August, and especially, the O Enterro do Senhor on Good Friday. Reis underscores the apparent paradox of these events: "Although several of Bahia's major religious festivals were based on the theme of death, they were also celebrations of life" (*Death,* 117). The reason behind this paradox, according to Reis, lies in the fact that these festivities marked the ultimate reuniting of the faithful with their beloved saints in the afterlife. A similar celebratory tone of anticipation imbued funeral processions, for then the dead were on the cusp of reuniting with the divine: "Festivals centering on effigies of corpses, these processions seem to have provided a model for Brazilian funerals, which were true spectacles. Christ's burial processions in particular dramatized the apotheosis of the funeral of a victorious God whom the faithful wanted to join after their own deaths. Funeral corteges reenacted the journey toward that reunion. The pomp of funerals, which might be called funerary festivities, anticipated the happy fate imagined for the dead and, by association, helped make it happen" (*Death,* 118).

Reis also makes the interesting point that, like death, the religious festa marks a rupture in the routine of everyday life. Both insert disorder and a degree of chaos into the prevailing social order. In this sense, the function of festas is analogous to that of carnival. The order that is lost during a festa is regained only at the conclusion of the festa, whereas the social order undermined by the arrival of death is restored through the communal healing process initiated by the funerary spectacle (118). To a large extent, the tradition of funerary festas was practiced outside the official ecclesiastic control of the church, which only begrudgingly tolerated the excesses associated with such spectacles: "In the name of a good death, the faithful broke Church regulations forbidding nocturnal funerals, the insistent tolling of bells, and music in the street" (*Death,* 119).

Representing the other end of colonial Brazil's social spectrum, the early-nineteenth-century illustrations and commentary of Jean Baptiste Debret, in his *Viagem pitoresca e histórica ao Brasil* (originally *Voyage pittoresque et historique au Brésil*), provide us with a portrait of African slave funerals that are, in their own way, equally as festive. The text accompanying the illustration "Enterro de uma negra" [The Burial of a Black Woman] describes the "rufo lúgubre" [mournful beat] created by a male lamenter on a *tambor* and the "clamores mágicos" [fantastic outcry] of the women in this procession. Debret adds, "along with this noisy funeral pomp was the sound of two small bells barely audible under the creaking of the rusty hinges that carried them" (2:184–85). In another such illustration Debret depicts the funeral procession of an African prince in which the body, carried in a hammock and shrouded in hearse cloth, is surrounded by what appear to be carnival revelers consisting of percussion players, a master of ceremonies, acrobats, and curious onlookers (3:175). The "espetáculo turbulento" [rowdy spectacle] of the procession eventually leads to a culminating burial at a church overseen by an Afro-Brazilian brotherhood: "During the burial ceremony the rumble of the fireworks, the noise of the clapping, and the deafening harmony of the African instruments accompany the songs of the Africans of both sexes and of all ages, reunited in the square before the entrance of the church. Finally, once the ceremony has ended, the police authorities disperse by force the last group of idlers, so that everything ends within the norms of Brazilian society" (3:186).

Debret's final comment shows how the carnivalesque revelry of many Afro-Brazilian funerals did not escape the attention of the Portuguese authorities, who viewed the syncretic rituals and apparent disorderliness of these events as a threat to the social order.[8] Even within the Afro-Catholic sects of the black brotherhoods, expressions of both the sacred and the profane often intermingled. A particularly carnivalesque gesture was contained in the crowning of a king and queen, a ritual often practiced by the Afro-Brazilian brotherhoods. As early as 1786 one of the black brotherhoods asked permission from the king of Portugal to preserve the use of traditional Angolan masks, dances, and songs in their religious festivities (Reis, *Death,* 57).

Ultimately, however, the carnivalized religious and funerary commemorations of the Portuguese themselves demonstrated that the colonizers shared their slaves' belief in the importance of ritualized festivals as a form of investing in the spirit world. The infiltration of profane elements in Portuguese Catholicism, and subsequently Brazilian Catholicism, stems from a much earlier time, according to Reis:

> The carnivalization of Bahian religious celebrations was not limited to Africans and their descendants, for the invasion of the sacred by the mundane was often color-blind. Dances and masquerades during religious festivals formed part of an ancient Portuguese tradition connected with the survival of strong pagan elements in the Catholicism of the Iberian Peninsula. . . . Despite purists' protests, this festive and even erotic religious experience would survive the Catholic reforms and be transported to colonial Brazil. (*Death,* 60)

Religious processions and festivities constituted the primary modes of publicly celebrating life for Brazilians of both European and African descent in nineteenth-century Brazil, particularly within the brotherhoods. The pervasive carnivalesque spirit of these religious events was instrumental in shaping the nature of funerary customs as well. This is one of the fundamental arguments put forth by João José Reis in his analysis of funerary customs in nineteenth-century Brazil, an argument that also serves as a crucial link, in my study, between Brazilian cultural history and the presence of the carnivalesque defunto in Brazilian literature produced during the nineteenth and twentieth centuries:

> This festive, showy, baroque Catholicism would also become the main vehicle for the celebration of death. And the brotherhoods played a vital role here too, as one of their main objectives was to give their members decent burials. In these confraternities, festivals and funerals built up group solidarity. In the symbolic economy of the confraternity, the production of funerals followed the same logic as the production of festivities. (*Death,* 64–65)

In other words, death and festas were by no means conceptualized as mutually exclusive in nineteenth-century Brazil. Moreover, the historical documents examined above suggest that religious festivals such as Our Lady of Good Death and Christ's ritual burial on Good Friday, infant burials celebrating the deceased "little angels," the rowdy spectacle of Afro-Catholic funerals, and the animated funereal processions of a uniquely baroque Brazilian Catholicism, in general, formed the carnivalesque elements of a pervasive cultural response to the social disorder brought about by death. As Reis sees it, "Old-time funerals were experienced as a rite of decompression whose effectiveness was directly proportional to the dissemination of signs, the production of gestures and symbolic objects, and the number of people in attendance" (*Death,* 118). Thus, the funerary "spectacle," on one level, served to distract the living from their loss and, by allowing mourners to experience their grief collectively, helped reestablish the social equilibrium jeopardized by the arrival of death. In short, the festivities surrounding death in Brazil enjoyed a distinct social function, one that resonates in unique and complex ways in many works of fiction.

Brazil's Death Culture in Transition

To what extent those characteristics of the relationship between the living and the dead outlined above have persisted into the twentieth century in Brazil is open to debate. Undoubtedly, many aspects of this relationship have been dramatically altered by broad modernizing trends and the influx of foreign value systems, such as positivism and notions of social hygiene. These factors have certainly changed the way Brazilians, particularly those living in urban areas, view death and the dead. It would be misleading, however, to assume that the traditional relationship described above has been simply substituted by a more modern one. Rather, it may be said that traditional and modern value systems have existed in a state of conflict and ongoing negotiation for quite some time.

The beginning of the nineteenth century saw the arrival of the Portuguese court in 1808 and national independence in 1822, two events that served as catalysts for the rapid infusion of European liberal and scientific ideals into the increasingly important urban centers in Brazil. Correspondingly, medical and public authorities, influenced by European, and particularly French, ideas of proper hygiene and health standards sought to regulate those traditional religious and social rituals that were perceived to be not only backward, but also a threat to the public and to social health as a whole. Following a trend that had already spread through much of Europe by the turn of the century, imperial legislation was passed in Brazil in 1828 that prohibited the burial of corpses in churches. The rationale behind this new public policy stemmed from the theory, promoted by health officials in France and later in Brazil, that a highly malignant, disease-bearing, atmosphere—a miasma—emanated from rotting corpses and other putrid matter. It was believed, therefore, that the burial of bodies near residential and public spaces posed a significant health risk to the population at large. This attempt by liberal-minded public officials (often in cooperation with the religious elite) to regulate the more sacred realms of private life in Brazil was not met, however, without resistance.

For example, when the city officials of Salvador extended a monopoly to private investors to construct a cemetery outside the city limits, thus violating the age-old practice of burying the dead inside local churches, an infuriated crowd, backed by members of the religious brotherhoods, marched on the city palace to demonstrate their grievances, and then promptly tore down the newly constructed cemetery, tombstone by tombstone. The so-called Cemiterada of 1836, thoroughly documented by João José Reis in *Death Is a Festa,* vividly illustrates the kind of popular and often contradictory uprising that can occur when two distinct moral universes collide. Indeed, the participants of the Cemiterada took their dissent to the streets to defend the most sacred aspects of their private life, that is, the right to choose one's burial site.[9]

The nineteenth century in Brazil is also characterized by the gradual disintegration of both the rural patriarchy and the uncontested autonomy of its casa-grande plantation system. Freyre's work *Sobrados e mucambos* [The Mansions and the Shanties] traces the evolving relationship of the white seigniorial class and their black servants in the urban context of city mansions and nearby shanties. Freyre points out, in the prefaces to both the first and second editions of *Sobrados e mucambos,* that vestiges of an earlier patriarchal prominence, rooted in colonial times, can be found in the elaborate sepulchers and mausoleums of nineteenth-century urban cemeteries. The patriarch's *jazigo,* or monumental tomb, erected as a physical reminder of his family's fading omnipotence, stood in contrast to the Afro-Brazilian's *cova rasa,* or unmarked grave. For Freyre: "The patriarchal tomb is, of all the forms of human occupation of space, the one that represents the greatest expression of permanence or survival for the family" (*Sobrados,* lx). This perpetuation of the family's presence, long after the death of its ancestors, is reinforced by the social immediacy of the dead: "The dead are, to some degree, still social beings" (lix).

Freyre originally envisioned "Jazigos e covas rasas" [Tombs and Common Graves] as the work that would conclude his study of the Brazilian family, beginning with *Casa-grande e senzala,* and eventually ending instead with *Ordem e progresso* [Order and Progress]. In the introduction to his second edition of *Sobrados e mucambos,* Freyre defined the primary focus of "Jazigos e covas rasas" as the "patriarchal rites of entombment and the influence of the dead over the living" (lix).

Freyre was particularly interested in examining these tombs as a manifestation of the patriarchal family's overall decline in Brazil during the nineteenth century. Freyre provides an anecdote that speaks to this decline, in which an old woman from Pernambuco, from a formerly prestigious family, dies with hardly the means to arrange for her coffin to be carried to the cemetery. Awaiting her body at the cemetery, however, is a monumental sepulcher, a vivid reminder of her family's aristocratic heyday (lxi–lxii).

Freyre's interests in the 1950s were increasingly directed at developing his theories of "Luso-tropicalism," with Brazil as the emblematic manifestation of successful miscegenation, on a physical, cultural, and spiritual level, between the Portuguese and the inhabitants of tropical societies. It is possible that this broader pursuit diverted Freyre's attention away from his plans to complete "Jazigos e covas rasas."[10] Nevertheless, the obvious importance he attributed to this project reflects his underlying belief that the dead, throughout Brazilian history, have exerted a profound influence on the living.

Spiritism According to Brazilians

> Há sessões como bailes improvisados. A verdadeira diversão da época é a conversa com o Além-túmulo. [The Spiritist sessions are like improvised dance parties. The true pastime of this age is conversation with those from beyond the grave.]
>
> —João do Rio, *Os dias passam . . .*

The above assertion, by Carioca writer and journalist João do Rio, is supported by the findings of Ubiratan Machado, in *Os intelectuais e o espiritismo: De Castro Alves a Machado de Assis* [Intellectuals and Spiritism: From Castro Alves to Machado de Assis], which traces the remarkable growth of Spiritism during the latter half of the nineteenth century in Brazil. Machado compares the relatively modest presence of

Spiritism among isolated groups and individuals in Rio de Janeiro and Salvador during the 1860s and 1870s, with the broad proliferation of that doctrine, in an often mutated form, throughout Brazil by the turn of the century. As formulated by Allan Kardec in France, Spiritism was predicated on the idea that God created immortal souls whose purpose is to reach spiritual perfection through a series of disincarnations and reincarnations. When souls reach a higher plane they no longer return to human form but instead become spirit guides, assisting, with the wisdom they have accumulated, lower souls in their journey up the spiritual ladder. Both guides and lesser-developed spirits can be evoked by the living, or incarnated souls, through mediumship.

The reasons why Brazilians in the mid-nineteenth century would become interested in Kardecian Spiritism are numerous and to some degree differ in significant ways from the motivations of Europeans and North Americans who adhered to the doctrine. In France, England, and the United States, Spiritists formed part of a larger movement toward mysticism in the nineteenth century. This movement was, in turn, a reaction against the eighteenth century's ascendancy of reason and scientific rationale, the Cartesian notion that the universe, human behavior, even God, could all be explained mathematically. While the works of Comte and the ideas of Positivism had certainly influenced intellectual circles in Brazil by the mid-nineteenth century, Brazilian culture as a whole still possessed a wide range of profound mystical leanings, ranging from a deep-rooted Portuguese Sebastianismo [King Sebastianism] to an African-influenced disposition toward fetishism and *curandeiros* [healers]. Ubiratan Machado points out that religious syncretism moved in both directions, shaping not only the religious expression of Afro-Brazilians, but also the Catholicism of European Brazilians: "The *mazombo,* or white population born in these 'Brazils,' gradually absorbed the blacks' superstitions, practices, and magical customs. This influence on the white master's religiosity, on top of Iberian superstitions, practices, and magical customs, shaped Brazilian popular Catholicism in an undeniable way" (25). According to Machado, the prestige, across social classes, of the feiticeiro in colonial Brazil stems from this multicultural amalgam of faith, superstition, mysticism, and apprehension (25).

Furthermore, Machado stresses the historical dualism of Brazilian Catholicism, combining a public and somewhat loose adherence to official Catholic doctrine, with a domestic, more personal devotion to magical and fetishistic solutions to life's problems. This fetishistic attitude extended to the adulation of the saints, who were commonly seen as possessing human attributes and whimsicalities. Despite attempts by Kardecian purists to dissociate their doctrine from the influences of popular Catholicism and Afro-Brazilian religious expression, Spiritism in Brazil quickly incorporated the activities of mesmerists, *adivinhas* [fortune-tellers], *videntes* [clairvoyants], *cartomantes* [card readers], homeopaths, as well as spirit-evoking mediums. Though varying in their methods, these agents of the supernatural were linked by the underlying belief, in large segments of Brazilian society, that the spirits of the dead governed the outcome of sessions with them. Machado points out that Allan Kardec's doctrine served to codify a deep-seated belief in supernatural phenomenology, and especially communication with the dead, that for centuries had been part of Brazilian daily life:

> All the trappings of the supernatural seemed to surround and threaten the patriarchal house. In haunted manors the rattling chains of deceased, martyred slaves clamored for revenge. Messages were transmitted from the beyond, and there were the unsettling occurrences of Africans entering into trance, seemingly possessed by the devil himself. In the house shamanesses exorcized evil spells cast on the slave master, warding off the evil eye. . . . In short, it was all this phenomenology that was being codified within Allen Kardec's doctrine, and that had for centuries been a part of the Brazilian's daily use of magic. (49)

The motivation, of course, behind specific individuals' involvement in Spiritism varied considerably, and was often linked to other pressing concerns of the late nineteenth century in Brazil. Abolitionists viewed Spiritism as a vehicle for social reform, whereas anticlerics viewed the doctrine as a means of moral reform. Some poets and writers, influenced by a romantic vision of the *homo religiosus*, were drawn to Spiritism by the promise of a universal and more egalitarian religious life. Others were attracted to Kardec's doctrines by their fascination with mysticism and Spiritism's intersection with the paranormal phenomena of magnetism, hypnosis, clairvoyance, and psychography (the act of receiving spirit messages through automatic writing). Still others were more inclined to view Spiritism as a science, particularly as a form of therapy or homeopathy. At the core, however, of each of these impulses was the underlying belief that communication with the dead was not only possible but also beneficial to the well-being of both individuals and Brazilian society as a whole.

Despite the constant disapproval of the church hierarchy (who viewed Spiritism as the work of Satan), repression by government and police authorities (who passed legislation in 1890 prohibiting Spiritism because of its association with popular cultural expressions), and dramatic political and socioeconomic changes taking place in late-nineteenth-century Brazil (namely the formation of a republic, the rise of a significant bourgeois class, expanded urbanization, and increased exposure to foreign ideas), Spiritism's popularity in Brazil, in fact, grew at the turn of the century. In contrast to the 1860s, when Kardec's works were first being translated into Portuguese and read by a handful of *espíritas* in Salvador and Rio de Janeiro, by the beginning of the twentieth century there were an estimated one hundred thousand Spiritists in Rio alone, and close to twenty journals that dealt with Spiritist matters nationwide (Machado, 210). Ubiratan Machado notes that, as late as 1912, João do Rio reported that Spiritism had taken over the city of Rio de Janeiro: "'It is not only bourgeois families that are conducting Spiritist sessions, but the masses as well. The Spiritist sessions are like improvised dance parties. The true pastime of this age is conversation with those from beyond the grave.' This dialogue with the other world, according to the chronicler, 'had captured the imagination of the city'" (227).[11]

The enduring appeal of Spiritism in Brazil during the first decades of the twentieth century, a time when the doctrine's popularity was already fading in Europe and North America, may be attributed to several factors. As has been already noted, Kardec's philosophy did not remain, for any significant length of time, the exclusive intellectual property of the elite in Brazil, but instead was assimilated and reconfigured into a preexisting amalgam of religious beliefs and folkloric traditions. Syncretizing with popular Catholicism, Kardecian spirit guides assumed the Catholic countenance of a guardian angel. Similarly, within the Afro-Brazilian religious pantheon of Umbanda, spirit guides mutated into the pipe-smoking *preto velho* [old black slave] and robust *coboclo* [Indian spirit]. These processes of assimilation endowed Brazilian Spiritism with a historical malleability and cultural relevance that has allowed it to withstand the test of time and overcome the secularizing and demystifying pressures of modern life. Furthermore, the convergence of Spiritist doctrine with homeopathic treatment was a development unique to Brazil, one that provided Spiritism with a practical, therapeutic appeal to Brazilians seeking remedies outside the realm of orthodox medicine. Homeopathic doctors were often also mediums who, through communication with their spirit guides, prescribed remedies for their patients.

Perhaps the most important reason for Spiritism's enduring appeal in Brazil, however, is the deep-seated belief in Brazilian society that communication with the dead can provide answers to the problems of daily life. The multifacetedness of this belief is outlined in the "Brazilian Catholicism" of D. Júlia, a character from the novel *Turbilhão* by the *maranhense* author Coelho Neto. As Ubiratan Machado describes: "I am referring here to a typically Brazilian Catholicism, such as that practiced by the character D. Júlia from the novel *Whirlwind,* who is highly devoted to the saints at home, only goes to church on rare occasions, solves her problems through the souls of the departed and prayer, and resorts to magical practices such as the use of *figas* [amulets] to ward off evil spells" (206). For Brazilians like D. Júlia, turning to the spirits to resolve one's problems was never perceived to be in conflict with their Catholic beliefs, or as a trivial superstition. Rather, it was a natural response from an individual living in a society that had long become accustomed to dialoging with the dead. In this sense, Spiritism, both in its Kardecian form and its more popular forms, provided an important alternative for Brazilians seeking moral and spiritual guidance. According to Machado,

> Any personal dilemma or tragedy, however, not alleviated by the priest's words or holy water, became excellent motive for resorting to Spiritism. The influential proponents of this doctrine, such as Felícia [a character in *Turbilhão*] lived in these homes and were ready to explain the Spiritist philosophy, its infallibility, and its consoling messages. But it was not only the servants who spread Spiritism in the bourgeois household, but also the gardeners, milkmen, bread suppliers, and other humble people who had free access into the Carioca household at the beginning of the twentieth century. (206)

Machado suggests that it is particularly in moments of crisis that Brazilians, of every social class, would seek the prophetic insight of cartomantes who, while employing methods quite different from Kardecian Spiritism, still acted as interpreters for the all-knowing spirits: "Hence, card readings, as a Spiritist phenomenon, became one of the most popular forms of communication with the spirit world" (219).

Perceptions of the Dead in Twentieth-Century Brazil: Continuity and Change

Some of the reasons discussed here concerning the rise of Spiritism take on particular relevance in light of its enduring popularity in contemporary Brazil. Indeed, Brazil is home to arguably the largest Spiritist movement in the world today. While this fact certainly does not discount the many substantial changes that have occurred in the past century, with respect to Brazilian society's relationship to the dead, it does speak to the tenacity of the spirit world as an integral part of modern life in this country.

Brazilian anthropologist Roberto DaMatta argues in his comparative essay on death in Brazil and the United States that, in contrast to North American society, Brazilians today continue to emphasize strong, personal relations with the dead, whereas they tend to reject death as an abstract or purely scientific concept:

> Well before becoming cognizant that death signifies nonbeing and nothingness, I believe that the majority of Brazilians become aware of the dead in their family, home, neighborhood, community, nation and century. They are the "people" who, in the form of spirits, specters, heroes, and phantoms, appear before their loved ones, friends, compatriots, and colleagues to ask for a prayer, mass, favor, or homage. I remember hearing about souls and spirits long before I became cognizant of death as something final and absolute in a person's existence. Because when one spoke about death it was to immediately comment about the existence of ghosts (and/or "wandering souls") that returned and demanded favors from their living relatives. (*Casa,* 119–20)

Mediators between this world and the next, the dead maintain as well as create social ties within modern Brazilian society. This preoccupation with the dead per se contains an inherent paradox, argues DaMatta: "On the one hand, it showed that people disappeared, but on the other hand, it reaffirmed a complimentary reality. That is, if people died and departed from the world of the living, they also went to *another world,* from which they could not only return, but also watch over, disrupt or aid the life of the living who remained here on Earth" (*Casa,* 120; emphasis in original). Death, therefore, in Brazil is perceived as a passage from *this* world to a highly immediate and complementary world, in contrast to American society's image of death as a journey that takes us beyond the limits of this universe. According to DaMatta, dealings between the two realms are conducted by way of warnings, omens, signs, mourning practices, and, of course, memory. The observance of birthdays, the date of a loved one's death, and the Dia de Finados (All Souls' Day) on November 2, are all ways in which Brazilians continue to cultivate the memory of the dead. Direct dialogue with the dead is not only accepted, but engenders the household "medium" with a degree of wisdom: "speaking periodically with the dead endows this individual with a certain wisdom, authority, and enviable and serene resignation toward the *world we live in*" (*Casa,* 120; emphasis in original).[12] Contrastingly, an overt preoccupation with the dead in North American society is viewed as irrational and even pathological. DaMatta argues that the kind of luto common to Brazilian society is impossible in an individualist system because social behavior such as the manifestation of grief must first "find support through so-called 'individual emotions' in order to be effectively legitimated" (118).

"The Feeling Is in the Color Black"

One recalls that it is precisely the validity of "individual emotions" that compels a young Brazilian woman in the 1960s to tell playwright Nelson Rodrigues that "the feeling is not in the color" of a widow's black dress. The value system reflected in this statement, and Rodrigues's complaint that "today, the pain of losing a loved one doesn't even merit a black tie," help us to put Roberto DaMatta's enthusiastic endorsement of Brazil's traditional connection to the dead in greater perspective. Indeed, it would be misleading to imply that the relationship between the living and the dead in Brazil has not undergone significant transformations during the twentieth century. Similarly, one has to be careful not to apply death related attitudes and belief systems universally, without taking into consideration the tremendous regional, socioeconomic, ethnic, and religious variations that exist in Brazilian society.[13]

Nelson Rodrigues's preoccupation with the gradual disappearance of traditional mourning rituals in modern Brazilian society may be found in a rather unlikely place, his *Crônicas de futebol* [Soccer Chronicles]. Throughout much of the 1950s, '60s, and '70s Rodrigues covered soccer matches as a sports editor, first in the magazine *Manchete Esportiva* and later in the newspaper *O Globo*. In his column these matches took on epic proportions between heroic *craques* [soccer stars] engaged in life-or-death struggles. One could say that Rodrigues's imagination elevated soccer games to the level of Greek drama, in which the full range of the human condition—its tragedy, heroism, and comedy—is played out on the field.

In one of his columns, dated February 11, 1956, and entitled "O craque na capelinha" [The Ace in the Chapel], Nelson describes the downward spiral of a *perna-de-pau* [peg leg or mediocre player] who, after quitting soccer, faded into anonymity until his funeral, which Nelson decides to attend. The Brazilian playwright remarks that, upon seeing the player's corpse, he is moved by its quiet dignity:

> Diante dele, diante do ser transfigurado, verifiquei o seguinte:—não há morto canastrão. Vestido de noivo, com sapatos engraxados, ele tem a face, o ríctus, o perfil do grande ator. Assim acontecera com o perna-de-pau:—no caixão, apresentava uma nobre e taciturna máscara cesariana.
>
> [Standing before him, before this transformed being, I realized that there is no such thing as a bad actor in death. Dressed like a groom, with polished shoes, he had the look, the expression of a great actor. Lying in his coffin, the former peg leg now wore the solemn and noble mask of a caesar.] (*Crônicas,* 21)

Unfortunately, according to Nelson, the solemn grandeur of the deceased perna-de-pau is undermined by the banality of the chapel. Nelson's description of the ambience inside the chapel is particularly telling:

> O diabo era o ambiente do velório. Eis a verdade:—nenhum morto devia ir para as capelinhas, jamais. Elas traduzem um sintoma terrível da nossa época. Antes de mais nada, significam um frívolo desamor à morte e aos mortos. Não sabemos morrer, nem enterrar. E pior do que isso:—não sabemos fazer quarto. Essa impotência diante da morte é o

melancólico e inevitável resultado das capelinhas. Antigamente, o defunto tinha domicílio. Ningúem o vestia às carreiras; ninguém o despachava às escondidas. Permanecia em casa, e pois, dentro de um ambiente em que até os móveis eram cordiais e solidárias. Armava-se a câmara-ardente numa doce sala de jantar ou numa cálida sala de visitas, debaixo dos retratos dos outros mortos.

[The damnedest thing was the setting of the wake. The truth is, the dead should never be brought to these little chapels. These places are a terrible sign of our times. First of all, they constitute a thoughtless aversion to death and to the dead. We don't know how to die, nor how to bury anymore. And worse, we don't know how to do a wake. This impotence in the face of death is the melancholy and inevitable result of these little chapels. Years ago, the dead had a home. No one dressed them in a hurry; no one dispatched of them furtively. The dead used to stay at home and therefore in a setting where even the furniture offered cordiality and solidarity. Their resting place was set up in an inviting dining room or a warm guest room, beneath the portraits of the other dead.] (21–22)

The "terrible sign of our times" that Rodrigues refers to here is precisely the depersonalization of death and the deceased that DaMatta identifies as a characteristic of modern societies, where individualism reigns as the predominant ethic. For Rodrigues, the *capelinha* symbolizes the coldness and impersonality of modern society's conduct when confronted with death. Whereas before, the deceased's body and, later, memory were brought into the intimate folds of the household, today direct contact with the dead is kept to a minimum, which Rodrigues denotes as a "thoughtless aversion" to death as well as the dead. However, what is most disquieting to Rodrigues is modern society's incapacity to hold a wake, that is, to preserve those rituals that give meaning to and glorify the life and death of a loved one.

Further on in "O craque na capelinha," Rodrigues recalls how, when he was a boy, he heard the incessant wailing of a neighbor who had lost her daughter to yellow fever.[14] After everyone else had stopped crying she continued to sob, an "insuperável solista" [unsurpassable soloist] (22). Rodrigues obviously laments the passing of these traditions in Brazilian society:

> Hoje, isto não é possível. A capelinha esvaziou a morte do seu conteúdo poético dramático e, direi mesmo, histérico. Preliminariamente, o defunto está fora do seu clima residencial. Como os demais, ele é um constrangido, um cerimonioso, um deslocado. Sim, todos, inclusive o cadáver, têm um ar de visita. Essa polidez impede a violência e a espontaneidade da dor que vem de dentro, das profundezas, como um gemido vacum. Bem que a viúva desejaria espernear, esganiçar-se, como uma canastrona do velho teatro. Mas eis a verdade:—a capelinha torna inexeqüíveis as histerias magníficas dos funerais antigos. Eu sei que o perna-de-pau era apenas um perna-de-pau. . . . Ainda assim. Qualquer morto é um césar.

> [Today, this would be impossible. The little chapel emptied death of its poetic, dramatic, and at times hysterical content. First, the dead is removed from its domestic setting. Like the visitors, he appears constrained, ceremonial, out of place. In fact, everyone, including the corpse, gives the impression of being mere guests. This politeness impedes the violent and spontaneous grief that emerges from the deepest part of our soul like the moan of an animal—even when the widow's urge is to flail and shriek, like the melodramatic actresses of old. The truth is that the little chapels have now rendered impossible the magnificent displays of hysteria seen at funerals years ago. I know that the peg-legged player was just a peg leg. . . . Even so, in death each of us becomes a caesar.] (*Crônicas,* 22)

Rodrigues's comment that the chapel has emptied death of its poetic and dramatic content is key to understanding the intimate link that the playwright establishes between theater and death. In death, even a perna-de-pau is able to embody the tragic qualities of a caesar, or take on the profile of "a great actor." Similarly, mourners become social actors and actresses as they go through the dramatic motions of grieving for their loved one. Rodrigues recognizes the drama inherent in such ritual gestures as luto, wakes, and fits of sobbing.

At the same time, underlying the criticism that Rodrigues levies in these *crônicas* at Brazilian society for having abandoned those traditions and rituals that ennobled the dead and kept their memories close to home, is a tacit disparagement of Brazil's rush to modernize in the 1940s, under Getúlio Vargas, and especially the 1950s, under Juscelino Kubitschek. Indeed, "O craque na capelinha" was written shortly after Kubitschek took office, announcing plans for a high-growth economic strategy, greater international visibility, and a new federal capital in the interior that would symbolize Brazil's flight into a bold new future. A hint of unease with Kubitschek's promise of "fifty years of progress in five" may be detected in Rodrigues's lamentations over the loss of certain "traditional" rituals and values.

Manifestations of a Contemporary Spirit Idiom in Brazilian Society

The prevalence of funeral processions, wakes, and other mourning rituals during the late nineteenth and early twentieth centuries suggests that death culture formed an integral part of daily life in early modern Brazilian society. As late as 1872 the life expectancy for free Brazilians was only twenty-seven years and for slaves a dismal eighteen years (Martins, 73). Undoubtedly, life expectancy was equally dismal for large segments of an indigenous population already devastated by epidemics and social upheaval. As mentioned earlier, infant mortality rates in Brazil at the turn of the century were staggering, with 30 percent of all newborns dying before a year had passed. Only half of those who survived this first crucial test lived to see twenty years (71–72).

Even in contemporary Brazilian society, anthropologists have noted that, due in part to a persistently high infant mortality rate, the ritual forms associated with the traditional enterro de anjinho continue to be practiced. Oscar Calavia Sáez, in his study *Fantasmas falados: Mitos e mortos no campo religioso brasileiro* [Spoken Ghosts: Myths and the Dead in Brazilian Religiosity] (1996), examines the sanctification of specific mortos buried in the Cemitério da Saudade in Campinas. Among those tombs that receive regular visits, thanksgivings, and offerings is one marked by a smaller gravestone painted blue, in which supposedly lie twin brothers, perhaps former slaves, who died a tragically premature death. The adults and children who visit the grave of the *Inocentes* [the Innocent Ones], leaving either candy, pacifiers, or plaster figurines of the twin saints Cosme and Damião, generally come seeking solace or remedies to child-related problems: "The tomb is visited in a more focused way than Antoninho's tomb, by children and adults who in general make requests having to do with children and their illnesses, or even problems that are less definable by medical criteria, such as unruly behavior or excessive crying and jealousy" (27). The abundance of infant tombs in the Cemitério da Saudade shows how precarious life is for infants in this community and clearly indicates why parents and siblings continue to seek help from the supernatural in the day-to-day upbringing of their children.[15]

The shrines that adorn the gravestones of certain individuals in the Cemitério da Saudade are a poignant and very current example of the natural convergence between the dead and saintliness in popular Brazilian culture. The other shrine mentioned above is that of Antoninho, a former house slave of the coffee baron Geraldo de Rezende, whose plantation was the largest of its kind in Campinas at the turn of the century. The presence of Antoninho's tomb, next to the baron's, in the most aristocratic part of the cemetery, has contributed to the myth of this former slave as a benevolent spirit, worthy of repeated offerings and favors. The candles and flowers routinely placed at his grave share space with smoking pipes and images of the good-natured and wise preto velho, whose spirit entered the Umbandist pantheon in the late nineteenth century, when the abolition of slavery and the socioeconomic challenges of integrating slaves into the free workforce required a redefinition of blacks in Brazilian society (Calavia Sáez, 26–27).

One other highly frequented tomb in Campinas's Cemitério da Saudade is that of Maria Jandira, a prostitute who, according to local myth, set herself on fire upon discovering that the only man she ever loved was married to another woman. Jandira's tragic spirit is, according to Calavia Sáez, intertwined with that of the *pomba-gira,* a kind of Mary Magdalene *santa-puta,* or feminine version of the trickster orixá *exu,* who uses her advantageous position in the afterworld to help other downcast or marginalized people. Each of the sanctified spirits studied by Calavia Sáez are linked by both misfortune experienced during life and the tragic circumstances surrounding their death. Their misery and social marginalization is easily identifiable for Brazilians who find themselves equally disenfranchised: "The misery experienced daily by the *povo* parallels that of these spirits, whose own misery makes them preferable to the bureaucratic church saints" (32).

An immediate spiritual connection to the dead, however, is not limited to the popular religious expression of socially marginalized Afro-Brazilians:

> What one finds with regard to observances around Jandira's tomb is not an extreme form of social or religious experience. Jandira is the patron saint of not only prostitutes, of women tarnished by love, or of women in general. Similarly, it is clear that not only blacks call upon Antoninho, nor only children who appeal to, or are seen to benefit from, the power of the Innocent Ones.
>
> Nor is this phenomenon limited to a private cult stemming from extremely dispossessed social levels that are, thus, distanced from the common ethical and religious makeup of the majority. Jandira's story—like that of other 'saintly' prostitutes, or pomba-gira—is the radical formulation and extreme manifestation of common tensions and social dramas found in everyday life. (Calavia Sáez, 49)

The same may be said for the widespread belief in Brazilian society that interaction with the dead occurs, not as the manifestation of an abstract sentiment, but rather as a social relationship interwoven into the fabric of daily interests and dilemmas. This interaction is cultivated by both Catholics and Umbandistas every Monday and once a year, on O Dia de Finados. Calavia Sáez makes the important point that, unlike any other day of the year, when this interaction with the beyond is taken for granted, on O Dia de Finados the cult of the dead appears on Brazilian society's center stage, receiving recognition in both local and national media sources (107). On this day, family tombs and anonymous graves alike are adorned throughout Brazil with flowers and candles, in addition to sweets and popcorn, items that serve as both offerings to the finados as well as fare for the children who visit them.

The cemetery also becomes a site where families reestablish kinship ties and ancestral continuity: "Groups of relatives who rarely gather outside their homes, walk together through the cemetery and reinforce, with their visits to the tombs, family ties that are normally loose. These visits are *guided* by the elderly or by extended family who explain, to the others, the family ties between their buried kin, or between the dead and those who have come to pay their respects" (111; emphasis in original). The people who congregate in the cemetery at the end of the afternoon come to light more candles, drink *cachaça* [sugarcane rum], smoke a cigar, or watch those who have fallen into a trance, possessed by an exu. Calavia Sáez observes that, while this behavior in a sacred space is not approved by all, few view the visitation of spirits with disbelief: "although more than a few bystanders condemn the rituals—because they perceive them to be intrinsically evil or practiced in a way or location that is inappropriate—rarely is the authenticity of the event itself doubted" (114).

Paradoxically, the isolating effects of modern life in Brazil, where impersonal relations and individual concerns increasingly supplant personal relations and family networks, may only compel a greater number of Brazilians to seek answers from the afterworld, as suggested in Calavia Sáez's conclusion:

> The religious consensus in Brazil is organized around mediumship—or, to avoid the doctrinal stigma of this concept, around the union of "this world" with "the beyond." There is a correlation between the proximity of the dead and the significant distances that exist between the living—hence the centrality of the dead in people's lives. The dead

> serve as mediators in this spiritual landscape, because it is through them and their processes—ranging from psychography to reincarnation—that it becomes possible to redraw relationships and conflicts that occur both within the family unit and the community. (186)

It is precisely the possibility of reconfigured social relations and conflicts, through the specificity of the carnivalesque defunto in modern Brazilian literature, that will be explored in the following chapters.

Chapter 2

Death and the Dead as Literary Motifs in Brazil and Beyond

But now is Christ risen from the dead,
and become the first fruits of them that slept.
For since by man came death, by man came
also the resurrection of the dead.
For as in Adam all die, even so in Christ
shall all be made alive.

—I Corinthians 15:20–22

Morto, o filho começava a ocupar o coração de Renata como quem se acomoda num quarto. Você é mais meu agora, sentia. Vou te dar o leite da minha dor, o leite da contemplação da tua morte.

[Dead, Renata's son began to occupy her heart like someone making himself comfortable in a room. Now you're more nearly mine, she thought. I shall give you the milk of my grief, the milk of my contemplation of your death.]

—Lya Luft, *O quarto fechado*

THE APPEARANCE OF the dead in Brazilian literature over the past two centuries, and specifically the topos of the *mortus redivivus,*[1] or resurrected defunto, is a vast subject, one characterized by extreme variations and multiple meanings. Certainly it would be unproductive to distill this figure's myriad of literary manifestations into a single composite, or to suggest that somehow a carnivalesque model is universally applicable. Instead, one observes a distinguishable tradition, a continuity of expression, a recurrent pertinence of the defunto topos in Brazilian fiction. In other words, the novels examined in subsequent chapters are not isolated examples of a lonely preoccupation with the dead, but rather part of a perennial literary discourse.

Of course, the topos of the resurgent dead is by no means exclusive to Brazilian social or literary history. It would be negligent, for example, to ignore the presence of Jesus Christ's resurrection as a ubiquitous reference for Brazilian authors dealing with this topos. Nevertheless, the fact that more universal references may appear, either explicitly or implicitly, in the selected texts at different times does not, in any way, undermine the relevance of specific Brazilian traditions and narratives, with respect to the image of the dead. Rather, they reinforce the interconnectedness of Brazilian death culture to a much broader spectrum of Western (and non-Western) religious and cultural traditions.

Ancient Apparitions and Biblical Resurrections

In classical times it was the necromancer who possessed the knowledge and methods necessary for summoning the spirits of the underworld, in order to consult with them about the future. In book 10 of Homer's *Odyssey,* Ulysses is given a crash course in necromancy by his seductress Circe, so that he may seek the advice of a dead prophet named Tiresias. Following Circe's instructions, Ulysses arrives at the gates of Hades and digs a small trench into which he pours honey, milk, wine, and barley; over this he offers prayers to the dead. He then sacrifices a ram and ewe and drains their blood into the hole. As Circe promised, ghosts fly out of Hades and gather around the hole, eager to drink from it. Ulysses, however, keeps them at bay with his sword until Tiresias arrives. After drinking the bloody mixture, the prophet peers into the hero's future. Before returning to his ship, Ulysses also speaks with the spirits of Achilles, Agamemnon, the mother of Oedipus, and his own deceased mother.

Similarly, Aeneas, the hero in Virgil's *Aeneid,* is visited by the ghost of his father while performing sacrifices at his tomb. Like Ulysses, Aeneas also makes a journey to the underworld, in this case to gain his father's advice concerning his destiny. The ghost as harbinger of future events is a common motif in both classical and contemporary literature. Yet, as we shall see, the defuntos that appear in Brazilian literature generally tell us more about the past than the future. In this sense, their messages are more memorial than necromantic.

A famous case of necromancy occurs in the Old Testament when Saul, the first king of Israel, asks the witch of Endor to conjure up the spirit of Samuel. Saul then learns from Samuel's disquieted ghost that both he and his three sons will be joining Samuel in the afterworld after their battle with the Philistines the following day. The appearance of Samuel's spirit was used frequently by early theologians as proof of the soul's immortality. Perhaps the best-known resurrection in the Bible, aside from that of Christ himself, occurs in the New Testament when Jesus raises Lazarus from the dead, one of many miracles Jesus performs to prove his identity as the Son of God.

Of course, a cornerstone of Christian faith is the belief in Christ's own resurrection on Easter Sunday, an event that completed his earthly mission and promised the eventual resurrection of all people, whose souls would be reunited with their risen bodies on Judgment Day. When Christ's imminent return did not occur after the first millennium, medieval scholars began to contemplate the possibility of an interim judgment at the moment of physical death, and then a waiting period in purgatory before final redemption.

The resurrections that occur in both Jorge Amado's *A morte e a morte de Quincas Berro Dágua* and Érico Veríssimo's *Incidente em Antares* contain numerous biblical allusions. It is no coincidence then, that the resurrection of seven corpses in Antares, for example, is perceived by some as apocalyptic and others as the moment of redemption.

By the High Middle Ages (eleventh–thirteenth centuries) the church routinely advocated prayer, masses, and alms giving as the surest means to assist the dead in purgatory. One of the underlying purposes of ghosts appearing in Christian liturgy and other literature during this period was, therefore, to confirm the existence of purgatory in the geography of the afterworld, as well as to affirm the imperative of prayers for the deceased. Ronald C. Finucane, in his study *Appearances of the Dead: A Cultural History of Ghosts,* points to three indicators of a relatively greater interest in *personal* salvation during the rise of lay piety in the later Middle Ages: (1) the image of the *danse macabre,* in which men and women confront their mortality in a dance with their own corpse; (2) the perpetuation of the memory of the deceased through elaborate tomb sculpture, rendering them "reanimate forever in stone"; and (3) the proliferation of chantries (endowments for masses and other indulgences) for the departed, in exchange for payments (51–54). In addition, it was the Abbot Odilo who, in the eleventh century, initiated the annual observance of the deceased on All Soul's Day.

Moreover, the notion of *ars bene moriendi,* or the art of dying well, became an increasingly popular theme in sermons and theological writings (Finucane, 55). Consequently, definitions of what constituted a good or a bad death were elaborated. Deathbed conflicts between angelic and demonic forces appear both in Machado de Assis's *Memórias póstumas de Brás Cubas* (in the delirium passage of chapter 7) and in Amado's *Quincas Berro Dágua* (in the struggle over Quincas's wake). Nevertheless, the treatment this theme receives in each novel extends well beyond its original Christian context and thus illuminates social dilemmas unique to their respective historical contexts.

According to Finucane, medieval ghosts assumed a far more concrete form than the ethereal apparitions of later centuries (81). Often confused with demons, the ghosts who traveled from hell or purgatory to warn, admonish, or make amends with the living often bore the physical signs of their torment in the afterlife. Furthermore, in conformity with religious and secular notions of propriety, nearly all medieval and modern ghosts appeared fully clothed. That makes Vadinho's frequently pornographic apparitions in Jorge Amado's *Dona Flor e seus dois maridos* all the more striking.

Protestant Specters and the Rise of the Gothic

> . . . bid me lurk
> Where serpents are; chain me with roaring bears
> Or hide me nightly in a charnel house,
> O'er cover'd quite with dead men's rattling bones,
> With reeky shanks, and yellow chapless skulls,
> Or bid me go into a new-made grave
> And hide me with a dead man in his shroud.
>
> —William Shakespeare, *Romeo and Juliet*

The Protestant Reformation put into question many of the fundamental tenets of Catholic dogma, one of which was the reality of purgatory and the related imperative of conducting masses for the souls of the dead. Although Protestant teachings categorized most spectral apparitions as either demonic or illusory, ordinary people continued to believe in the possibility of souls returning in ghostly form. As Finucane points out, the ghost in Shakespeare's *Hamlet* incorporates the ambiguities of Elizabethan England that had passed from Catholic to Protestant thought but had not fully given up on the existence of purgatory and its ghosts. This uncertainty is evoked by the questions Hamlet directs at the ghost of his father:

> Be thou a spirit of health or goblin damn'd,
> Bring with thee airs from heaven or blasts from hell,
> Be thy intents wicked or charitable.
>
> (*Hamlet,* act 1, sc. 4)

The prototype of the revenge-seeking ghost, so common in European literature during the Renaissance, may be traced back to Seneca, who made good use of the figure in his classical drama during the first century AD (Finucane, 111). The demonization of ghosts by Protestants was met by a renewed, post-Trident affirmation by Catholics that "there is a purgatory and . . . souls there detained are helped by the intercession of the faithful" (Finucane, 113). Throughout the seventeenth century in Europe ghosts became increasingly important pawns in this ideological war. Paradoxically, confronted by unorthodox and sectarian views within their own ranks, Protestants themselves turned to ghost stories as proof of immortality. These specters, in contrast to their medieval purgatorial counterparts, often mirrored the social goings-on of *this* world. As Finucane observes, "Cut free from the purgatorial matrix, apparitions reflected more accurately the anxieties of the people who experienced them" (150).

The tremendous technological and scientific advancements of the seventeenth and eighteenth centuries created an intellectual environment in Europe in which rationalist thinking became paramount. Consequently, during much of the Enlightenment belief in the supernatural was subjugated by an unmitigated faith in reason as the essential instrument of human progress. Gradually, however, those who had become disenchanted with rationalism's choke hold on epistemological inquiry, as well as with the pressures of capitalism and industrialism, began to seek answers to society's problems beyond the scope of reason. By the latter half of the eighteenth century a reactionary art of *unreason* had begun to emerge, for example, in the paintings of Francisco Goya and the writings of William Blake and the Marquis de Sade. A renewed interest in supernaturalism during this period is similarly manifested in the sudden popularity of so-called gothic literature. The publication in 1764 of Horace Walpole's novel *The Castle of Otranto: A Gothic Story* (the term *gothic* here referred to the story's medieval setting) is generally regarded as the inauguration of gothic fiction in the eighteenth century. The novel's representation of its protagonist's fear, as she is pursued through the dark cloisters of the Otranto castle, created an archetypical aesthetic of horror. The success of Ann Radcliffe's *The Mysteries of Udolpho* (1794), Matthew Lewis's *The Monk* (1796), and especially Mary Shelley's *Frankenstein* (1818), further demonstrated the degree to which this particular genre, with its emphasis on the forces of unreason, resonated with readers during the Enlightenment. Though the gothic tradition flourished most in the

Protestant milieu of England, many of its core elements were borrowed from Roman Catholicism. As Emma McEvoy comments in her introduction to *The Monk:* "The crux of the matter is that *The Monk,* like many Gothic novels, feeds off a 'Catholic' aesthetic, though it takes its morality from its Protestantism" (xxix). In other words, there exists an inherent paradox in the gothic tendency to both uphold and condemn belief in the supernatural.

Shelley's *Frankenstein* joins Robert Louis Stevenson's *The Strange Case of Dr. Jekyll and Mr. Hyde* (1896), Oscar Wilde's *The Picture of Dorian Gray* (1891), and Bram Stoker's *Dracula* (1897) as nineteenth-century English novels in which there is a pronounced awareness of the divided nature of the self. The demonic forces that surface within gothic narratives are ultimately generated from within this fragmented self. Rosemary Jackson discusses this breakdown of the self that occurs within the more mature works of gothic fiction:

> As Gothic undergoes transformations through the work of Ann Radcliffe, M. G. Lewis, Mary Shelley and Charles Maturin, it develops into a literary form capable of more radical interrogation of social contradictions, no longer simply making up for a society's lacks. It is progressively turned inwards to concern itself with psychological problems, used to dramatize uncertainty and conflicts of the individual subject in relation to a difficult social situation. The subject is no longer confident about appropriating or perceiving a material world. Gothic narrates this epistemological confusion: it expresses and examines personal disorder, opposing fiction's classical unities (of time, space, unified character) with an apprehension of partiality and relativity of meaning. (*Fantasy,* 97)

The ghost figure, in particular, is a source of epistemological confusion, for it disrupts "the crucial defining line which separates 'real' life from the 'unreality' of death" (69). Moreover, the return of the dead or, better yet, undead in gothic fiction marks the resurfacing of repressed desires during the Victorian period, with its myriad of social taboos.

The concept of the ghost or demon as a projection of the tormented psyche was also consistent with early-twentieth-century psychological theories of the unconscious. Freud's notion of *das Unheimlich,* the uncanny, in particular offered a useful psychoanalytic interpretation of the psyche's preoccupation with the supernatural. On the broadest level Freud designates the uncanny as "related to what is frightening—to what arouses dread and horror. . . . It tends to coincide with what excites fear in general" ("Uncanny," 219).[2] More specifically, the uncanny refers to the disquieting transformation of what is familiar and comforting to what is unfamiliar and discomforting. According to Freud, it is not so much the introduction of a novel or alien figure, but the unconscious projection of "something which is familiar and old—established in the mind and which has become alienated from it only through the process of repression" (241).

Rosemary Jackson relates the effect of the uncanny to that of fantasy literature, which, she argues, also works to "uncover all that needs to remain hidden if the world is to be comfortably 'known'" (65). The obscure areas revealed by the uncanny are, according to Freudian theory, those of concealed desire and anxiety. Thus, gothic literature's obsession with ghosts, the undead and tormented double selves signals, in Freudian terms, the return of these repressed desires, in opposition to those cultural taboos constructed as a bulwark against the libidinal and primitive drives of the unconscious. Though they were writing before the proliferation of Freud's ideas on the unconscious, many of the authors of gothic fiction mentioned above, as well as other authors of the Victorian period, such as Henry James and Rudyard Kipling, represented ghosts in their narratives as the projection of their characters' inner psychological states.

The Collective and Carnal Spirit of Brazilian Ghost Stories

In contrast to gothic fiction's tendency to turn inward in its exploration of its subjects' psychological problems, the focus of the Brazilian "ghost stories" I will be examining is directed outward, toward the community's *collective* attempt to ascribe meaning to the defunto's disruptive and untimely appearance. Absent are the psychological development of their character's inner conflicts and the subsequent projection of this conflict upon the figure of the ghost. Instead, the defuntos exist on their own account and, in a form that is frequently both carnalized and carnivalized, their return is emblematic of larger social issues that remain collectively unresolved. In this sense, they fall more under the narrative category of "cultural haunting" proposed by Kathleen Brogan (see chapter 5). It is worth noting here that within recent American literature there has emerged a new brand of ghost story that stems not from the gothic tradition, but instead from the attempt by certain minority writers to recover and rewrite their respective ethnic identities through a narrative confrontation with the supernatural. Notwithstanding the many functional differences that exist between these stories and the Brazilian fiction explored in my study, the representation of the ghost as emblematic of collective social dilemmas is, I propose, consistent in both traditions.

This is not to say that the history of Brazilian literature is totally void of certain gothic elements, or that manifestations of the uncanny or the fantastic have not appeared at particular moments. On the contrary, a cornerstone of my argument in this study is that the image of the defunto has been both a frequent and profound literary motif in Brazil since the second half of the nineteenth century. It is possible that the defunto's presence has been overlooked by critics, however, due to the relatively underdeveloped tradition of the fantastic in Brazilian literature. In his anthology *O conto fantástico* [The Fantastic Short Story] (1959), Jerônimo Monteiro explains this dearth:

> The truth is that I was not fully aware of the scarcity of fantastic short stories in Brazilian literature. When the idea of the anthology emerged, I expected there to be an abundance of usable material, given the popularity of this mode in a society that so often recounts fantastic stories that contain apparitions, mysteries, and wandering souls. . . . It seemed to me that, over the years, I had read quite a bit of this sort of literature.

> After confronting this apparent contradiction, however, I confirmed that the fantastic literature read in this country is, on the whole, translated, especially from English. It is the English who adore haunted houses, and their authors who, through literature, provide what is not frequently found in real life. Among Brazilians the opposite seems to be true: there are countless legends, superstitions, and hauntings in these parts and few who make use of these themes in their writing. (1)

Monteiro's discovery of the absence of a gothic tradition in Brazilian literature, in contrast to the rich English literary tradition of haunted tales, is, while perhaps overstated, nonetheless revealing. This apparent paradox would suggest, if we were to apply the Freudian model outlined above, that literature, particularly in the English case, has functioned at given historical moments as a release for otherwise repressed, perhaps unconscious, fears and beliefs. Following this line of thinking, then, Brazilian society would already possess inherent religious and cultural outlets in which interaction with the supernatural is not only possible but expected, and therefore literature need not perform the same cathartic function.

Death and the Dead: Recurring Images in Brazilian Literature

The absence of a strong gothic tradition in Brazil does not necessarily imply the paucity of a literary interest in the dead per se. Rather, it is the characterization of the dead in Brazilian literature that has developed largely independent of the gothic model. Nonetheless, examples of a gothic aesthetic do exist, as we shall see. More important, a sweeping glance at Brazilian literature over the last two centuries suggests that Machado de Assis was not alone in his fascination with the dead or their lingering voices and occasional resurrections. Aluísio Azevedo, a contemporary of Machado, infused his novel *Mortalha de Alzira* [Alzira's Shroud] (1894) with spectral figures. In this story the cynical

Countess Alzira falls in love with and seduces Father Ângelo, a young priest who is as remarkably naive as he is angelic. Alzira's seduction and Ângelo's subsequent temptation, however, do not cease after her death. Alzira's ghost returns to him at night in his dreams and leads the conflicted priest to the land of the dead, where spirits indulge in an uninterrupted orgy of sensual pleasures.[3]

Aluísio Azevedo is perhaps best known for his novels *O mulato* [Mulatto] (1881) and *O cortiço* [Slum] (1890), works that confirmed his place as a leading figure of naturalism in late-nineteenth-century Brazil. He also produced a considerable number of romantic works, like *Mortalha de Alzira,* of lesser literary merit intended for mass consumption. The popularity of these works by Azevedo, one of the few authors of his time who could live off his writing, suggests that romanticism, and its frequent preoccupation with the theme of death, still attracted a wide audience in Brazil at the turn of the century.

Frei Álvaro, the central character of Azevedo's short story "O Impenitente" [The Unrepentant], is, like Father Ângelo, a clergyman who has fallen irrevocably into sin.[4] Equally tormented by the desire to possess the forbidden fruit of a woman's body, Frei Álvaro slips away from his monastery at night to be with the object of his passion, a beautiful young woman named Leonília. Then, on another evening, as the monk is gazing out his window, he sees her figure, dressed in white, suddenly in the courtyard of the monastery. When he runs down to greet her she has already made her way into the street. He pursues her through the streets, always a block behind her gliding ethereal figure. Finally she leads him to her apartment, which, upon entering, he discovers is the scene of a wake. There in the coffin, surrounded by flittering candles and black velvet curtains, is the cadaver of Leonília, the woman he had just been chasing through the streets.

This combination of terror and primal desire, so characteristic of gothic fiction, also appears frequently in Álvares de Azevedo's collection of short stories *Noite na taverna* [A Night at the Tavern] (1878).[5] Highly influenced by Lord Byron and Alfred de Musset, Álvares de

Azevedo is better known for his poetry, which, consistent with the aesthetics of ultraromanticism, cultivates a sense of discontented love and the desire to escape from reality. For romantic poets such as Azevedo the ultimate form of escape, from which there is no return, is death. In *Noite na taverna* six inebriated students each recount bizarre personal stories, including bacchanal sexual adventures, murders, incest, and encounters with the supernatural. One of the stories, "Solfieri" (also the narrator's name), is set in Rome, which the narrator describes as a city that blends fanaticism and perdition, "o beijo lascivo à embriaguez da crença!" [the lewd kiss with the rapture of faith] (169). On one moonlit night the narrator notices the shape of a woman, in white, appear in a solitary window. She quickly disappears but he then hears a melancholy song emanate from the window. His description of her voice combines the elements of both romanticism and gothicism: "aquela voz era sombria como a do vento à noite nos cemitérios cantando a nênia das flores murchas da morte" [her voice was ominous like the night wind in the cemeteries, lamenting with her elegy the shriveled flowers of death] (170). He then follows the figure to a local cemetery, where she kneels crying before a cross. As if from a dream, the narrator awakens the next day alone in the cemetery.

A year later, after a night of debauchery, the young man happens to make his way to a neighborhood chapel. Inside the chapel is a coffin wherein lies the corpse of the woman he had seen the year before, now draped in a hearse cloth. Impetuously, he lifts the woman out of the coffin and, holding her in his arms, kisses her ardently on the lips. In the heat of the moment her corpse begins to stir: "Àquele calor de meu peito, à febre de meus lábios, à convulsão de meu amor, a donzela pálida parecia reanimar-se. Súbito, abriu os olhos empanados" [Through the warmth of my chest, my feverish lips, and the convulsions of my love, the pale maiden seemed to come to life. Suddenly she opened her hazy eyes] (171). Believing the woman to be a victim of catalepsy, he carries her barely conscious body out of the chapel and to his house. A patrol officer, who happens to pass by, also mistakes her for a cadaver, until the man points out her faint breath. At his house the woman breaks into a delirious fever and, after two days and nights of suffering, dies a second death. After having a wax statue made of her form, he buries her in a tomb he has dug under the tiles of his room, over which he then places his own bed. The young man only discovers a year later that, according to the man who made her wax statue, she had been dead long before he first saw her in the cemetery. As we can see here, the motif of the resurrected corpse returning momentarily to the world of the living is one that substantially precedes both Amado's *Quincas Berro Dágua* and Veríssimo's *Incidente em Antares* in Brazilian literature.

"What Is There between Life and Death? A Short Bridge"

The last delirious moments of a dying person, skirting that tenuous line between life and death, has also appeared frequently in Brazilian fiction.[6] Brás Cubas experiences a fantastic journey on the back of a hippopotamus to "the origin of time," where he witnesses the endless march of human history before succumbing to the "undiscovered country." "Delírio" [Delirium] is also the title of Afonso Schmidt's short story, set in a hospital room, in which a young man suffering from tuberculosis is visited by the spirit of his godfather and other inhabitants of the afterlife.[7] During his feverish state he learns from his godfather that life and death are two sides of the same coin: "entra-se pela Morte e sai-se pela Vida . . . Uma questão de nome apenas. . . . Dois filósofos que num café falam sôbre a morte, parecem dois fetos gêmeos, no seio materno, conversando sôbre a vida" [we enter through Death and leave through Life . . . A question merely of wording. . . . Two philosophers who converse in a café about death resemble twin fetuses, in the mother's womb, talking about life] (136). The godfather's description of an endlessly rotating life and afterlife, as two relatively neutral spaces, is reminiscent of Machado's sarcastic treatment of reincarnation in his short story "A segunda vida" [A Second Life].

Moribund delirium is also the central focus of Graciliano Ramos's "Paulo." Published in 1947 in his collection entitled *Insônia* [Insomnia], this short story is narrated by a dying man suffering intense pain and delirium in a hospital. Passing in and out of consciousness, the narrator projects his suffering onto the space and people around him: "A minha carne, que apodrece, suja a gaze e o algodão, espalha-se no teto e nas paredes" [My flesh, which rots and soils the gauze and cotton, spreads across the ceiling and walls] (51). His wife appears and disappears like a ghost at his bedside. In this semiconscious, anguished state he is visited by a Spiritist whose "forbidding eyes can see spirits" and by Paulo, the faceless figure of death who looms over his bed and twists a knife deeper into his mortal wound. Strikingly similar, Ramos's short story "O relógio do hospital" [The Clock in the Hospital] is told from the point of view of a man who spends his last agonizing days in a hospital. Death also relentlessly pursues Fabiano and his family through the parched *sertão* [backlands] in Ramos's novel *Vidas secas* [Barren Lives] (1938). The pathos evoked by the death of the family's dog stems largely from the consequences of a socioeconomic and regional situation that has also transformed the wandering family into animals. And in *São Bernardo* (1934) the death of Madelena marks the inevitable culmination of Paulo Honório's brutish and all-consuming jealousy.

The principal character of Henrique Maximiano Coelho Neto's short story "Duplo" [Double], from his collection *Contos da vida e da morte* [Stories of Life and Death] (1927), recounts an out-of-body experience that occurs while he is sitting on a streetcar. Peering above his newspaper, lost in thought, the narrator suddenly sees an exact replica of himself. Believing it to be his soul that has recently departed from his body, he envisions the commotion his sudden death will cause: "todos os passageiros de pé, a verificação da minha morte, o reconhecimento do meu cadaver pelo conductor e a minha entrada funebre em casa" [all the passengers standing up, the verification of my death, the recognition of my cadaver by the conductor, and my funereal arrival at home] (115). Spurred by his will to live, he stands up and the double vision suddenly disappears. Stupefied, he retells this story to a friend, who simply advises him, "Essas coisas, meu amigo, não se explicam" [My friend, these things one cannot explain] (116).

We find a peculiar twist on the danse macabre motif in the short story "Os olhos que comiam carne" [The Eyes that Consumed Flesh] (1935) by poet and short story writer Humberto de Campos.[8] The story begins as its central character, the eminent scholar Paulo Fernandes, is waking up the morning after the publication of the last volume of his series "The History of Human Knowledge." As he begins to open his eyes he notices that, strangely, no light seems to be entering his room. He calls the housekeeper, who confirms that light is indeed entering the room. It is the writer who, to his own horror, has gone blind. The news of his sudden blindness travels through the city, leaving his friends and admirers in great despair. Local doctors, however, hold out hope that a renowned German surgeon might be able to restore the scholar's sight by treating the damaged optical nerve with X-rays. Confident of the success of his method, the doctor leaves Brazil after the operation, ordering Paulo to remove the bandages in two weeks. Two weeks pass and, in a moment of great anticipation, Paulo's friends and supporters gather around him for the decisive moment.

Upon removing the bandages, Paulo's face begins to contort with terror. His sight has returned, but instead of seeing as he did before, his eyes, influenced by their exposure to X-rays, now see through skin, exposing only the skeletal structures of those around him:

> E o que enxerga, na multidão de médicos e de amigos que o aguardam lá fora, é um turbilhão de espectros, de esqueletos que marcham e agitam os dentes, como se tivessem aberto um ossuário cujos mortos quisessem sair. Solta um grito e recua.
>
> [And what he sees, in the multitude of doctors and friends that await him outside, is instead a whirlwind of specters, of skeletons that march and move their teeth about, as if an ossuary had opened up and the dead were clamoring to get out. He lets out a scream and retreats.] (Monteiro, 197)

Horrified, he rips his newly restored eyes from their sockets,

> esmagando nas mãos aquêles olhos que comiam carne, e que, devorando macabramente a carne aos vivos, transformavam a vida humana, em tôrno, em um sinistro baile de esqueletos.
>
> [crushing in his hands those eyes that consumed flesh, and that, in their macabre devouring of the flesh of the living, transformed human life around him into a sinister ballet of skeletons.] (198)

In this short story, as in *Frankenstein* and so many other works of gothic fiction, the limitations of human knowledge and man's "vision" for the future are revealed in our vain and often disastrous attempt to control the course of nature.

In Lima Barreto's short story "Sua Excelência" [His Excellency], from his collection *Histórias e sonhos* [Stories and Dreams] (1920), a minister of state, after delivering a triumphant speech, makes an unexpected journey in his coach through a hellish afterworld. After fainting, he awakes to find himself back at the front steps of the palace he had just left, but this time dressed as a pauper. Death's ability to relativize all social positions and aspirations similarly appears in narratives possessing a carnivalesque ethos.

The Defunto Returns

Machado de Assis's interest in the defunto as a literary motif appears to have caught the attention of a contemporary of his, poet and novelist Carlos Magalhães de Azeredo. In a short story dedicated to Machado de Assis, "De além-túmulo" [From Beyond the Tomb], Azeredo makes clear allusions to several of Machado's works.[9] The story is told in the first person by a lawyer (with a side-interest in the occult), who is sitting in his apartment alone contemplating a failed love affair. Suddenly he hears the sound of slow footsteps making their way up the stairs to his apartment. He opens the door to find an extremely pallid young man in a black cape standing there. With the candidness of Brás Cubas, the strange visitor informs the narrator that he has come from beyond the grave. He then assures the frightened man that he means him no harm. He has come instead to inquire about a woman who, during his life, he loved deeply and, for a few brief years, made his wife. However, a shadow had crept into his feelings for her, that of jealousy:

> era o ciúme . . . ciúme mais cruciante quanto mudo e concentrado . . . Eu tinha, por meias razões unicamente—mas essas bastavam para me torturar—a desconfiança de que não era amado quanto merecia. Foi sob essa impressão que expirei.
>
> [it was jealousy . . . jealousy that was as torturous as it was silent and concentrated. . . . I suspected, for only half-formed reasons—but those were enough to torture me—that I was not as loved as I deserved to be. It was with this impression that I expired.] (Monteiro, 246)

For this distrustful defunto the proof of his former wife's betrayal lies in her decision to marry again only a few months after his death. From the apartment window they are able to view the happy couple together. The narrator tells how, overwhelmed by the presence of this scorned spirit, he fainted with a high fever and awoke alone in his room again. Only years later has he summoned the courage to tell the story. Written in 1893, thirteen years after *Memórias póstumas de Brás Cubas,* "De além túmulo" not only clearly echoes Machado's creation of a dead man who carries his jaundiced nature into the afterlife but also prefigures the consuming jealousy embodied by Bento in Machado's later novel *Dom Casmurro* (1899).

Before Coelho Neto had published his *Contos da vida e da morte,* the diplomat, poet, and novelist Thomaz Lopes published his own *Histórias da vida e da morte* [Stories of Life and Death] in 1907. In this volume is a short story written in 1899 entitled "O defuncto," in which a man awakes to discover that he has been buried alive.[10] Initially the narration is sufficiently vague as to leave the reader wondering whether the man is alive or, as the title indicates, actually deceased and just stirring in his deathly slumber: "Passou os frios dedos pelo rosto e retirou-os espantado, sentindo a face morta como a de um cadaver" [He touched his face with his cold fingers and pulled them away in fright, feeling the dead face of a cadaver] (12). He throws off the lid of his coffin only to discover that he is trapped within the cold, dark walls of a marble tomb. There is a tiny vent that lets in a sliver of light during the day and just enough air to condemn him to this perpetual hell. Calling for help is useless. He makes several desperate, insane attempts to push aside the marble tombstone, to no avail. Half mad, his only escape is through sleep, during which he dreams of the woman who was to be his bride. Yet even his dreams are invaded by death:

> Passou por cemitérios, e à sua passagem os defunctos erguiam-se, cobertos de pó e de segredo, acompanhando-o fantasticamente por dilatados e dolorosos momentos. As arvores tomavam assombradoras formas de avejões e as estrellas apagando-se no céu deixavam o céu cinzento e frio como o mármore da sua sepultura tão fria e tão cinzenta! E entretanto, no silencio, na noite e na treva o Defuncto caminhava.
>
> [He walked through the cemetery, passing by defuntos that rose up, covered in dirt and secrecy, fantastically joining him in these endless, agonizing moments. The trees became huge specters and the vanishing stars left the sky gray and cold, like the cold, gray marble of his tomb! And so, in silence, through the darkness of the night, the defunto walked.] (15–16)

Though still alive, he is already very much a defunto. The marble walls of his tomb are a gothic refrain throughout the story. Starved, dying of thirst, and bloodied from his futile attempts to escape, his horrific figure at the end of the story is pure gothic:

> Ajoelhou-se, rilhou os dentes, entrelaçou os dedos sobre as mãos n'uma prece maldicta,—e ficou morto, immovel, rigido e nú, coberto de sangue escarlate.
>
> [He kneeled down, clenched his teeth, clasped his fingers together in a cursed prayer—and became dead, immobile, rigid and naked, covered in scarlet blood.] (21)

As the story closes, although still breathing, he is as dead as the other corpses in the surrounding sepulchers.

Other Incarnations of the Dead in Brazilian Poetry and Prose

Any attempt at providing an overview of death and the dead as recurring motifs in Brazilian literature would be remiss not to mention the poetry of Augusto dos Anjos. With lines like "Ah! Um urubu pousou na minha sorte" [Ah! A vulture perched on my fortune], Augusto dos Anjos's verse exemplifies a certain malaise in Brazil during the first decade of the twentieth century, stemming as much from popular revolts at home as from the global conflict of World War I looming ahead. Combining both a romantic sense of melancholy and a naturalist use of scientific terminology, Augusto dos Anjos's poetry reveals an obsession with the themes of death and disintegration, as in "Idealisação da humanidade futura" [Idealization of Future Humanity] (1909):[11]

> E, em vez de achar a luz que os Ceus inflama,
> Somente achei moléculas de lama
> E a mosca alegre da putrefacção!
>
> [And, instead of finding the light that illuminates the heavens,
> I found only molecules of mud
> And the joyful fly of putrefaction!]
>
> (*Poesia,* 66)

A glance at his complete works of poetry shows an elaborate mosaic of death-related themes. Often the dead themselves are empowered with a voice to express their grief, as in "Monólogo de uma sombra" [A Shadow's Monologue] (1912) or the sonnet "Vozes de um túmulo" [Voices from a Tomb] (1905), quoted here in its entirety:

Morri! E a Terra—a mãe commum—o brilho
Destes meus olhos apagou! . . . Assim,
Tantalo, aos reaes convivas, num festim,
Serviu as carnes do seu proprio filho!
Porque para este cemiterio vim?!
Porque?! Antes da vida o angusto trilho
Palmilhasse, do que este que palmilho
E que me assombra, porque não tem fim!
No ardor do sonho que o phronéma exalta
Construí de orgulho enea pyrámide alta . . .
Hoje, porém, que se desmoronou
A pyrámide real do meu orgulho,
Hoje que, apenas, sou materia e entulho
Tenho consciencia de que nada sou!

[I died! And the earth—our common mother—shut out
the light of my eyes! Thus did
Tantalus, who, to the royal guests at a feast,
Served the flesh of his own son!
Why to this cemetery have I come?
Why?! I would as soon continue my anguished
Journey through life than follow this path
That frightens me so, because it has no end!
In the passion of a dream that phronema exalts
I proudly constructed anew this tall pyramid . . .
Now, however, that the real pyramid
Of my pride has collapsed,
Now, that I am only material and debris,
I realize that I am nothing!]

(*Poesia*, 113)

Montgomery José de Vasconcelos, in *A poética carnavalizada de Augusto dos Anjos* [The Carnivalized Poetics of Augusto dos Anjos], identifies a confluence of the carnivalesque with the theme of death in this sonnet and in other poetry of Augusto dos Anjos: "The focus of carnivalization in this sonnet is death, nature's daughter, all-knowing in Earthly affairs and possessing supernatural powers, causing at will the end of human existence" (207).

In *Macunaíma* (1928) Mário de Andrade's puckish central character visits the land of the dead. Similarly, in the poem "Menipo," Manuel Bandeira portrays the arrival of the infamous Greek cynic to the underworld, beginning with his journey across the River Styx where, instead of the traditional coin, Menippus offers the boatman Charon his ironic smile as payment for passage.[12] Furthermore, narratives such as *Vida e morte de M. J. Gonzaga de Sá* [The Life and Death of M. J. Gonzaga de Sá] (1919) by Lima Barreto, *Menino de engenho* [Plantation Boy] (1932) by José Lins do Rêgo, and *A república dos sonhos* [The Republic of Dreams] (1984) by Nélida Piñon commence with the swift announcement of a prominent character's demise, an event that has repercussions throughout the rest of each novel.

Mário de Andrade's short story "O peru de natal" [The Christmas Turkey] portrays how one Brazilian family manages to come to terms with the death of the head of the household.[13] Narrated years later by the son of the deceased father, the story revolves around the family's decision to indulge in a turkey dinner on the first Christmas following the patriarch's death. Still in mourning and under the shadow of the father's joyless ways, the family is at first unable to allow themselves the pleasure of such a treat. Chagrined by the defunto's ability to diminish the family's joie de vivre, the son finds a way to appease the father's spirit by pointing out his virtues and the pleasure he would take in seeing the family united. Once the father's memory is ostensibly sanctified, the family is able to free itself of the guilt associated with mourning and eat the turkey with a new lack of inhibition. According to the narrator, that turkey dinner was the beginning of a much happier and intimate family dynamic, at peace with the former patriarch but also free of his somber overbearance.

Striking similarities exist between the psychological intricacies of one family's mourning in Mário de Andrade's story and the multitude of domestic mourning scenes that one encounters in *Velórios* [Wakes] (1936) by Rodrigo M. F. de Andrade. This volume of short stories represents the only fiction produced by Rodrigo de Andrade, who spent most of his career as director of the Instituto do Patrimônio Histórico e Artístico Nacional, dedicating himself to the recovery and collection of historical documents and art objects. Written in a fluid and deftly understated prose, each of the eight stories in *Velórios* portrays a different family or individual's response to death. The stories are tied together by the often contradictory, sometimes liberating, but always indelible institution of luto in Brazilian society.

Literary Reverberations of the Carnivalesque Defunto

Rodrigo de Andrade's literary mosaic of the dead in Brazilian society did not go unnoticed. The modernist Aníbal Machado dedicated one of his own meditations on the topic to Andrade, in the short story "O defunto inaugural: Relato de um fantasma" [The First Corpse].[14] Of all the *fantasmas* and resurrected corpses we have considered so far in Brazilian literature, it is perhaps the deceased narrator in "The First Corpse" that best approximates the particular suborder of the dead that lies at the core of this study—the carnivalesque defunto. Like Brás Cubas, this story's narrator comments from the other side of life. Unlike Brás, the link between his soul, or metaphysical consciousness, and his body remains quite close. In other words, though free to wander about, his soul generally does not stray far from its corpse.

The story begins as the defunto (an expired cattle driver named Fagundes) is being carried in a hammock over a ridge by two *sertanejos* (cowboys from the Sertão region) he affectionately calls Bigode and Careca. "Moustache" and "Baldy" have a special interest in this defunto. News has spread that a local town named Arraial Novo is opening its first cemetery, but is in need of a good cadaver to inaugurate the grounds. Moreover, the transporters of the inaugural corpse will be paid well for their services. Knowing that surrounding areas may be sending their own corpses, Fagundes urges his mercenary pallbearers on: "Engulem a cachaça, disse eu, já impaciente. E toquem depressa!"; "Eh, Bigode! . . . Eh, Careca! Depressa!" (*A Morte,* 57, 59) ["'Swallow your rum and get going!' I said impatiently; 'Hey, Moustache! Hey, Baldy! Hurry up!'"] (K. Jackson, *Oxford Anthology,* 173–74). The defunto even gloats when they pass another exhausted couple whose "merchandise" is already at a more advanced stage of decomposition, unlike Fagundes's tanned and well-preserved body. Throughout their journey the defunto expresses a gleeful satisfaction: "Que bom este passeio! Tudo tão fluído que posso perceber o que se faz e acontece na área mais próxima de meu corpo" (59) ["What a pleasant journey this was! It was so clear that I could see all that went on in the vicinity of my body"] (173).

When they arrive in Arraial Novo the defunto is given a mixed reception. The older women of the town, who have long advocated for a cemetery, are satisfied with this corpse and begin preparations for its burial. The town's adolescent boys, however, whose soccer field has been chosen as the new cemetery site, conspire against the strange corpse. They complain to the elders: how can a town have a cemetery with only one corpse, and one who was not even a resident to begin with? How can they practice for their club's upcoming match against a rival town? Death, however, settles in permanently with the arrival of Fagundes. Previously unknown words such *esquife* [bier], *féretro* [coffin], and *funeral* are used in conversation for the first time. For the girls of the town there is one consolation: "o enterro valeria a pena como festa" (62) ["they had the funeral (festa) to make up for it"] (175). The defunto's presence becomes larger than life and consumes the town's imagination: "Para todos eu era um defunto imenso e difuso, presidindo à noite do Arraial" (62) ["An immense, omnipresent dead man presided over the Arraial night"] (176).

Like Brás Cubas, the narrator witnesses his own funeral the following day. In contrast to the pathetic turnout for the former's burial, the entire town of Arraial appears for Fagundes's celebratory ceremony: "O ambiente é festivo" (63) ["The atmosphere was festive"] (176). The still slightly disgruntled boys take advantage of the atmosphere by making advances on their coy girlfriends: "Aqui não, diz uma. Olha o morto!" ["'Not here,' said one of the girls. 'Look at the dead man!'"] The defunto's encouragements add to the funeral's carnivalesque atmosphere:

> Deixa, deixa que ele te aperte, moça,—insuflo aos ouvidos dela. Não te preocupes com o que vai lá na frente; aquilo é apenas um corpo abandonado, arranjo de velhas que só pensam na morte. Parece que a moça me atendeu. (63)
>
> ["Go ahead and let him," I whispered in his ear. "Don't worry about that fellow up front; he's just an abandoned corpse fixed up by old women with nothing to think about but death."] (176)

Similarly, when a group of girls surrounds his coffin before it is to be lowered into the ground, Fagundes's lascivious behavior is as carnal as Vadinho's in *Dona Flor e seus dois maridos:*

> As môças me cercam e eu me surpreendo numa onda de alegria indefinida. Aura de juventude emanando delas! Que fazer de tanta primavera desaproveitada? Meus fluidos roçam-lhes o colo. Somente os fluidos. A invisível carícia arrepia-lhes a pele, enquanto a musiquinha toca uma coisa triste debaixo das árvores. Que se passou com elas que erubesceram de repente? Algumas cruzam os braços ou tapam com o xale o busto arrepiado; outras se escondem, pertubadas, no meio do povo. (64)
>
> [The girls surrounded me and a wave of happiness washed over me. The aura of youth emanating from them! What to do with so much springtime going to waste? My ectoplasm brushed their necks. Only my ectoplasm. The invisible caress raised shivers on their skin, while the little band played a mournful tune under the trees. What came over them that made them blush suddenly? Some crossed their arms or covered a tingling bust with a shawl; others, agitated, hid themselves among the multitude.] (177)[15]

As we shall see later in this study, sensuality and carnal desires are often part of the carnivalesque defunto's unique features in Brazilian literature. The underlying humor contained in Fagundes's whimsical sense of competitiveness and personal eccentricities lends this corpse an endearing quality that, in turn, serves to reanimate him even more. Over time the town becomes accustomed to its deceased guest and begins to express pride in the ghostly sounds that seem to emanate from the cemetery at night: "Que todos respeitassem agora o cemitério com as almas que nele transitam!" (66) ["Everybody must respect the cemetery now, and the souls that passed through it"] (178). Strangely, as Fagundes affectionately adds, the souls always add up to twenty-two—eleven on each side of the field. He does not hide his approval of the boys who are desecrating his burial site by sneaking into the cemetery at night to play soccer. In fact, Fagundes fancies himself a spectral referee: "Eu adorava ficar ali. Acompanhava o movimento do jogo. Torcia. Metia-me no meio dos jogadores. Só faltava gritar" (67) ["I loved it there then. I would take part in the game, get into the play. I did everything but shout"] (178). The ending of the story suggests that a carnivalesque regeneration will stem from the cycle of life and death that now has a place in Arraial Novo. Just as the vital force of Fagundes's soul is beginning to fade away, a second cadaver is brought into the cemetery, symbolically, a woman named Maria who has died while giving birth.

"The First Corpse" contains themes that overlap with several other short stories by Aníbal Machado. The profound impact of a stranger's arrival in a new town, especially for the children, is one that Machado eloquently explores in "O iniciado do vento" [The Wind's Apprentice]. The dead are also an integral part of the story narrated by the elevator operator in "O ascensorista" [The Lift Operator] who tells how on several occasions he has had to bring defuntos down through the building. On one occasion the power fails on the way down, stopping the elevator in the dark for a few unpleasant minutes: "Parecia que íamos ficar sepultados ali, além do defunto, eu e seus parentes"

[It seemed like the defunto, his relatives, and I would all be entombed there] (76). In Machado's story "A morte da porta-estandarte" Rosinha's corpse becomes the central focus of the narrative as the deliriously jealous boyfriend holds her tenderly in his arms, after having slain her with a knife during carnival. Her corpse seems to respond to his murderous affection: "Ela parecia sorrir. . . . A qualquer momento ela poderia se erguer para dançar. Nunca se viu defunto tão vivo" (232) ["She seemed to be smiling. . . . At any moment she might get up and dance. No one ever saw such a live corpse"] (K. Jackson, *Oxford Anthology*, 170). Once again carnival and death collide.

Death and the dead have also frequently emerged as important motifs in Brazilian theater. Joaquim Manuel de Macedo, one of the most prominent playwrights of the nineteenth century, incorporated the figure of the menacing ghost (that turns out to be a fake) in his satirical play *O fantasma branco* [The White Ghost] (presented in 1851 and published in 1856). Staged as a dramatic opera in three acts, *O fantasma branco* has also been viewed as an example of Macedo's social criticism of the oppression of women in Brazil during the nineteenth century.[16]

The highly influential modern playwright Nelson Rodrigues viewed theater as a form of social ritual, much like a church Mass or deathwatch.[17] The innovative dramatic techniques that he employs in his groundbreaking *Vestido de noiva* [The Wedding Dress] (1943) emphasize this constant juxtaposition of theater, ritual, and death. In the play Rodrigues manipulates three levels of experience: reality, hallucinatory fantasy, and memory. The protagonist, Alaíde, who is dying on an operating table after having been run over by a car, attempts to reconstruct her past by searching through each of these three levels for some clue that would explain her inner turmoil. Frequently, Rodrigues inverts those rituals that give shape to both life and death—for example, when Alaíde imagines Madame Clessi (and herself) buried in her bridal gown.

The motif of the dead also surfaces in the work of another important modernist Brazilian playwright, Ariano Suassuna. In his play *Auto da compadecida* [The Rogues' Trial] (1955), Suassuna combines the tradition of classic European drama with the folk theater and *literatura do cordel* of the Brazilian northeast. A commedia dell'arte of the sertão, *Auto da compadecida* blends tragic and comic elements in its story of a picaresque and mischievous rogue named João Grilo who is determined to undermine the dealings of his *patrão* [boss]. Halfway through the play many of the principal characters have died, including the patrão, a corrupt priest, a *cangaceiro* [outlaw], and João Grilo himself, and are judged in a circuslike atmosphere involving the Devil and Jesus Christ. Near the end of the play, João Grilo "returns from the dead" (we discover that he was only injured and unconscious), much to the comical surprise of his companion, Chicó, who is solemnly carrying his body to be buried.

The prominence of death in the backlands of the Brazilian northeast is also evoked in the fiction of João Guimarães Rosa. For example, Augusto Estêves, the protagonist in Guimarães Rosa's "A hora e vez de Augusto Matraga" [The Hour and Turn of Augusto Matraga], dies a symbolic death when, after a life of cruelty to others, his family abandons him and his fellow *jagunços* [armed hands] beat him senseless, then throw him off a cliff. Augusto miraculously survives and is nursed back to health by a black couple who teach him the meaning of compassion. Before Augusto's complete physical and moral recovery can occur, he must journey, figuratively speaking, through the geography of the afterlife—that is, hell, purgatory, and paradise. When his real death occurs at the end of the story, following his fight with the bandit Joãzinho Bem-Bem, Augusto has incorporated both good and evil into his life and has, in the process, become more human.[18] Some of the numerous short stories by Guimarães Rosa in which death and scenes of mourning are prominent include "Sorôco, sua mãe, sua filha" [Sorôco, His Mother, His Daughter], "A menina de lá" [The Girl from Beyond], and "Os irmãos Dagobé" [The Dagobé Brothers] from *Primeiras estórias* [First Stories] (1962).

A study concerning death and the dead in modern Brazilian literature cannot fail to mention João Cabral de Melo Neto's poem "Morte e vida severina" [Death and Life of a Severino] (1956). As in many of João Cabral's other poems, death is a principal subject of this *auto* set in the drought-ridden northeast. The poem is told from the point of view of a *retirante* [migrant] named Severino, whose generic name evokes the severity of the region's physical and socioeconomic environment. As Severino says, a "morte severina" is one in which one dies of old age before turning thirty (71). During his odyssey through the sertão, Severino encounters two men carrying a defunto in a hammock, visits a house in which alms are being sung for a defunto, attends the burial of a field worker, and listens in on the conversation of two grave diggers. Seeking work, he encounters a woman whose vocation is to pray for the souls of the dead. She explains to him, "só os roçados da morte compensam aqui cultivar" [only the fields of death are worth cultivating here] (85). Severino's search for meaning in this parched world is also very much a journey through the mosaic of mortuary rituals and mourning traditions of the Brazilian northeast.

Manifestations of the Dead in Contemporary Brazilian Literature

Perhaps no other female voice in contemporary Brazilian literature, since Clarice Lispector's existential contemplations on the subject, has focused more intently on the theme of death than Lya Luft. In *O quarto fechado* (1984) the figure of death permeates each page and, like the casket containing Camilo's corpse, literally lies at the narrative's epicenter.[19] Both death and the dead are personified in the opening pages of the novel, giving each a "life" of its own. The novel's first line suggests that *o morto* [the dead one] and *a Morte* [death] are inextricably linked to one another in a kind of maternal relationship: "Ele dava os primeiros passos em sua Morte, abraçado a ela, que o instruía devagar" (13) ["He took the first steps in his Death, embraced by Death, who instructed him slowly"] (*Island,* 5). The image of the morto as a child similarly conveys a sense of rebirth through death, which, in turn, evokes its own carnivalesque connotations. The first line in the second paragraph reinforces the personification and subtle renascent qualities of the morto: "Nada o incomodava: vozes, tosses discretas, portas abrindo-se e fechando" (13) ["Nothing bothered him—not voices, not discreet coughs, not doors opening and closing"] (5).

The characters mourning Camilo's death, namely his sisters and separated parents, also experience death as a living presence. The grieving father, for example, imagines himself grappling with this unwanted intruder who has taken his son away:

> a qualquer momento poderia levantar-se da cadeira e golpear com punhos o peito ossudo d'Aquela que, sem sua permissão, reinava na casa. (14)

> [as if he might momentarily rise from the chair with clenched fists to batter the bony chest of Death, who, without his permission, was ruling his house.] (6)

Renata, the mother, finds herself reflecting on the figure of death ferrying passengers to a lonely island, in a painting entitled *Ilha dos mortos.* Camilo, when he was alive, felt death's attractive lure when a close childhood friend died:

> Na memória de Camilo o rosto da criança morta se desfez, nem um perfume sobrou, um gesto. Tudo fora transferido para aquele espaço maior de atração: na Morte estão as coisas mais belas, que um dia possuirei. (24)

> [In Camilo's memory, the face of the dead child dissolved, not even his scent remained, not even a gesture. All now belonged to that larger, more attractive realm. What is most beautiful is to be found in death, that I shall possess one day.] (14)

By the end of the novel, when the morning's first rays signal the end of Camilo's wake, death's transformation from mother figure to seductress is complete:

> Sobre as copas das árvores negras pulsou o novo dia, abrindo na bruma uma cunha de luz que pousou na sala, onde o morto se enlaçava em seu Amor: e atracavam no cais. (133)
>
> [Over the black treetops the pulsations of a new day forced light into the thick fog, and the light struck the living room, where the dead boy embraced his Lover as they docked.] (106)

Cristina Ferreira-Pinto, in her article examining gothic and fantastic elements in contemporary Brazilian women's fiction, suggests that the themes of death, madness, the repression of desires, and the absurdity of life tie together Lya Luft's novels *O quarto fechado* and *As parceiras* [The Partners] (1980): "Death is the starting point of the two novels, as the narrative compensates for the void left by the absence of the dead (in both novels, the protagonist's son). But while the narrative—in the form, mainly, of the characters' thoughts and memories—serves to fill in the space left by a loss, it will also reveal other losses and absences, the *death in life* experienced by each character in their daily existences" (73; emphasis in original). It is this recrudescence of death in life that partly explains the intrusion of supernatural forces in the daily existence of these characters, Ferreira-Pinto suggests. The other female Brazilian author whose incorporation of the fantastic and the gothic is explored by Cristina Ferreira-Pinto is Lygia Fagundes Telles. According to Ferreira-Pinto, these elements are most evident in Telles's short fiction and in her novels *Ciranda de pedra* [Stone Circle] (1954) and *As horas nuas* [The Naked Hours] (1989). It is worthwhile also mentioning the frequently morbid short stories of the contemporary author Dalton Trevisan, in which a corpse appears prominently. These include "O morto na sala" [The Corpse in the Parlor], "Meu avô" [My Grandfather], and "Últimos dias" [Final Days] from his collection *Novelas nada exemplares* [Novels Not at All Exemplary], as well as "Angústia do viúvo" [The Widower's Anguish] and "Uma vela para Diário" [A Candle for Diário] in *Cemitério de elefantes* [The Elephants' Graveyard].

In *The Female Voice in Contemporary Brazilian Narrative,* Susan Quinlan argues that the contemporary gothic novel in Brazil works to expose the hidden abnormalities of societal norms, revealing as much about "the silent, mad places of a collective consciousness" as they do about the dark secrets of the protagonist's individual psyche (83). Through a consideration of the supernatural and the fantastic, female protagonists move from a complacent acceptance of the "real" to an imaginative and self-disclosing creation of the "unreal" (85). Concurrently, the limitations and inconsistencies of certain social structures, especially those prescribing a fixed role for women in Brazil, are brought to light. Commenting on Lya Luft's novel *As parceiras,* Quinlan underscores the sociopolitical relevance of the gothic element: "Defining women's place in society by illustrating past experiences through the device of horror, the protagonist is able to discover herself in nontraditional ways" (82). Quinlan points out that, in reality, Luft's narrative "underexpresses," or recounts offhandedly, the story's fantastic occurrences and ghostly apparitions (in contrast to the traditional gothic model) and in so doing brings the female protagonist's real struggle for self-definition to the forefront (98).

Susan Quinlan and Cristina Ferreira-Pinto's identification of gothic elements in contemporary women's fiction sheds light on one form of feminist discourse that has emerged in response to traditionally male-dominated discourses in Brazilian society. By referencing their studies, however, I do not mean to propose that Lya Luft's novels, or that of any other contemporary author, represents either the emergence of a full-fledged gothic movement, or the resurgence of a deeply rooted gothic literary tradition in Brazilian literature. Nor am I suggesting that the works of nineteenth- and twentieth-century poetry and fiction I have outlined in my overview of the defunto motif constitute a gothic tradition per se. While undoubtedly certain works discussed above fit into this narrative mode, their individual parts do not equal a whole. A more constant preoccupation in Brazilian literature, beginning in the latter half of the nineteenth century and continuing through the twentieth, has been directed at the figure of the dead, independent of any formal gothic trappings. Moreover, it is the personified carnality and the highly accessible nature of the renascent defunto, in many of the texts we have considered so far, that give this figure its unique quality.

Carnival and Literary Ghosts in a Comparative Context

Before examining the specific manifestations of the carnivalesque defunto within modern Brazilian literature, it is important to keep in mind the extent to which this topos overlaps with other literary and cultural traditions, particularly within the Western Hemisphere. It would be misleading to claim, for example, exclusivity or absolute uniqueness for the Brazilian figure of the dead or death, endowed with a ludic, trickster, or carnivalesque quality. Indeed, we can identify within this figure certain thanatological archetypes that are undoubtedly transcultural, such as the image of laughing death, the ghost as trickster, and death as seducer. Carnival traditions intersecting with death and the dead are numerous and include (but of course are not limited to): (1) the performance of symbolic burials, testaments, and reincarnations at Entroido festivals in rural Spain; (2) the pre-Lenten ritualistic death and resurrection of the Dionysian Kouker figure in Bulgaria; (3) the honoring of Supay, the spirit of the underground mines (later diabolized by the Catholic Church) during carnival in Oruro, Bolivia; (4) the omnipresence of Gede, the bawdy, top hat–wearing master of death and libido in Haiti's Vodou-infused carnival celebrations; (5) the "joyful noise" of African American jazz funerals in New Orleans, intended to "cut the body loose" through dance, music, and humor; (6) the festivities and tangible offerings to the dead surrounding Mexico's Día de los Muertos, in which the image of death is routinely treated with humor, disdain, and familiarity; (7) the often erotic Death and the Maiden motif portrayed by northern Renaissance artists such as German painter Hans Baldung Grien and Swiss painter Niklaus Manuel

Deutsch; (8) the bombastic Midnight Robber character in Trinidad's carnival who, through his "robber talk" and macabre garb, promises death and destruction to all.[20]

The Midnight Robber, for example, served as the central masquerade, or *mas,* in *Danse Macabre,* the 1980 carnival band conceived and created by Trinidadian artist Peter Minshall. Worn by carnival king Peter Samuel, this tall, skeletal masquerade of the Midnight Robber underscored death's underlying presence within Trinidadian carnival. The Jamaican writer Nalo Hopkinson similarly employs this figure as a unifying theme in her novel *Midnight Robber* (2000), a hybrid work of science fiction and fantasy in which elements of traditional Caribbean folklore (stick fighting, the *douen,* and the jumbie bird, for example) blend with futuristic elements such as nanotechnology and alternate dimensions. Eshu, the trickster deity of Yoruba mythology, for example, is represented as a holographic source of artificial intelligence, frequently appearing as a dancing skeleton or other guise of death in Hopkinson's utopian/dystopian vision. Other Caribbean novels in which carnival features prominently include Trinidadian Earl Lovelace's *The Dragon Can't Dance* (1979) and Guyanese Wilson Harris's highly imaginative and experimental *Carnival Trilogy,* consisting of *Carnival* (1985), *The Infinite Rehearsal* (1987), and *The Four Banks of the River of Space* (1990). A repeated feature in Harris's trilogy is the spirit of a deceased individual (or universalized, transhistorical "ghost") that serves as the protagonists' guide in a Dantesque spiritual journey and postcolonial revision of history.

In *An Echo in the Bone* by Jamaican playwright Dennis Scott (first produced in 1974), the action revolves around the dual forces of spirit possession and historical (re)possession, as the wayward spirit of a black man named Crew, accused of murdering a white plantation owner, returns during a nine-night ritual and, through the possession of different members of his family and friends, evokes a greater level of historical understanding for the oppression his community has suffered in Jamaica. The laughing, singing, storytelling, sexual comments, drinking, and smoking of marijuana by the living during this midnight wake, depicted in *Echo,* speak to some of the more festive elements of this Jamaican ritual honoring the temporary return of the dead.

Afro-Caribbean and African American spiritual traditions meet at the crossroads in Erna Brodber's *Louisiana* (1994). The novel is set in the 1930s and written in a fragmented, first-person narrative by a young Afro-Caribbean woman from Jamaica named Ella who, after some academic training in the United States, is sent to St. Mary District, near New Orleans, to record the oral history of Sue Anne King, otherwise known as Mammy, one of the community's elderly keepers of knowledge. Ella's interviewee, however, dies midway through the fieldwork; but that does not end the dialogue between the two women, because Ella has been chosen to be the medium for the community's spiritual voices. The narrative left by Ella, in the form of autobiographical field notes and transcribed messages from the dead, recounts her gradual transformation, while living in New Orleans surrounded by Afro-Caribbean immigrants, African American jazz musicians, and other mediums, from rational social scientist to spirit-channeling Hoodoo priestess. Her initial misgivings and fear—"What was my head into?—anthropology of the dead? Celestial ethnography? Crazy"—give way to an acceptance and embracing of her calling as a conduit between not only the living and the dead, the past and the present, but also the deeply enmeshed but often unrecognized cultural ties between Afro-Caribbeans and African Americans (61). While not necessarily carnivalesque, Mammy's spirit is often described as playful, full of "tricks up her sleeve," and as a spirit guide whose messages rarely are delivered "plain and straight" (109).

In fact, Brodber's *Louisiana* is just one example of a number of important works of fiction in which Hoodoo fuses with African American spirituality. In *Faithful Vision: Treatments of the Sacred, Spiritual, and Supernatural in Twentieth-Century African American Fiction,* James W. Coleman argues why spirituality plays such an important role in the lives of people throughout the African diaspora: "I would argue that many—perhaps most—African Americans have faith in the sacred, spiritual, and supernatural because belief is the only thing possible, in the final analysis, in the context of the African cultural background and black American culture and history" (2). In addition to *Louisiana,* Coleman explores the various inflections and tensions between African American Christianity and Vodou/Hoodoo practices and belief systems in novels such as Ellease Southerland's *Let the Lion Eat Straw* (1979), Gloria Naylor's *Mama Day* (1988), and Ishmael Reed's *Mumbo Jumbo* (1972). In a similar vein is the collection *Mojo: Conjure Stories* (2003), edited by Nalo Hopkinson, consisting of short stories tied together not only by the thematic element of mojo (a form of personal magic existing throughout the African diaspora), but also the historical context of racial segregation and oppression (as in the stories "Trial Day" by Tananarive Due and "Daddy Mention and the Monday Skull" by Andy Duncan). Repressed histories of abuse and trauma also emerge as a central theme in the collection, as in "Rosamojo" by Kiini Ibura Salaam, in which a girl uses mojo first to put a hex on her father, who has violated her, and then, after his death, to communicate with his spirit about the possibility of forgiveness.

One example of a story from *Mojo* that engages the intersection of death and the carnivalesque is "Daddy Mention and the Monday Skull." Set in a southern prison where most, if not all, of the prisoners are black, the story tells how one prisoner, Daddy Mention, conjures the powers of the Monday Skull to assist him with his breakout. Based in southern American folklore, Daddy Mention is the emblematic escape-artist convict, while the Monday Skull is the malevolent spirit of a dead man who dwells in the swamps in the form of an alligator. By conjuring and harnessing, to some degree, the powers of the Monday Skull, Daddy Mention gains the temporary gift of exquisite song, which he uses to gain the audience of the state's governor and other white citizens. During the performance, however, Monday Skull's unbridled demonic and transformative force is set loose on the audience, spreading mayhem on all those who come in contact with its song. The lyrics of this song give voice to the lascivious, carnivalesque nature of this trickster spirit:

> Uncle Monday's been dead for many a year
> But he keeps hanging round 'cause he like it here . . .
> Uncle Monday likes to crawl up onto the land
> Go two-legged dancing like a natural man . . .
> Uncle Monday goes a-strolling on the second day
> He'll let you keep your money, steal your soul away . . .
> Uncle Monday has so many teeth sharp as a file
> Can take you seven days just to watch him smile . . .
> . . . .
> His breath blows hot but his blood runs cool
> And his nuts swing low like a Georgia bull . . .
> When Uncle Monday wants a woman he just gives her a shout
> She goes skipping into the swamp and never comes out . . .
> . . . .
> Uncle Monday made a raw head and bloody bones
> Rise up and be a-walkin' just to hear it moan . . .
> Uncle Monday, there's a poor man got no legs
> Yes, I swum up beneath him, cut him down a peg . . .
> Uncle Monday took a trip down to hell and back
> Toting seven governors in a croker sack . . . (15–16)

Embedded in the death-wielding, sexually charged bravado of Uncle Monday's song (much like the Midnight Robber's robber talk) is a subversive, relativizing tone, audacious enough to drag morally and politically corrupt white governors to hell and back. No one is spared Uncle Monday's wrath, however, and, in typically carnivalesque fashion, both the governor and the "poor man" become his victims. The ensuing chaos, upon the release of Uncle Monday's spirit into the realm of the living, underscores the carnivalesque impact of the event, one in which the societal norms are inverted, people's lives take a radically different course, and the world is turned on its head.[21]

Another work of fiction that combines African American music with the supernatural and, as we shall see, shares certain relevant qualities with Jorge Amado's *Dona Flor e seus dois maridos* is Tananarive Due's recent novel *Joplin's Ghost* (2005). Alternating between Los Angeles in the present and St. Louis in the early 1900s, the novel's main narrative thread follows the sudden pop stardom of a young, talented black artist named Phoenix Smalls, who has put aside her musical roots and abilities as a composer in order to succeed within the fast-paced, overly commercialized, and sometimes violent world of Los Angeles's hip-hop music industry. Concurrently, the novel traces the exuberant musical career, and ultimately tragic end, of Scott Joplin, the King of Ragtime, in turn-of-the-century St. Louis. The two plot developments converge after Pheonix visits Joplin's former home, now a museum, and subsequently is visited by and, in some instances, possessed by the ragtime king's spirit. While most of these supernatural occurrences follow the formulaic conventions of popular ghost stories (with apparitional sightings behind windows and doors, the intervention of psychics, and other paranormal activity), the inclusion of particularly erotic dream sequences involving Joplin's ghost endow the spirit world with an unusually transgressive, sensual quality reminiscent of Vadinho's spectral seduction of Dona Flor in Amado's novel.

It is evident that elements of Uncle Monday's trickster persona and encoded discourse (that is, non-European-based) emerge in Joplin's erotic haunting through African American music, Crew's unpredictable yet instructive spirit possession in *Echo in the Bone,* Mammy's cryptic spirit vernacular in *Louisiana,* as well the boastful speech of the Midnight Robber, Trinidadian carnival's bombastic agent of death. It is precisely this connection that interests Henry Louis Gates Jr. in his seminal study *The Signifying Monkey,* in which he uses African mythology to understand the connection between black vernacular tradition and African American literary tradition. In his search for the structures that inform and organize these traditions, Gates points to two trickster figures—Esu-Elegbara, of Yoruba mythology, and the Signifying Monkey—within African American culture:

> At first glance, these two tricksters would seem to have little in common. Esu, both a trickster and the messenger of the gods, figures prominently in the mythologies of Yoruba cultures found in Nigeria, Benin, Brazil, Cuba, and Haiti, among others. The Signifying Monkey, it seems, is distinctly Afro-American. Nevertheless, the central place of both figures in their traditions is determined by their curious tendency to reflect on the uses of formal language. The theory of Signifyin(g) arises from these moments of self-reflexiveness.
>
> Whereas Esu serves as a figure for the nature and function of interpretation and double-voiced utterance, the Signifying Monkey serves as the figure-of-figures, as the trope in which are encoded several other peculiarly black rhetorical tropes. . . . Together, the two tricksters articulate the black tradition's theory of its literature. (xxi)

Brazilian Carnival and the Dialectics of Malandragem

The trickster is an important component of the Brazilian carnivalesque defunto's personality as well, a parallel that suggests possible cultural and aesthetic affinities with a wider African diasporic expression (as is clearly the case in Amado's fiction), or perhaps the broader, less easily traceable, cultural currency of Brazil's own streetwise trickster, the *malandro,* or rogue, who, as has been argued, is the central protagonist in Brazilian carnival.[22] The malandro's sphere of activity in Brazilian society oscillates between the fringes of work, leisure, crime, and a bohemian lifestyle, and it is the malandro's guile and adaptability that enables him to resist full integration into any particular social realm. The malandro's ethos of *malandragem* is the focus of an essay, "Dialectic of Malandroism," by noted Brazilian critic Antonio Candido, who identifies it as a fundamental operating principle in the mid-nineteenth-century Brazilian novel *Memórias de um sargento de milícias* [Memoirs of a Militia Sergeant] (1852) by Manuel Antônio de Almeida and, by extension, within Brazilian society as a whole. According to Candido, the malandro operates between two distinct, yet ultimately permeable, social spheres—the world of order (work, family, civic, and religious authority, and financial and social stability) and the world of disorder (vagrancy, popular culture, festivities, and behavior otherwise deemed immoral)—and, in so doing, exposes the frequently comic slippage of hierarchical forms into the realm of disorder, and vice versa. The flexibility inherent in these social (and corresponding moral) spheres, in the case of Brazil, is compared with American society's puritanical foundation, with its rigidly demarcated social, religious, racial, and moral spheres, as expressed most poignantly in Nathaniel Hawthorne's *Scarlet Letter* and the Salem witch trials (Candido, 99).

Moreover, Candido stresses that the malandro in Almeida's novel springs less from erudite sources, such as the European picaresque tradition, than it does from both the universal trickster archetype and Brazilian popular culture (83). He also adheres to the notion of the malandragem dialectic (with its malandro antihero) forming part of a lineage unique to the formation of Brazilian literature, one that can be traced from Almeida's novel to modernist works such as *Serafim Ponte Grande* (1933) by Oswald de Andrade and, most emblematically, *Macunaíma* (1928) by Mário de Andrade. In this respect, Candido agrees with the statement of Walnice Nogueira Galvão, which he quotes in his essay: "It is in this mode that Manuel Antônio de Almeida described the character Leonardo, which results in a *hero without any character,* or better, one who represents the fundamental traits of the stereotype of the Brazilian. Manuel Antônio de Almeida is the first to fix in literature the national character of the Brazilian, which then will have a long life in our literature . . . I believe that we meet in Leonardo the ancestor of *Macunaíma*" (102; emphasis in original).

To this deep tradition within Brazilian literature of the trickster or antihero (or both), who is simultaneously pushing the boundaries of order and disorder and promoting moral indeterminacy, one could arguably add Machado de Assis's Brás Cubas, João Grilo in Ariano Suassuna's play *Auto de compedecida,* Vadinho and Quincas Berro Dágua in Jorge Amado's novels, Luis Galvez in Márcio Souza's *Galvez, imperador de Acre,* Max in Chico Buarque de Hollanda's *Ópera do ma-*

landro, and even, to some degree, Riobaldo in Guimarães Rosa's *Grande sertão: Veredas.* Furthermore, carnivalization, masked characterizations, and inverted realities serve as key narrative features in an even broader range of Brazilian literature by authors such as João do Rio, Augusto dos Anjos, Manuel Bandeira, Aníbal Machado, Lima Barreto, Roberto Drummond, Rubem Fonseca, Moacyr Scliar, Lygia Fagundes Telles, Silviano Santiago, João Ubaldo Ribeiro, and Sônia Coutinho, to name only a few.[23] In his article concerning the use of parody and carnivalization in Souza's *Galvez, O Imperador de Acre,* Luiz F. Valente echoes Candido's and Galvão's assertion of Brazilian fiction's pervasive carnivalesque tradition:

> In bringing back laughter to contemporary literature, Márcio Souza is upholding a truly national trait: the capability Brazilians have always had of laughing at themselves, that is, the paradoxical Brazilian ability of talking about serious issues in an outwardly non-serious way. But, more importantly, he is restoring a truly national literary tradition, which lay seemingly dormant in the dark years of the late 1960's and the 1970's: the carnivalesque tradition that is as old as Brazilian literature itself, going all the way back to Gregório de Matos and Manuel Antônio de Almeida, and culminating in Oswald de Andrade. ("Parody," 792)

It is the anthropologist Roberto DaMatta who has given the most systematic attention to the connections between carnival and malandragem in Brazilian society. Using terms very much in tune with Antonio Candido's "Dialectic of Malandroism," DaMatta differentiates between two broad social spheres in Brazil: the *casa* [home], where personal relations dominate, and the *rua* [street], where impersonal laws and institutions preside. The malandro, however, oscillates between the two spheres and in fact frequently applies the logic of one in the context of the other. It is the malandro's personal connections, for example, that enable this social actor to circumvent an impersonal law, when necessary. The malandro's primary tool for social navigation is the *jeitinho,* the improvised, highly personal, intermediary solution residing halfway between "yes, you may" and "no, you may not" (*O que faz,* 100). The malandro, according to DaMatta, is the paradigmatic figure, or "marginal hero," of carnival because of his ability to operate outside the laws that normally govern social structures (*Carnivals,* 208–9).[24]

Carnival, with its prevailing ethos of malandragem, therefore, is more than a tangential aspect of Brazilian social identity, as DaMatta explains: "We know that in the case of Brazil such a feeling of singularity is deeply marked by Carnival as a moment when we can make sense of a series of actions, attitudes, and relations that are perceived and experienced as creating and building not just a mere festival, but our very heart. Carnival, then, is one of those perpetual institutions that has enabled Brazilians to sense and feel (more than abstractly conceive) their specific continuity as a distinct social and political entity through and over time" (*Carnivals,* 15).

Any discussion of national traits or broad social modes of living runs the risk of upholding certain essentialist myths regarding national identity that, in turn, can form part of an official discourse intended for both internal and external consumption. In *Third World Literary Fortunes: Brazilian Culture and its International Reception,* for example, Piers Armstrong argues that the discourse and image-making, by Brazilian socioanthropologists and government officials, surrounding carnival, and particularly Rio de Janeiro's manifestation of this event, have eclipsed other social traditions, differences, and artistic forms within Brazil, resulting in "the conventional wisdom that Brazil can be represented as a happy, racially democratic tropical town during carnaval" (202). He offers, as a counterpoint to this, the Bahian carnival, as more participatory and sociopolitically relevant in a postmodern, globalized world. To the extent that this is true (no one would argue that Rio's carnival has not become highly commercialized and, as a result, drained to some degree of its sociopolitical edge), it is also debatable whether Bahian carnival remains on the margins of cultural production within, or even beyond, Brazil. Significantly, the next largest, and highly recognized, carnival tradition in Brazil takes place in the neighboring cities of Recife and Olinda in the state of Pernambuco, a tradition that, for the most part, shares Bahia's participatory ethos. And, according to Bakhtin, as well as DaMatta, it is the communal, dialogic aspect of this social ritual that is at the heart of carnival. In this sense, Bahia's participatory ethos has, for some time now, permeated carnival festivities throughout Brazil, even before the first *blocos* and *trio-elétricos* appeared in Salvador. Indeed, according to DaMatta, what distinguishes Brazil's carnival (with few exceptions) is its refusal to be localized in one area, one city, or social sphere (*Carnivals,* 118). A recognition of this national scope does not, by any means, obscure the many regional expressions of carnival in Brazil. On the contrary, the multitude and variety of regional carnivalesque "dialects" confirm the deep-felt connection that Brazilian society, in all its plurality, has with this complex ritual. I have argued here, in chorus with Candido, Galvão, Valente, DaMatta, and others, that this deep-felt connection has found fertile ground within nineteenth- and twentieth-century Brazilian literature, even when those narratives concern sociopolitical and historical issues that are profoundly serious.

Consequently, Armstrong's statement that "it is significant that Brazilian literature does not reflect the steady rise of carnival as a cultural icon" seems peculiar, unless he is using the terms *carnival* and *icon* in a very restrictive, literal sense, rather than as a concept that broadly encompasses parody, ambiguity, the seriocomic, communal participation, dialogism, trickster discourse and characterizations, transgression, mocking laughter, erotic celebration, subversion, among other elements (12). David Jackson's comment, for example, that the Brazilian short story is characterized by its "plasticity, adaptation, syncretism, and movement" is a reflection of traits he sees as significant within Brazilian society as a whole (*Oxford,* 3). The twentieth-century literary and ideological paradigm for this syncretic tendency stems, he says, from Oswald de Andrade's "Cannibal Manifesto" (1928), which proclaimed a strategy "of incorporating the alien with the indigenous, the cooked with the raw, while disguising resistance or converting aggression into play" allowing for, like the *jeitinho,* "a creative synthesis and a turning of Western tables" (*Oxford,* 11). Another, more recent theoretical articulation of Brazilian literature's syncretic dynamic is, as Jackson points out, Silviano Santiago's notion of "the space in-between," a hybrid zone in which an intersection of dominator and dominated, European and local, discourses emerge and are tested, subverted, and rearranged (10). Within this logic, Macunaíma's journey represents Brazil's original journey of discovery in reverse—from the interior to the sea (Santiago, *Space,* 91).

In a more directly comparative mode, Judith A. Payne and Earl E. Fitz propose that Brazil's relative sociopolitical unity, in contrast to Spanish America's political fragmentation during the nineteenth century, enabled Brazilian literature to evolve in a more cohesive fashion and, therefore, to develop a stronger tradition of iconoclastic, experimental expression early on. They assert that Machado de Assis's groundbreaking use of metafiction, intertextuality, unreliable narration, gender deconstruction, as well as other Brazilian examples of atypically self-conscious narration in the latter half of the nineteenth century, set in motion a cultivation of ontological, aesthetic, and especially gender related "ambiguity" in Brazilian literature (2–3).[25] As we have seen, the revenant represents perhaps the literary figure par excellence of ambiguity. For this reason, a comparative consideration of the literary ghost, particularly in light of Brazilian literature's cultivation of the carnivalesque and malandragem, brings into focus some of the distinctive ways that Brazilian and Spanish American literary traditions have grappled with, expressed, or negated forms of ambiguity.

An "Ancestral Impulse" and "American Books of the Dead"

In *The Usable Past,* Lois Parkinson Zamora begins her discussion of ghostly apparitions in the literature of the Americas (both North and South) by quoting Flannery O'Connor: "Ghosts can be very fierce and instructive" (Zamora, 76). With the intention, then, of exploring what it is that ghosts can teach us, as readers, Zamora then outlines the full semantic and functional richness of this figure:

> Ghosts in American literature may serve as carriers of metaphysical truths, as visible or audible signs of atemporal, transhistorical Spirit. Or, they may carry historical burdens of tradition and collective memory: ghosts often act as correctives to the insularities of individuality, as links to lost families and communities, or as reminders of communal crimes, crises, and cruelties. They may suggest displacement and alienation or, alternatively, reunion and communion. . . . They may signal primal and primordial experience, the return of the repressed, or the externalization of internalized terrors. They are always double (here and not) and often duplicitous (where?). They mirror, complement, recover, supplant, cancel, and complete. Which is to say that literary ghosts are deeply metaphoric. They bring absence into presence, maintaining at once the "is" and the "is not" of metaphoric truth. (76–77)

Zamora then traces the multifarious trope of the ghost (in a very broad sense) through the works of Jorge Luis Borges, Gabriel García Márquez, Isabel Allende, Carlos Fuentes, Juan Rulfo, and Elena Garro, as well as North American writers such as Nathaniel Hawthorne, William Faulkner, Toni Morrison, and the Texan writer William Goyen, to name a few. She contrasts, for example, the "culturally specific" and historically repeating ghosts in Márquez's fiction (such as the successive José Arcadios and Aurelianos, as well as Melquíades's ghost in *Cien años de soledad*) with the universalizing and archetypal "wraiths" (ones that embody "ideas, figures of philosophy or dream") expressed by Borges in his short stories "La muerte y la brújula" [Death and the Compass], "Las ruinas circulares" [The Circular Ruins], and "La otra muerte" [The Other Death] (81–84). To these examples we could add his "El Immortal" [The Immortal], "Diálogo de muertos" [Dialogue between Dead Men], and "His End and His Beginning," as stories by Borges in which the boundaries of death and the dream state are blurred, leaving the protagonist drifting from one realm to the other.

The predominant trait identified by Zamora in twentieth-century Spanish American literary ghosts, however, is what she describes as an "ancestral impulse" that seeks to recover lost, sacrificed, or oppressed oral/visual narratives, through a literary mode that transcends realism (123). Novels and short stories of this sort, which excavate ancestral presences and privilege local cultural knowledge over European sources, constitute for Zamora "American books of the dead, necrogeographies of the buried traces of indigenous cultural identity in a shared region of America" (79). To exemplify this idea, Zamora points to two Mexican novels in which the collective voices of the dead, inhabitants of towns long since deceased, serve as narrator—Elena Garro's *Los recuerdos del porvenir* [Recollections of Things to Come] (1963), set during the postrevolutionary confusion of the Cristero rebellion in southern Mexico, and Juan Rulfo's *Pedro Páramo* (1955) set in Comala, a ghost town frozen in time, ostensibly in the Jalisco region of Mexico, but in fact more mythically situated, as Zamora proposes, at the intersection of "Mexican Catholic and indigenous afterworlds" (100–101).

Mexican society has cultivated a deep and frequently festive relationship with the idea and figure of death that resonates with Brazil's own thanocratic traditions. The prominence of Mexico's Day of the Dead, with its profusion of *ofrendas* [offerings], *calaveras* [candy skulls], public celebration of the deceased, and often ironic domestication of death is a well-recognized aspect of Mexican cultural identity. The Mexican writer and poet most responsible for articulating the Mexican connection to death, even in modern times, is Octavio Paz, who, in his essay "The Day of the Dead" in *The Labyrinth of Solitude* (1950), states: "The Mexican . . . is familiar with death, jokes about it, caresses it, sleeps with it, celebrates it; it is one of his favourite toys and his most steadfast love" (49). Claudio Lomnitz, in his comprehensive *Death and the Idea of Mexico* argues that "the three great totems of Mexican national history" are "Guadalupe, (Benito) Juárez, and the playful skeleton" (43). According to Lomnitz, Mexico's intimate, ironic, and often lighthearted relationship to, and representation of, death contrasts sharply with other cases of a nationalized death, such as nineteenth-century Russia's romantic and tragic "sublimation of suffering," and late-imperial Japan's "fearlessness before death," stemming as much from Buddhist conceptions of life's brevity as from the country's militarism at the time (20). Instead, the smiling face of death has become a national symbol in Mexico, one that has not only withstood modernity's broad denial of death, but has become a common feature of everyday life there. Lomnitz traces the origins of this "nationalization of a playful familiarity with and proximity to Death itself" as far back as pre-Columbian Mesoamerican cosmology (with regard to death, the afterlife, and mortuary rituals), through the devastating holocaust of sixteenth-century Spanish conquest and the subsequent colonial administration of death by both church and state, to the impact of the Mexican Revolution (1910–20) and the modernist movement on the cultivation of a broad, national familiarity with death (36). Paradoxically, macabre imagery and Day of the Dead festivities, celebrated in both traditional rural settings as well as the paseos of urban centers, flourished during the nineteenth century, precisely when enlightened rationalists in Mexico (as in Brazil) were trying to rid the country of its "backwardness" and "superstition" (283). As Lomnitz observes, "Baroque Catholicism proved to be a tar baby for Mexican rationalists: the more they struggled against it, the more they were mired in it" (291).

Equally fascinating are the ways in which death became a template for Mexican modernist strategies of identification and cultural pride. Diego Rivera's mural *Day of the Dead—City Fiesta,* at the Ministry of Education in Mexico City, depicting a bustling urban fiesta in which every segment of Mexican society—the worker, peasant, revolutionary soldier, priest, student, capitalist, and the throng of popular masses—is represented as an active participant in the Day of the Dead, thereby suggesting a form of "national reconciliation in death" (Lomnitz, 46). Similarly, the mestizo illustrator José Guadalupe Posada's satirical engravings of the Mexican upper class, in the guise of skeletons, during the progress-driven reign of Porfirio Díaz of the late nineteenth and early twentieth centuries, resonated with the modernists' affirmation of cultural *mestizaje*. Rivera's mural and the modernists' rediscovery (along with French artist Jean Charlot) of Posada's illustrations acknowledged the viability of a Mexican "social pact," albeit an uneasy one shaped by cyclical historical conflict. Inherent in this pact, signed by death, was also the possibility of temporal and ethnic reconciliation, as Lomnitz indicates: "Thus Mexican attitudes toward death, as they are instantiated in the Days of the Dead, came to be paradigmatic example not only of cultural *mestizaje* and its revolutionary potential but also the formula that would give voice to Mexico's singularity by way of an artistic expression that fused pre-Columbian and popular elements" (50).

It is the deadly weight of the past, and the impossibility of the future, that most characterizes Juan Rulfo's introspective *Pedro Páramo*. Comala is haunted not only by the lingering voices of the dead, but also by what Lomnitz calls "negative reciprocity," that is, a community founded on rape, murder, illegitimacy, and patriarchal authoritarianism, as embodied by the cacique Pedro Páramo (407). The return of Páramo's son, Juan Preciado, to Comala does not, in fact, bring reconciliation and forgiveness but rather further incorporation into the realm of the dead, frozen in time. Death does not bring about change in Comala. Rather, the novel suggests that there are forces from Mexico's past, such as its violent origins, religious conservatism, and rural patriarchy, that continue to hold a grip on the present.[26] The murmurs of the dead that echo throughout Comala, as if rising from the ground itself (the word *páramo* refers to bleak highland terrain), are, to use Zamora's terminology, the subterranean traces of "ancestral presences" that bring with them "buried belief systems that still resonate in contemporary culture" (Zamora, 125).

Indeed, the list provided by Zamora of Boom and post-Boom Latin American writers whose work foregrounds "ancestral apparitions" and disinterred memories of "what the West sacrificed in other cultures" (quoting Fuentes) is particularly long and includes Miguel Angel Asturias, Alejo Carpentier, José María Arguedas, Rosario Castellanos, Julio Cortázar, Carlos Fuentes, Luisa Valenzuela, Eduardo Galeano, Mario Vargas Llosa, and Isabel Allende.[27] Zamora also acknowledges those U.S. "minority" writers who similarly "give the earth voice" and listen to its indigenous, ancestral presences, namely, William Goyen in his collection of short stories *Ghost and Flesh* (1952), Leslie Marmon Silko in her novel *Ceremony* (1977), Susan Power's novel *The Grass Dancer* (1994), Louise Erdrich's novel *Tracks* (1988), among others.

It would undoubtedly be an exaggeration to claim that death in Brazil enjoys the same degree of prestige that it does in Mexico. The dancing skeleton and laughing skull, personifications of an ironic, domesticated death, do not appear in Brazil, as they do in Mexico, where death has become a national sign. If we recall, Roberto DaMatta observes that Brazilians tend to cultivate strong, personal relations more with the dead than with death per se, although still not to the degree that Mexicans have celebrated this relationship. In fact, the social ritual in Brazil that most approximates Mexico's Día de los Muertos, in terms of its national scope and cultural currency, is arguably carnival. Indeed, it is the national vitality of carnival that partly explains why the defunto so frequently appears in Dionysian garb in Brazilian literature.

Moreover, the respective colonial endeavors of Spain and Portugal in the New World are characterized by vastly different historical scenarios, circumstances, and approaches, despite their many parallels. To use Mexico as a point of comparison, important differences emerge with regard to the nature of the indigenous society conquered and assimilated (the highly developed civilizations of the Mayas and Aztecs in and around Mexico, in contrast to Brazil's partially sedentary and dispersed Tupi tribal groups and other diverse nomadic peoples); the respective systems of forced labor (Brazil's importation of large numbers of African slaves versus the Spanish use of forced indigenous labor through its *encomienda* system); and the significantly more centralized, structured colonial model employed by the Spanish (intended to replicate institutional forms of church and state in the New World), in contrast to Portugal's more decentralized colonial approach, characterized by immediate gains, an absentee crown, and a particularly weak presence of church hierarchy within the Brazilian colony. This last factor is widely recognized as having contributed to the flourishing of unorthodox religious practices and values in colonial Brazil. One might speculate that the relative permeability of Brazilian religiosity, plus the contribution of African cosmologies, during colonial times would create the kind of conditions within which the carnivalesque defunto might appear as a modern literary manifestation of a colonial vestige.[28]

However, it would seem more likely, or at least more easily traceable, to return to the fundamental differences, in the case of Brazil and Mexico, between the most important collective social rituals respectively in each society. Whereas for Brazilians carnival signifies a temporary moment of Dionysian subversion, a final indulgence of the flesh and libido, the festive celebrations of Mexico's Day of the Dead are endowed with a very specific restorative, totemic (rather than subversive) purpose, namely the reunion of the living with the dead, the distribution of offerings, and the restoration of communal ties and familial, national, and cultural allegiances. Whereas Brazilian carnival is intended, in theory, to turn the world on its head and imagine alternative social relations, the Day of the Dead reinforces ancestral relations and the reuniting of two worlds (that of the living and the dead) through celebration.

Latin American Literature and the Carnivalesque

To the extent that other parts of Spanish America (not including those Caribbean cultures whose histories of African slavery run more parallel to Brazil's) have developed diverse but comparable strategies and rituals for restoring and celebrating ties with their indigenous heritage, it is not surprising then that an "ancestral impulse" stands out as a salient feature of the literary ghost within these societies as well. Zamora's omission of Brazilian narratives within her "Latin American" framework for discussing the ghost, however, excludes a somewhat diverging manifestation of this literary trope—the carnivalesque revenant, with its unbridled laughter, playful irreverence, and expressions of sensuality. Indeed, many of the defining qualities of the Brazilian apparitions discussed in the following chapters—Brás Cubas's whimsical narrative and moral ambiguity, Vadinho's malandro obscenity, Quincas's bohemian carnality, and the subversive, mocking discourse of Verissimo's protesting defuntos—are conspicuously absent in the Spanish American variant of the literary ghost.

This is not to suggest that the carnivalesque does not appear in twentieth-century Spanish American fiction. David K. Danow, for example, in *The Spirit of Carnival,* explores precisely the varied and numerous manifestations of the carnivalesque and the grotesque in magical realist works from Spanish America, as well as in fantastic literature written in response to the Holocaust during World War II. As such, Danow's study is attuned to both the "bright, life-affirming, magical side" of the carnivalesque mode, as well as "its dark, death-embracing, horrific aspect" (5). While generally attributing the former to Latin American works and the latter to Holocaust literature, Danow recognizes, for example, the coexistence of both "carnival heaven" and "carnival hell" (per Bakhtin's distinction) in a number of Spanish American magical realist works (6). A quintessential example of this confluence of carnival eros and thanatos occurs in García Márquez's *Cien años de soledad* during a scene of "bloody carnival," quoted by Danow:

> Innocent of the tragedy that threatened it, the town poured into the main square in a noisy explosion of merriment. The carnival had reached its highest level of madness. . . . Suddenly, during the paroxysm of the celebration someone broke the delicate balance. . . . The rifle shots drowned out the splendor of the fireworks and the cries of terror drowned out the music and joy turned into panic . . . and there were

> many dead and wounded lying on the square: nine clowns, four Columbines, seventeen playing-card kings, one devil, three minstrels, two peers of France, and three Japanese empresses. (8)

Carnival appears as a "theater of cruelty" with even more force in García Márquez's novel *El otoño del patriarca* [The Autumn of the Patriarch] (1975), in which the protagonist, a ruthless dictator whose power frequently extends into the supernatural, embodies murderous despotism in Latin American history (17). The country has been transformed into "a realm of doom" by its patriarch's brutal and magical forms of oppression, a place where, as Danow observes, even death is carnivalized when the general's double is assassinated and his own funeral is staged, "amidst the delirious howls and the roar of fireworks celebrating the carnival of my death" (Danow, 47–48). Another carnivalesque dictator who, like a specter, defies normal chronology is Paraguay's nineteenth-century Eternal Dictator, José Gaspar Rodríguez de Francia, the loquacious narrator in Augusto Roa Bastos's *Yo, el Supremo* [I, the Supreme] (1974). Similarly, death is made into a mockery in the novel's opening pages when an anonymously posted document nailed to the door of a church announces, in the feigned words of El Supremo himself, that upon his death his decapitated head will be held on public display, to the ringing of church bells and the hanging of all his regime's servants. The document's mocking tone is, in fact, in tune with El Supremo's own whimsical repression and timeless grandiosity. Another Spanish American work of fiction described by Danow as a "veritable textbook of the carnivalesque" is the Guatemalan Miguel Angel Asturias's *Mulata* (1963), a novel infused with "grotesque laughter" and an assortment of devils, demons, ghosts, sorcerers, and other supernatural creatures (22). The novel's extravagant use of fantasy is, however, grounded in Guatemalan myth and folklore and is, in this sense, driven by a similar "ancestral impulse" that Zamora identifies in *Pedro Páramo* and other Latin American narratives that feature literary ghosts.[29]

A comparative perspective also reveals that Brazilian literature, most significantly in the case of Brás Cubas, is not unique within Latin America in its use of deceased narration as a rhetorical device. In fact, Sandra Messinger Cypress in her dissertation, "The Dead Narrator in Modern Latin American Prose Fiction" (1968), calls attention to a fairly significant range of Latin American writers and works that, beside Machado de Assis and *Memórias póstumas,* utilize posthumous narration, albeit in diverse manifestations. Examples of works narrated by a highly "self-conscious narrator," aware of both his own deceased state and narrative/literary voice, include the short story "El fusilado" [The Firing-Squad Victim] by the Mexican José Vasconcelos, and Machado's *Memórias póstumas* (23). Recognition of deceased narration comes to the reader of "El fusilado" only halfway through the story as it becomes evident that the man "about" to be executed by a firing squad is, in fact, recounting his past experience with the moment of death. The second category of deceased narration outlined by Cypress involves those prose works in which the narrator addresses the reader directly and from a posthumous position, but without any claim to the act of writing (86). These works include the short story "El condenado" [The Condemned Man] (1951) and the novels *Anticipación a la muerte* [Anticipation of Death] (1939) and *La muerte de Pamilo* [The Death of Pamilo] (1964) by Mexican authors Juan José Arreola, José Rubén Romero, and Ernesto Ramos Meza, respectively; the short story "El espectro" [The Specter] (1921) by the Uruguayan Horacio Quiroga; and *Un muerto de mal criterio* [A Dead Man of Bad Judgment] (1926) by the Chilean Jenaro Prieto. Finally, Cypress addresses a third category in which deceased narration occurs not as a direct conversation with the reader but as part of a dialogue with the narrator's own fictive world (166). Examples of this narrative voice (or voices) include Quiroga's short story "Más Allá" [Further On] (1935), Rulfo's *Pedro Páramo,* the Uruguayan Enrique Amorim's novel *La desembocadura* [The Opening] (1958), and the Chilean María Luisa Bombal's *La amortajada* [The Shrouded Woman] (1938).

Despite the multitude of narrative positions, degrees of self-consciousness, thematic insights, and sociohistorical commentaries expressed by the many Spanish American deceased narrators examined by Cypress, it is notable that none possess the highly ironic, unreliable, Menippean whimsy of their Brazilian counterpart, Brás Cubas. In short, what is missing is the subversive, mocking, trickster element of the carnivalesque defunto. Moreover, the carnivalesque defunto dissolves the notion of a dichotomy between carnival heaven and hell by fusing the two poles through a protagonist-narrator that is both life affirming and death embracing.

The comparative framework outlined in this section is not intended to assert the total absence of a carnivalized literary ghost in the Spanish American tradition. It more than likely exists or, as the examples given above allude to, is expressed partially. The point is that this figure does not emerge as a recurring, predominant topos the way it does in modern Brazilian fiction. While the reasons for this difference may be difficult to identify with any absolute certainty, I have underscored the relative weight attributed to carnival (and its ethos of malandragem) in Brazilian culture, both as a national sign and ritual and as an identifying literary mode characterized by playful subversion, syncretic ambiguity, and a dialectic of malandragem. In contrast to this mode, modern Spanish American literature is characterized by a pertinacious and often consuming "ancestral impulse" that requires a creative reassessment of historical awareness, especially when confronted with the figure of the literary ghost.

Piers Armstrong makes some interesting comparative observations that shed further light upon this important distinction. He argues that Brazilian modernism, following the initial "revolutionary" rupture of the Week of Modern Art, is noteworthy for its "spirit of subjective individualism," as exemplified by Clarice Lispector, João Guimarães Rosa, João Cabral de Melo Neto, and Carlos Drummond de Andrade, among other modern Brazilian writers (with some obvious exceptions such as Jorge Amado) for whom political convictions were secondary to their aesthetic goals (21). In contrast to this trend, Armstrong points to Spanish American modernism's "strong tendency of essentialism," (particularly during the Boom years but also dating as far back as the Nicaraguan Rubén Darío's turn-of-the-century innovations) characterized paradoxically by a greater cohesion among modernist intellectuals from various nations, a more urgent sense of political purpose, and "above all by the sense of an historic mission to rewrite history" (21).[30] This overarching ethos of political conscientization in Spanish American *modernismo* and Boom writers stems from the region's history of "revolutionary moments," including the nineteenth century independence movements and Simón Bolivar's dream of a pan-Hispanic republic, the Mexican Revolution, the Mexican-American War, the Spanish-American War, the Cuban Revolution, the oscillation between socialist experiments and brutal authoritarian regimes, and the post–World War II resistance to neoimperialist forces.[31] One of the outcomes of these historical experiences is what Armstrong describes as a distinctive preoccupation among Boom writers to portray "a polarized Utopian-dystopian duality in the perception of Latin America" (38).

Most important for our understanding of the underlying differences between the Brazilian carnivalesque defunto and the Spanish American "ancestral apparitions" is Armstrong's subsequent observation that, given these historical circumstances (to which we may add the initial destruction and fragmentation of highly developed indigenous civilizations during the Spanish *conquista*): "the Spanish American literary discourse of Latin American identity is consistently one of trauma" (40). Notwithstanding notable exceptions, such as Euclides da Cunha's *Os sertões,* Graciliano Ramos's *Vidas secas,* and a number of historical novels of social protest following the 1964 military coup, it would appear true that this sense of acute, historical trauma is "conspicuously absent in the greater part of Brazilian writers" (40), relative to their Spanish American counterparts.[32] In this regard, the Spanish American concern with ancestral apparitions shares more in common with works such as Toni Morrison's *Beloved,* Louise Erdrich's *Tracks,* or Cristina García's *Dreaming in Cuban*—ethnic literature in the United States in which the haunting figure of the ghost signals a collective history of oppression, marginalization, and unresolved trauma.[33] The same may be said for much of the Afro-Caribbean and African American literature considered in the first part of this comparative discussion. It is clear, for example, in the aforementioned works by Dennis Scott, Andy Duncan, Erna Brodber, and Tananarive Due that the community's ancestral apparitions extend far back in time and are associated with the trauma and oppression of a specific ethnic or racial group. As we shall see, a similar specificity, at least with regard to ethnicity, marginalization, and traumatic origins, cannot be claimed in the case of the Brazilian carnivalesque defunto. At the same time, the strong tradition of the Eshu/trickster figure in Afro-diasporic literature, as demonstrated by Gates, presents compelling overlapping parallels with the Brazilian malandro.

The relatively greater focus of Spanish American literary discourse on ancestral trauma has, I believe, an important repercussion on both the mode and function of their literary ghosts. Saddled with the twin burdens of signaling the pain of past, historical traumas and of evoking the ancestral presence of buried indigenous, mythic voices, playfulness is largely emptied from the figure of the Spanish American literary ghost. In other words, the unencumbered Dionysian spirit finds little space or reception within this dual burden. As we shall see, it is precisely this spirit of carnival subversion that serves as the modus operandi of the deceased reveler in modern Brazilian fiction.

Chapter 3

The Carnivalesque Defunto in Memórias póstumas de Brás Cubas

> Vi-a, pela primeira vez, no Rossio Grande, na noite das luminárias, logo que constou a declaração da independência, uma festa de primavera, um amanhecer da alma pública. Éramos dous rapazes, o povo e eu; vínhamos da infância, com todos os arrebatamentos da juventude.
>
> [I saw her for the first time on the Rossio Grande, the night of fireworks celebrating the declaration of independence, a springtime festival, the dawn of the public soul. We were a couple of youths, the people and I. We were coming out of childhood with all the ecstasy of youth.]
>
> Onde estão elas, as flores de antanho? Uma tarde, após algumas semanas de gestação, esboroou-se todo o edifício das minhas quimeras paternais.
>
> [Where are they, the flowers of yesteryear? One afternoon, after a few weeks of gestation, the whole structure of my paternal dreams crumbled.]
>
> —Machado de Assis, *Brás Cubas*

The Work of a Dead Man . . .

IN 1880, WHEN Joaquim Maria Machado de Assis wrote his fifth novel, *Memórias póstumas de Brás Cubas,* Brazil was, to borrow Gayatri Spivak's expression, "learning to live at the seam of the past and the present."[1] The transition to a republican form of government, following nearly sixty years of a constitutional monarchy, loomed close on the horizon. Six years earlier, the Brazilian emperor Pedro II dictated the first message by telegraph from Brazil to Europe. This achievement constituted a kind of technological manifestation of the symbolic connection that existed between Brazil's capital city, Rio de Janeiro, and the cultural centers of Europe. It was a time, for example, when pianos were being imported in great numbers from France and England for the enjoyment of the Carioca elite.

Yet it was this same social class that clung stubbornly to a slave-based economy, the last of its kind in the Western Hemisphere. The disjointedness of a society that professed the ideals of enlightenment and liberalism, but whose way of life depended largely on slave labor was not lost on Machado de Assis. Perhaps more so than any author of his era, Machado de Assis delved deeply into the underlying incongruences of a Brazilian elite caught in the liminal state of a developing modern nation with an unresolved colonial past.

Nearly all Machado's bourgeois characters, to some degree, germinate from the disjointedness of this particular social milieu, but none more than Brás Cubas. A self-professed dilettante, Brás Cubas embraces the privileges bestowed on a slaveholding class accustomed to a maximum of social advancement with a minimum of actual effort expended. Consequently, he also embodies the moral pitfalls of an elite whose ideological bearings were determined by its desire for cultural ornamentation and social recognition. As many of Machado's critics have pointed out, Brás Cubas's narrative tone is steeped in the impertinence of the class from which the narrator springs, all the more so because he has had the audacity to return from the grave to compose his memoirs. For the reader discovers at the outset of the novel that Brás Cubas's memoirs are posthumous in the literal sense of the word. The narrator is indeed dead, but rather than laying his soul to rest, Machado has Brás Cubas appear to us as a restless soul anxious to reconstruct his life's story.

The short chapters that make up *Memórias póstumas* were published originally in the literary periodical *Revista brasileira* in 1880 as a series of individual vignettes.[2] A year later it was published in its entirety as a novel. For his contemporaries, however, the work was radically unnovelesque. Although the staccato chapters were a trademark of Machado's style, the level of digression and circuitous narration broke down all conventions of common literary sensibility in Brazil. Alternating between memorialist reflections and philosophical excursions, the story meanders in a seemingly purposeless way that may best be described as antinarrative.[3] Caught between the ebb of Brás Cubas's autobiography and the flow of his witticisms, the reader finds precious little narrative footing. It is no wonder that *Memórias* has been described as the watershed in Brazilian literature between plot-driven fiction and poetic fiction (Teixeira, 93).

The story begins at the end, with Brás Cubas satirically narrating his own funeral, attended by only eleven friends on a drizzly afternoon. He can hardly conceal his amusement when a "friend" eulogizes that nature is weeping over the loss of one of humanity's finest characters. Shortly thereafter, we learn how Brás Cubas died. Obsessed with the idea of inventing an antihypochondriacal poultice aimed at curing humanity of its melancholy, and driven by a final quest for personal glory, Brás Cubas ultimately neglects his own health and dies after a bout with pneumonia brought on by a "strong draft." If his death seems pointless, ironically so is the "remedy" which indirectly caused it, and, as we soon discover, both are reflections of a life remarkable for its futility. During the course of his narrative (which extends from his birth in 1805 to his death in 1869), we learn of his amorous escapades during adolescence, his life as a bachelor while attending university in Portugal, an ill-fated maneuver by his father to simultaneously furnish his son with a bride and a prestigious political appointment, a brief stint into oppositional journalism, and a long, drawn-out love affair with a married woman named Virgília. By the time Brás Cubas dies, so have most of the people who exerted any influence on his life.

Ultimately, *Memórias póstumas* derives its poetic force and psychological insights not from the content of its narrative but rather from the fecundity of its narration. Brás Cubas's memoirs are, we are warned in his preliminary note to the reader, the work of a dead man, "obra de finado," written with "a pena da galhofa e a tinta da melancolia" (29) ["a playful pen and melancholy ink"] (*Posthumous,* 5).[4] Death offers distinct advantages, particularly for a narrator inclined to expose and then dissect the moral and psychological inconsistencies of his countrymen (as well as his own). In the following passage he explains in a typically garrulous fashion why this is so:

> Talvez espante ao leitor a franqueza com que lhe exponho e realço a minha mediocridade; advirta que a franqueza é a primeira virtude de um defunto. Na vida, o olhar da opinião, o contraste dos interesses, a luta das cobiças obrigam a gente a calar os trapos velhos, a disfarçar os rasgões e os remendos, a não estender ao mundo as revelações que faz à consciência; e o melhor da obrigação é quando, à força de embaçar os outros, embaça-se um homem a si mesmo, porque em tal caso poupa-se o vexame, que é uma sensação penosa, e a hipocrasia, que é um vício hediondo. Mas, na morte, que diferença! que desabafo! que liberdade! Como a gente pode sacudir fora a capa, deitar ao fosso as lentejoulas, despregar-se, despintar-se, desafeitar-se, confessar lisamente o que foi e o que deixou de ser! Porque, em suma, já não há vizinhos, nem amigos, nem inimigos, nem conhecidos, nem estranhos; não há platéia. O olhar da opinião, esse olhar agudo e judicial, perde a virtude, logo que pisamos o território da morte; não digo que ele se não estenda para cá, e nos não examine e julgue; mas a nós é que não se nos dá do exame nem do julgamento. Senhores vivos, não há nada tão incomensurável como o desdém dos finados. (87–88)

> [Perhaps I'm startling the reader with the frankness with which I'm exposing and emphasizing my mediocrity. Be aware that frankness is the prime virtue of a dead man. In life the gaze of public opinion, the contrast of interests, the struggle of greed all oblige people to keep quiet about their dirty linen, to disguise the rips and stitches, not to extend to the world the revelations they make to their conscience. And the

> best part of the obligation comes when, by deceiving others, a man deceives himself, because in such a case he saves himself vexation, which is a painful feeling, and hypocrisy, which is a vile vice. But in death, what a difference! What a release! What freedom! Oh, how people can shake off their coverings, leave their spangles in the gutter, unbutton themselves, unpaint themselves, undecorate themselves, confess flatly what they were and what they've stopped being! Because, in short, there aren't any more neighbors or friends or enemies or acquaintances or strangers. There's no more audience. The gaze of public opinion, that sharp and judgmental gaze, loses its virtue the moment we tread the territory of death. I'm not saying that it doesn't reach here and examine and judge us, but we don't care about the examination or the judgment. My dear living gentlemen and ladies, there's nothing as incommensurable as the disdain of the deceased.] (52)

Like Menippus in Lucian's *Dialogues of the Dead,* Brás Cubas finds in death a unique vantage point from which to ridicule the living and reflect on his past. In the chapter entitled "Óbito do autor" [The Author's Demise] he offers the following clarification concerning his location as narrator: "não sou propriamente um autor defunto, mas um defunto autor, para quem a campa foi outro berço" (31) ["I am not exactly a writer who is dead but a dead man who is a writer, for whom the grave was a second cradle"] (7). Here Brás Cubas introduces himself not as a deceased author whose memoirs are published posthumously, but rather as an author who happens to be deceased and is thus able to send memorialist dispatches from the afterworld.

Deceased Narration in Memórias póstumas

While there has emerged a fairly broad consensus within Machadian criticism that *Memórias póstumas* represents a turning point, both artistically and philosophically, for Machado de Assis, the specific relevance of deceased narration as a rhetorical strategy in this novel and, correspondingly, the purpose behind its narrator's markedly ironic tone has been the subject of diverse interpretations by Machado's critics since its publication in 1880.

In 1897 Sílvio Romero wrote a critical review of Machado's work, *Machado de Assis,* which is notable for its thinly veiled personal attack on Machado. In it Romero describes Brás Cubas's turn of phrase "autor defunto e defunto autor" as a mere play on words ("trocadilho") and an example of Machado's poorly executed humor (123). In a similarly disdainful tone, Romero questions the originality of Brás Cubas's posthumous perspective:

> Esta espécie de espiritismo litterario póde ser para muita gente o signal de grande profundeza; mas lhe não descubro a menor significação. Com originalidade é de genero inferior.
>
> [This brand of literary spiritism may be for many a sign of great profoundness; but I find it to be lacking in any significance. With respect to originality it is of inferior quality.] (119)

Romero's description of *Memórias póstumas* as a kind of "literary spiritism" contains both a negative association with the Spiritist movement, very much in vogue in late-nineteenth-century Brazil, as well as a recognition that many readers found Brás Cubas's deceased narration profoundly engaging. We will return later in this chapter to the influence of Spiritism on Machado de Assis's work.

João Peregrino Júnior, in *Doença e constituição de Machado de Assis* (1938) [The Sickness and Well-Being of Machado de Assis], echoes Romero's preoccupation with reading Machado's work as an externalization of the author's epilepsy. In a chapter entitled "Instinto de Morte," Peregrino Júnior interprets deceased narration in *Memórias póstumas* as a manifestation of Machado's own "death instinct" brought on by his epileptic condition:

> Machado de Assis possuía, pois, em alto grau, o "instinto de morte" que Schilder descreveu nos epilépticos, e é sobretudo nos romances da sua última fase que podemos observar melhor as suas tendências de destruição e renascimento—a sedução nietzschiana do "eterno retorno."

> [Machado de Assis possessed, to a large degree, the "death instinct" that Schilder described in those suffering from epilepsy, and it is especially in his later novels that his tendency toward destruction and rebirth is expressed most clearly—the Nietzschean seduction of the "eternal return."] (107)

In her critical biography of Machado, Lúcia Miguel Pereira creates a similar, though more psychologically oriented link between Machado and his character Brás Cubas when she confronts the question, "Quem é, afinal, esse Brás Cubas? O primeiro dos tipos mórbidos em que Machado extravasou as próprias esquisitices de nevropata" [Who, ultimately, is this Brás Cubas? The first of these morbid types within whom Machado expressed his own neurological peculiarities] (195). In contrast, I am interested in exploring the emergence of deceased narration in Machado's second phase, not as a physiological symptom brought on by a disease or nervous condition, but rather as a rhetorical strategy motivated by the author's awareness of the dead's symbolic force in the collective imaginary of Brazilian society.[5]

Within more recent works of criticism two general tendencies have stood out as ways of reading Brás Cubas's posthumous narration: as symbolic of some universal or sociological theme and as the manifestation of an identifiable philosophical position or literary mode that is characteristic of Machado's second phase of writing.

Helen Caldwell challenges the common interpretation of *Memórias póstumas* as an exclusively "pessimistic work" and instead focuses attention on the many comic elements to be found in its pages, in the relatively harmless vanities of its characters, and principally in the "carefree" manner of its narrator: "He is about as carefree a corpse as one is likely to come across. Even the worm of his dedication, that is, death (perhaps his critics also), is patted on the back, so to speak, with a certain camaraderie, and one suspects that Braz's tomb was a snug affair with hot and cold running water and a good library" (85). Caldwell recognizes, however, that if one scratches beneath Brás Cubas's tireless wit and the often amusing hypocrisies of his compatriots, traces of pessimism surely appear. The reemergence of the once lovely but vain Spanish girl Marcella, later in the novel, as a pockmarked and demoralized woman inserts a dose of melancholy that ultimately contributes to Brás Cubas's failure to court Virgília as his wife. Similarly, the ignominy surrounding the death of Dona Plácida, the woman who begrudgingly served as confidant to Brás Cubas and Virgília's adultery, produces little comic effect. For Caldwell, the root of the novel's "tinta de melancolia" lies in the specter of "self-love" dwelling in the heart of its narrator and in the hearts of the majority of its characters (104). Brás Cubas proves himself incapable of love and therefore constitutes the living-dead. Even in life, his was a dead soul (110). Caldwell accordingly finds echoes of dead souls throughout the novel (Marcella's soul was eaten away by the worms of her love for material things), and throughout his work, as in *Resurrection* (1872), Machado's first novel, where Felix's heart is briefly resurrected only to sink back into the grave forever (86, 41).

The concept of dead souls, and especially wandering souls, is, I believe, important for understanding both the author's stance in *Memórias póstumas* and the unique liminality of its narrator's highly capricious voice. Caldwell's conceptualization of deceased narration as a metaphor for Brás Cubas's "dead soul," condemned to perpetual egotism, however, does not extend beyond the universal symbolism of life/death, love/self-love, good/evil. These are universal themes that undoubtedly are essential to Machado's work, but that ultimately tell us very little about how the dead, or for that matter, dead souls, were viewed in late-nineteenth-century Brazil, or why Machado, being a product of that specific culture, might be compelled to tell his story from a posthumous perspective.

A radically different kind of symbolic reading of deceased narration in *Memórias póstumas* is offered by Roberto Schwarz, who places Brás Cubas's noted comic wit and carefree style under the scrutiny of a sociological analysis, with the aim of identifying how certain narrative strategies utilized by Machado parody strategies of hegemony employed by the Brazilian elite in the late nineteenth century. According to Schwarz, "the voice from beyond the grave automatically puts parody into everything it says," by which he means the very improbability ("inverossimilhança") of deceased narration sabotages the narrator's credibility and contributes to his overall impertinence (*Master,* 10). Credibility is further diminished by Brás Cubas's narrative "volubility," that is, his constant ideological waffling and indiscriminate usage of disparate narrative modes, which Schwarz argues are reflective of the inconsistencies of a slaveholding elite professing to the nineteenth-century ideals of positivism and enlightenment.

Schwarz rejects the distinction, often made by critics, between the deceased narrator's privileged perspective and the earthbound one available to the characters, including Brás Cubas when he is still alive: "the comedy is to be found precisely in the earthly passions of this dead man, who is very much alive" (*Master,* 38). Thus, Brás Cubas's personal claim to intoxicating freedom and unaccountability in the "undiscovered country," far from the gaze of public opinion, is, Schwarz proposes, merely a portrait of the ideological recklessness and *social* unaccountability enjoyed by the ruling class in Brazil.

While Schwarz argues, on the one hand, that the Brás Cubas speaking to us from beyond the grave and the Brás Cubases of this world are essentially one and the same, on the other hand, he admits that the narrator's posthumous voice is problematic for his readers. This voice, he observes "is contrived to deprive fiction and its reader of an easy relation to one another, and this itself becomes an object of constant teasing" (*Misplaced Ideas,* 88). Schwarz here stresses the improbability of the situation and the parody that naturally results from it.

I believe, however, that the relationship between reader and narrator in *Memórias póstumas* goes far beyond improbability. Although I agree that Brás Cubas's parodic tone is a central feature of his narrative, one that has multiple ramifications for the reader's relationship to the text, I contend that the voice of the dead was anything but improbable to Machado's readership more than a hundred years ago. Though never easy, this relationship between the living and the dead was a highly familiar one in the day-to-day lives of most Brazilians. The degree to which this proximity exists in Machado's text and the impact that Brás Cubas's posthumous dialogue has on the relationship forged between reader and text constitutes a pivotal question in this study.

Although arriving from radically different places, Schwarz's and Caldwell's interpretations of deceased narration in *Memórias póstumas* do have one thing in common—they are both fundamentally symbolic readings of Brás Cubas's posthumous voice, with Caldwell's "dead souls" functioning on a universal level, and Schwarz's "defunto volúvel" [fickle defunct] operating on a sociological level. Both serve as important references for my own symbolic reading of *Memórias,* a reading that differs from theirs in that it is culturally driven, that is, its analytical scope is demarcated by the sociohistorical parameters of Brazilian death culture.

Before looking more closely at some of these cultural parameters, it is apropos to briefly consider another pervading critical approach toward understanding Brás Cubas's deceased status. The salient feature of this approach is that it attempts to link Brás Cubas's worldview with a particular philosophical orientation, as well as the literary mode that has historically served as a vehicle for that orientation. A recent example of this approach may be found in José Raimundo Maia Neto's *Machado de Assis: The Brazilian Pyrrhonian,* in which the author forms a connection between Machado's fiction and the ancient Pyrrhonian tradition of skepticism, by way of the influence exerted on the Brazilian author by the sixteenth- and seventeenth-century skeptics Montaigne and Pascal, respectively. According to Maia Neto, the evolution of Machado's fiction can be described in terms of a "gestation," then a maturation of a skeptical "life-view," that is, the philosophical stance that allows one to question the inconsistencies of social life, including all forms of dogmatic thought, and then reach some level of tranquility by suspending all judgment in the search for truth in the world (10). As Maia Neto sees it, the skeptical viewpoint becomes an increasingly important alternative for the "homem de espírito" [man of spirit] who, in Machado's earlier fiction, repeatedly fails to come to terms with the human condition, usually in the form of a female counterpart.

Maia Neto also makes a point of rejecting Schwarz's interpretation of deceased narration in *Memórias póstumas.* To begin with, Maia Neto does not recognize an inherent incompatibility in its narrator's ideological stances; rather they are all consistent with a skeptical worldview. Second, he upholds the conventional critical distinction made between the ordinary perspective of Brás Cubas the character and the brutally sincere and ruptured perspective of Brás Cubas the narrator. This distinction, he argues, is crucial to the deceased writer's ability to "denounce the duality" of our inner and outer selves, as well as to "unmask himself to reveal the falseness of social appearances" (96). Because he must be dead, Maia Neto argues, in order to remove himself from social hypocrisy, Brás Cubas has not fully reached *ataraxia,* the state of tranquility achieved, for example, by a living and socially engaged Counselor Ayres in *Memorial de Aires* (164–165).

Ultimately, Maia Neto's approach views deceased narration not only as a philosophical attitude that radically removes Brás Cubas from social life but also as a giant step for Machado toward Pyrrhonian skepticism. The distance afforded Brás Cubas by death allows him to expose his own vanity and subsequent misery while alive, along with the very precariousness of life. Maia Neto's argument, however, is essentially linear. By insisting that Machado's maturation as a writer is strictly linked to the gradual adoption of a philosophical orientation, thereby excluding any and all sociohistorical influences, Maia Neto detaches Machado's preoccupations from the cultural milieu in which Machado lived. One of the objectives of the present study is precisely to reinsert the stance of both narrator and author into the social lives from which they sprang.

The final critical work that discusses deceased authorship in a way that is particularly relevant to my own argument is *O calundu e a panacéia: Machado de Assis, a sátira menipéia e a tradição luciânica*

[Petulance and Panacea: Machado de Assis, Menippean Satire, and the Lucianic Tradition] by Enylton José de Sá Rego. Much like Maia Neto, Rego is interested in identifying the source of Machado's new "world vision" that emerges in his fiction's second phase. Similarly, Rego locates this source in antiquity, in the form of Menippean satire, made famous by Lucian of Samosata. Born in Syria around AD 117, Lucian earned his living as a public speaker and was best known for his scathing satires of the philosophers, kings, gods, and canonical works of his time. One of the central figures in his *Dialogues of the Dead* is the skeptic Menippu, who, upon his arrival in Hades, takes pleasure in ridiculing the vanity of kings who desire to bring their wealth with them into the afterworld.

In his analysis of *Memórias póstumas,* Rego identifies in Brás Cubas's unique perspective a series of characteristics that are consistent with the Lucianic "spirit" and Menippean satire, including (1) a mixture of literary genres; (2) the use of parody and fragmented quotations, particularly to other satirical works; (3) a heightened sense of narrative freedom and imagination; (4) a distanced point of view; and, perhaps most important, (5) the coexistence of comic and serious elements (*Calundu,* ch. 2). According to Rego, it is only with the distanced point of view of the "defunto autor," and the resurrection of his "fixed idea" (the "emplasto," or universal panacea for man's melancholic condition) in the form of a posthumous, seriocomic narrative (also seen as a cure-all for melancholy in the Menippean-satire tradition), that Brás Cubas is able to fully embody the Lucianic spirit. Brás Cubas's memoirs, therefore, constitute an innovative and ironic rewriting of the epic genre in comic form and, in so doing, transcend what Machado de Assis perceived to be the intrinsic limitations of romanticism and naturalism for addressing Brazilian reality in the late nineteenth century. Rego concludes:

> através do conhecimento e do uso da poética implícita na tradição luciânica, Machado de Assis produziu em seus romances da chamada segunda fase textos híbridos nos quais re-escreveu os mais importantes

gêneros narrativos da tradição literária ocidental. Sendo sua obra profundamente brasileira, pertence a obra de Machado de Assis ao mesmo tempo a uma corrente literária tão antiga e tão universal quanto a própria instituição da literatura ocidental: a tradição menipéia, ou luciânica.

[through his knowledge and use of the poetics implicit in the Lucianic tradition, Machado de Assis produced hybrid novels during his second phase in which he reinterpreted the most important narrative genres of the Western literary tradition. Machado's works are at the same time both profoundly Brazilian and part of a literary vein as old and universal as the institution of Western literature itself: the Menippean or Lucianic tradition.] (188)

Despite the originality of Rego's treatment of Machado's fiction, he, in fact, offers no explanation for why Machado's work is "profoundly Brazilian." Is there a connection between Machado's use of the Lucianic tradition and the fact that he is a Brazilian author living and writing at the end of the nineteenth century? Was Machado's appropriation of Menippean satire motivated by some specific occurrence in Brazil during this period? In Machado's own life? To what extent did Lucian's emblematic *Dialogues of the Dead* influence Machado's choice of deceased narration in *Memórias póstumas?* I argue that Brás Cubas's resurrection as a dead narrator, and the reader's subsequent "dialogue" with the dead through his posthumous memoirs, is closely linked to the common belief in nineteenth-century Brazil that the dead routinely intervened on behalf of the living. Moreover, I propose that Brás Cubas's attempt to restore his past through writing speaks to Brazil's necessity, on the eve of its transition to a modern republic, to resurrect and reinterpret its own sociohistorical past.

Each of the critical explanations for deceased narration described above offers a provocative reading of Machado's rhetorical strategy in *Memórias póstumas.* Universally missing from their analyses, however, is a consideration of Brás Cubas's posthumous voice in light of the cultural context from which the narrator emerges. The prevalence of deaths and funerals in *Memórias póstumas* alone suggests that Machado was inclined to incorporate elements of death culture into his stories. Placing *Memórias póstumas* within the larger question of the social relationship between the living and the dead in Brazil gives us a better understanding of why Machado elected to make use of deceased narration in this particular novel.

An Untrustworthy Specter

What sort of revenant is Brás Cubas? To begin with, he is curiously uninterested in the spirit world to which he belongs. No mention is made of his fellow deceased, nor for that matter of God, angels, or saints. Rather, his attention is focused almost exclusively on the affairs of the living, their ambitions, hypocrisies, and idiosyncrasies. Brás Cubas does not enjoy any particular clout in the afterworld, nor does he exhibit any interest in forming a reciprocal relationship with the living. In this sense, he is more spectral than spiritual, and as such his involvement with *this* world comes at the expense of the living. Throughout the novel the reader is addressed in a tone ranging from playful indifference to outright mockery. Brás's dedication is brazenly sarcastic and sets the tone for the rest of the book: "Ao Verme Que Primeiro Roeu as Frias Carnes do Meu Cadáver Dedico Como Saudosa Lembrança Estas Memórias Póstumas" (25) ["To the Worm Who Gnawed the Cold Flesh of My Corpse I Dedicate These Posthumous Memoirs As a Nostalgic Remembrance"] (2). If we understand "cadáver" to mean also the body of his memoirs, the implication is that we the readers are the worms gnawing through the chilly remnants of his life.

Interspersed through his meandering narrative are pauses in which Brás addresses the reader directly. These narrative intrusions are notable because they remind us that he is not merely an omniscient narrator, but rather a voice speaking directly from the beyond. They are often confessional and suggest a level of intimacy that is, nevertheless, later violated when the narrator's relentless sarcasm becomes apparent.

Such otherworldly interventions constitute heightened narrative moments in the novel that serve to either uphold or undermine the relationship between narrator and reader. Halfway through, Brás takes the liberty of undercutting his own narrative, which he now finds tedious, all the while blaming the reader for any defects it might possess:

> Começo a arrepender-me deste livro. Não que ele me canse; eu não tenho que fazer; e, realmente, expedir alguns magros capítulos para esse mundo sempre é tarefa que distrai um pouco da eternidade. Mas o livro é enfadonho, cheira a sepulcro, traz certa contração cadavérica; vício grave, e aliás ínfimo, porque o maior defeito deste livro és tu, leitor. Tu tens pressa de envelhecer, e o livro anda devagar; tu amas a narração direita e nutrida, o estilo regular e fluente, e este livro e o meu estilo são como os ébrios, guinam à direita e à esquerda, andam e param, resmungam, urram, gargalham, ameaçam o céu, escorregam e caem. (154)

> [I'm beginning to regret this book. Not that it bores me, I have nothing to do and, really, putting together a few meager chapters for that other world is always a task that distracts me from eternity a little. But the book is tedious, it has the smell of the grave about it; it has a certain cadaveric contraction about it, a serious fault, insignificant to boot because the main defect of this book is you, reader. You're in a hurry to grow old and the book moves slowly. You love direct and continuous narration, a regular and fluid style, and this book and my style are like drunkards, they stagger left and right, they walk and stop, mumble, yell, cackle, shake their fists at the sky, stumble, and fall.] (111)

Brás Cubas's haughty claim that the book's primary defect resides in the reader is a double-edged sword: he is condescending both to traditional, linear narratives as well as to those readers who lead their lives as they read their romances, anxious to arrive at the conclusion.

As these examples illustrate, Brás Cubas's return does not signal the reestablishment of communal ties or the benevolent intervention of a spiritual benefactor. Instead he makes a parody of the intimacy, expectations, and trust generally reserved for the dead when acting as celestial advocates and, consequently, his provocations serve to systematically abuse the reciprocal and emotional ties that constitute the traditional relationship between the living and the dead in colonial and imperial Brazilian society. The ambivalence created by such an untrustworthy specter contributes greatly to the irony of the novel. Moreover, the reader perceives him as an ironic narrator, not only because he flaunts a rhetorical style based largely on confabulations, but also because he invalidates the expectation of proximity between the living and the dead.

Spiritism and Machado de Assis

An inquiry into late-nineteenth-century religious movements and cultural trends in Brazil raises the interesting prospect that much of Machado's irony in *Memórias póstumas* stems from his own skepticism in regard to those doctrines laying claim to a close connection with the spirit world. One of the most visible doctrines of this kind to arise in Brazil during the latter half of the nineteenth century, particularly among intellectual circles in Rio de Janeiro, was Spiritism. Fashioned after Allan Kardec's Spiritist movement in France, and inspired by his book *Le livre des esprits* (1857) (translated into Portuguese as *O livro dos espíritos* in 1860), the Spiritist movement in Brazil became increasingly organized in the decade leading up to the publication of *Memórias* in 1880. In August 1873 the first Spiritist society was founded in Rio de Janeiro: Sociedade de Estudos Espiríticos—Grupo Confúcio [Society of Spiritist Studies—Confucius Group]. A year later the society elected Antônio da Silva Neto, a prominent republican and abolitionist, as its first president. In January 1875 the first Spiritist journal (*Revista espírita: Publicação mensal de estudos psicológicos*) [Spiritist Journal: A Monthly Publication of Psychological Studies] was published by Silva Neto and other society members. The following year a splinter Spiritist group with more evangelical leanings formed its own society called the Sociedade de Estudos Espíritas Deus, Cristo, e Caridade [God, Christ, and Charity Society of Spiritist Studies], which by 1879 possessed more than eight hundred members. As David Hess points out, there was an inherent ambiguity to the "scientific religion" of nineteenth-century Brazilian Spiritism, which claimed both a "purely scientific orientation" and a belief in Jesus as "the divine master" (*Spirits and Scientists,* 193).

Spiritist activity only increased in the decade following *Memórias póstumas.* In 1886 a medical doctor and politician by the name of Adolfo Bezerra de Menezes announced his belief in Kardecian Spiritism before a large gathering of Rio's elite. His dramatic public conversion grabbed the city's attention and helped spawn an even wider interest in Spiritism. Menezes later became president of the Federação Espiritista Brasileira [Brazilian Spiritist Federation] and a leading figure in the movement. It was largely through Menezes's efforts that some reconciliation was found between the movement's religious and scientific tendencies in the late nineteenth century.

In his influential book *A loucura sob novo prisma* [Insanity in a New Light] (ca. 1897), Menezes concluded that in cases of mental illness where there are no signs of a physiological ailment, the patient suffers from a "spirit obsession," that is, the person becomes obsessed by a wayward spirit who has not yet reached a higher spiritual plane. A spirit medium is able to "disobsess" the patient by communicating with the spirit and persuading it to abandon the obsessed person in favor of obtaining a higher moral existence. Menezes and his followers, paradoxically, viewed disobsession treatment as an alternative to orthodox medicine, yet still grounded in scientific reasoning and methodology. The movement's scientific affirmations were at least in part motivated by the desire of Kardecian Spiritists to differentiate themselves from what they considered to be the "low spiritism" of Candomblé, with its elements of magic and animal sacrifices.

An avid reader of Rio de Janeiro's newspapers and scholarly journals, Machado undoubtedly stayed abreast of Spiritism's growing popularity both inside and outside the academy. Evidently, Machado held Spiritists and Spiritist doctrine in low regard, judging by the numerous disparaging references he makes to the movement in his novels, chronicles, and short stories. Shortly after Menezes had publicly embraced Spiritism, Machado observed, "não se pode servir a dois senhores, ou ao Baependi ou a Allan Kardec" [one cannot serve two masters, that is, both Baependi and Allan Kardec], alluding to Menezes's ties to the conservative Senate leader, Baependi (*Diálogos,* 44). In a chronicle that appeared in the *Gazeta de notícias* newspaper on June 7, 1889, Machado sarcastically evokes the spirit of Nostradamus, who, through the mediumship of a fictitious friend, José Basílio Moreira Lapa, predicts the dissolution of the emperor's cabinet ministry and with it, the end of the monarch's rule over the country.[6] Machado uses his fictitious friend to poke fun at the progressive stages of a Spiritist's development. In the first stage of Spiritism (José's current level) the Spiritist is still unable to summon some of the higher spirits and gradually loses the ability to reason clearly. After four or five years of this initial stage, "pure dementia" sets in and with it greater contact with the spirit world. Machado even provides some "statistics" to support his theory:

> Tem-se calculado que, dos espíritos evocados durante um ano, 28 por cento o foram por espíritas ainda meio sãos (primeira fase); 72 por cento pertencem aos mentecaptos. Alguns estatísticos chegam a conceder aos últimos 79 por cento; mas parece excessivo.
>
> [It has been calculated that, of the spirits invoked during this year, 28 percent were summoned by Spiritists still slightly sane (the first phase); 72 percent by total lunatics. Some statistics go so far as to claim 79 percent for the latter, but that seems excessive.] (*Bons dias,* 192)

In this chronicle Machado also proposes a way of cultivating Spiritism in Brazil. He would create a law whereby Spiritists recognized as having succumbed completely to the second phase would be wedded together. Their offspring, endowed with an extraordinary degree of "idiocy" and "cretinism," would carry a weighty responsibility: "preparariam as bases de um excelente século futuro" [they would prepare the foundations for an excellent next century] (192). Published just months before the military's overthrow of Pedro II's imperial regime, Machado's chronicle portrays the growth of Spiritism in Brazil as a symptom of the collective dementia of those carrying out Brazil's transition from an empire to a republic. It is, in other words, a biting denouncement of those who would "prepare the foundations for an excellent next century" in Brazil. Similarly, contained in Machado's satirical description of Spiritism's evolutionary stages and the creation of a race of Spiritist leaders is an implied criticism of positivism's affirmation of social progress, so in vogue during the fall of the empire and the inauguration of the republic.

Machado reiterates his association of Spiritism with dementia in "A segunda vida" [A Second Life].[7] The short story begins with a conversation between Monsenhor Caldas and a man named José Maria, who claims to be leading his "second life," having died once before, on March 20, 1860, at 5:43 in the morning. The monsignor, alarmed by the man's self-delusions, discreetly arranges for the police to come and then continues to listen to the man's story. José describes his soul's ascension into the heavens and directly into the sun without burning because, as he explains, "as almas são incombustíveis" [souls are incombustible] (*Obra completa,* 441). He then excitedly recounts his reincarnation, maladjusted youth, and tumultuous relationship with a woman named Clemência. By the end of the story José's delusions become more vivid as he imagines the monsignor to be his wife, who is at this point the object of his hate. We hear the sounds of help arriving as the monsignor retreats in fear from this menacing man.

One of the central components of Spiritism is the belief in reincarnation. According to Kardec the spiritual evolution of human beings occurs over a period of incarnations during which karma is accumulated through one's virtue and goodness in each life. Throughout this process the individual's free will acts as a guiding principle. When asked in the afterlife whether he wishes to be reincarnated as a prince or a trolley operator, José Maria responds, "declarei que me era indiferente nascer mendigo ou potentado, com a condição de nascer experiente" (441) ["I declared that it made no difference whether I was born a beggar or a potentate, as long as I could be born experienced"] (*Devil's Church,* 53). José's seemingly noble request reflects a Kardecian notion of spiritual and moral evolution. The general reaction in heaven, however, is that of incredulous amusement:

> Não imagina o riso universal com que me ouviram. Jó, que ali preside a província dos pacientes, disse-me que um tal desejo era disparate; mas eu temei e venci. (441)
>
> [You can't imagine the universal laughter with which they heard me. Jo, who presides over the province of the patient, told me that such a wish was ridiculous, but I persisted and won.] (53)

The spirit world laughs with good reason, for, in his "second life," José not only fails to accumulate wisdom, his degree of suffering increases to the point that he has become paranoid and hostile to others. Machado's negative portrayal of reincarnation in this short story is representative of a larger skepticism with which he viewed Spiritist doctrine.

The frequency with which Machado lampoons Spiritism in his writings suggests that the movement represented a lightning rod for some of the broader social issues that preoccupied this author at the end of the nineteenth century. From Machado's perspective Spiritism was ushered in, along with other professedly enlightened European schools of thought, such as positivism and naturalism, as a substitute for Brazilian society's colonial heritage of superstitions and backward mentality. Machado generally problematized the Brazilian elite's slavish imitation of European models through sarcasm, as in this statement in another chronicle that satirizes Spiritism: "Eu em geral creio em tudo aquilo que na Europa é acreditado" [In general, I believe in everything that the Europeans believe].[8] One senses that, for Machado, blind acceptance of such models as the absolute truth represented a greater threat to Brazil's "development," than the continued existence of "backward" beliefs. Spiritism, therefore, was emblematic of Brazil's cultural dependency becoming a form of collective social dementia. It represented the most absurd example of this troubling relationship and illustrated the negative consequences for a society that substituted its own powers of criticism for a doctrine wherein the solutions to humanity's problems were acquired through communication with spirits.

This opposition between Spiritism and critical thinking also appears in Machado's short story "Uma visita de Alcibíades" [A Visit by Alcibiades] in which a court judge (*o desembargador X*) writes to the court's chief of police about a bizarre incident that occurred earlier that day. While reading Plutarch's biography of Alcibíades, the Athenian statesman and general, the judge asks himself, "Que impressão daria ao ilustre ateniense o nosso vestuário moderno?" [What impression would this illustrious Athenian have of our modern apparel?] (*Obra completa,* 2:352). In response to this rather innocuous question, Alcibíades suddenly appears before the judge, as seemingly alive as when he addressed the Athenian assemblies more than two thousand years ago:

> Não se demorou Alcibíades em acudir ao chamado; dous minutos depois estava ali, na minha sala, perto da parede; mas não era a sombra impalpável que eu cuidara ter evocado pelos métodos da nossa escola; era o próprio Alcibíades, carne e osso, vero homem, grego autêntico, trajado à antiga, cheio daquela gentileza e desgarre com que usava arengar às grandes assembléias de Atenas.
>
> [It did not take long for Alcibiades to respond to this appeal; two minutes later, there he was, in my room, next to the wall; but it was not the impalpable shadow that I expected to invoke using the methods of our school; it was Alcibiades himself, in flesh and blood, a real man, an authentic Greek, in ancient garb, and full of that gentility and elegance that he used while addressing the great assemblies of Athens.] (353)

The school to which the *desembargador* refers is, of course, Spiritism, with its "methods" of spirit communication through mediums. We may ask ourselves then, what sort of medium is the desembargador X? He describes himself as a novice whose motivation for adopting Spiritism was driven as much by cynicism as anything else:

> Sou espiritista desde alguns meses. Convencido de que todos os sistemas são puras niilidades, resolvi adotar o mais recreativo deles. Tempo virá em que êste não seja só recreativo, mas também útil à solução dos problemas históricos; é mais sumário evocar o espírito dos mortos, do que gastar as fôrças críticas, e gastá-las em pura perda, porque não há raciocínio nem documento que nos explique melhor a intenção de um ato do que o próprio autor do ato. E tal era o meu caso desta noite. Conjeturar qual fôsse a impressão de Alcibíades era despender o tempo, sem outra vantagem, além do gôsto de admirar a minha própria habilidade. Determinei portanto, evocar o ateniense; pedi-lhe que comparecesse em minha casa, logo, sem demora.
>
> [I have been a Spiritist for some months now. Convinced that all belief systems are pure nihilisms, I decided to adopt the most amusing of all. The time will come when this doctrine will be not only recreational but also useful for solving the world's problems; it is more efficient to invoke the spirits of the dead than to waste energy thinking critically, to absolutely no avail, because there is no line of reasoning or document that can better explain the intention of an act than the author of that act himself. Such was the case this very evening. To hypothesize about Alcibiades's impression would be to squander time, with no advantage other than to admire my own talents. I decided, therefore, to invoke the Athenian; I asked him to appear at my house at once.] (352–53)

In this passage Machado levies a thinly veiled criticism at those who would rather invoke the spirits of the dead before expending any energy in critical reflection. The fact that the judge, after only a few months as a Spiritist, is even capable of summoning a spirit as ancient and venerable as Alcibíades speaks little of the doctrine's validity and methods. The judge himself confesses that, from all the possible philosophical systems, he chose Spiritism because it was the most "amusing." Machado's sarcasm is thus targeted both at Spiritism, whose doctrine he considers chimerical, as well as those who renounce historical and social critical analysis in favor of the most recent philosophical fad.

The judge's motive for invoking Alcibíades is, after all, to see what the Athenian's opinion of modern clothing would be. Generally, the spirit guides evoked by Spiritist mediums are figures of great distinction (such as Victor Hugo, the Jesuit Manuel da Nóbrega, or the Spiritist Bezerra de Menezes) who shed light on weighty moral, religious, or scientific problems. While Alcibíades certainly fits this bill, the judge's question makes a mockery of mediumship. After the judge brings the Athenian up to speed on the ill fate of Greece and the pantheon of gods who once inhabited Mount Olympus, Alcibíades decides that he will accompany the desembargador to the casino that evening. Failing to dissuade his now unwanted spirit guide, the judge exhibits the kind of contemporary attire Alcibíades must wear in order to fit in at this social event. Shocked by the drab colors of the judge's suit and tie, the Athenian general concludes, "O mundo deve andar imensamente melancólico, se escolheu para uso uma côr tão morta e tão triste. Nós éramos mais alegres; vivíamos" [The world must be quite a melancholy place now, if they have chosen to wear such a sad and lifeless color. We were happier; we lived] (357). When the judge puts on his hat, the finishing touch of melancholy, the illustrious spirit swaggers a bit and then drops dead, that is, "morto pela segunda vez" [dead twice over] (357). Thus the desembargador gets an answer to his initial question, in the form of a dead Athenian waiting to be transported to the morgue. That the great spirit's demise was apparently caused by the shock of seeing modern dress constitutes a biting satire of Spiritism's "usefulness in finding solutions to historical problems."

Spiritists during the late nineteenth century in Brazil were sure to distance their scientifically minded belief in human spirits from Afro-Brazilian religions such as Candomblé and other popular beliefs or customs involving the supernatural. In Machado's novel *Esaú e Jacó,* when Santos expresses his disapproval of Natividade's visit to an "adivinha" [fortune-teller], his wife answers back, "Mas você é espírita" [But you are a spiritist]. Santos's paternalistic and disparaging response indicates that Machado was keenly aware of the distinctions claimed by Spiritism:

> "Perdão, não confundamos," replicou ele com gravidade. Sim, podia consentir numa consulta espírita; já pensara nela. Algum espírito podia dizer-lhe a verdade, em vez de uma adivinha de farsa. (47)
>
> ["Excuse me, let us not confuse the two things," he replied. Yes, he might consent to consultation with a spiritist. He had already thought of it. Some spiritist might tell him the truth instead of a fake fortune-teller.] (*Esau and Jacob*, 24–25)

Ironically, when Natividade and her sister return from their visit to the "cabocla do Castelo" [mestiza from Morro do Castelo] Santos can hardly contain his curiosity, particularly concerning the destiny of their twin boys, Pedro and Paulo. Thrilled with the fortune-teller's rather ambiguous prediction of "coisas futuras" [future things] in store for his sons, but somewhat vexed by her knowledge that they had also "fought in their mother's womb," Santos decides to consult his Spiritist master, Plácido. The scene demonstrates the kind of religious malleability that existed (and still exists) in Brazilian society's relationship to the supernatural. Santos does not recognize the inherent contradiction in consulting his Spiritist master about information he has received from a fortune-teller he has just written off as a farce.[9]

Ultimately, both Natividade and Santos invest a great deal in the prophetic words of the cabocla. As the twins grow older their rivalry only intensifies. As adults, the battle that once took place in their mother's womb now shifts to the political arena where the twins represent the two poles of political life in late-nineteenth-century Brazil: Paulo is a staunch republican and Pedro a stubborn monarchist. Ironically, it is a street fortune-teller who sets the foreboding tone for the two conflicting faces of political life in late-nineteenth-century Brazil. Nevertheless, any real promise for the twins' future greatness (and by implication, Brazil's) is eventually squelched by their unyielding and frequently petty ideological conflicts. In this sense, they represent a microcosm of Brazil's political woes during the country's transition from a monarchy to a republic.

A Parody of the Spirits

Machado's satire of Brazilian society's (and particularly its elite's) blind faith in the spirit world, whether in the form of Spiritism or the occult, is perhaps exemplified most succinctly in the short story "A cartomante" [The Fortune-Teller]. The opening scene, where Rita tells of her visit to an adivinha to her incredulous lover, Camilo, so closely resembles the opening scene in *Esaú e Jacó* that one suspects Machado used the short story as a model for the later novel. Like Santos, Camilo looks down on the cartomante and her methods. Also like the desembargador he has grown to form a passive disbelief in all philosophical and religious systems. This was not always the case, however:

> Também êle, em criança, e ainda depois, foi supersticioso, teve um arsenal inteiro de crendices, que a mãe lhe incutiu e que aos vinte anos desapareceram. No dia em que deixou cair tôda essa vegetação parasita, e ficou só o tronco da religião, êle, como tivesse recebido da mãe ambos os ensinos, envolveu-os na mesma dúvida, e logo depois em uma só negação total. Camilo não acreditava em nada. Por quê? Não poderia dizê-lo, não possuía um só argumento; limitava-se a negar tudo. E digo mal, porque negar é ainda afirmar, e êle não formulava a incredulidade; diante do mistério, contentou-se em levantar os ombros, e foi andando.
>
> [He too was superstitious, for, as a child and even later, he carried with him a full assemblage of beliefs that his mother had inculcated him with, but that disappeared when he turned twenty. On the day that he allowed all this parasitic vegetation to fall away, leaving only the trunk of religion, and convinced that he had received both forms of belief from his mother's teachings, he wrapped them in the same shroud of doubt, and soon after, abolished both completely. Camilo did not believe in anything. Why? He wasn't able to say why, he didn't have an underlying reason; he simply rejected it all. In fact, that is not entirely correct, because to reject is still to assert one's beliefs, and he did not formulate his disbelief; in the face of the unknown, he resigned himself to shrug his shoulders and continue on his way.] (478)

The symbolic gesture of approaching the unknown with a shrug of the shoulders reflects the kind of intellectual and moral apathy that one detects in so many of Machado's characters. As the reader discovers, however, in "A cartomante," the parasitic vegetation has a tendency to creep back. Camilo's fears of his affair with Rita being discovered by her husband, Vilela, are compounded when he receives an urgent note beckoning him to their house. Increasingly nervous, he sets out in his coach, only to be delayed by an accident ahead. While waiting for the road to clear, Camilo notices the fortune-teller's house and realizes that never in his life had he wished so much to believe in what the cards have to tell him: "A agitação dêle era grande, extraordinário, e do fundo das camadas morais emergiam alguns fantasmas de outro tempo, as velhas crenças, as superstições antigas" [His agitation was astoundingly great, and from the depths of his moral being began to emerge the ghosts of his past, the old beliefs, the former superstitions] (481). The superstitions that come back to haunt Camilo at this critical juncture in his life are the ones his mother infused him with as a boy, the ones he claimed to have outgrown as an adult. They are also Brazil's phantoms, that is, the colonial legacy of religious syncretism, popular Catholicism, and the pervasive cultural influence of the African wet nurse on the colonizer's children, which, like *vegetação parasita* [parasitic vegetation] continued to wind its way around the trunks of both official Catholicism and nineteenth-century positivism. This underlying vegetation, Machado seems to suggest in both "A cartomante" and *Esaú e Jacó,* emerges particularly during moments of either personal crisis, in Camilo's case, or social crisis, as in the case of the quarreling twins.

The cards, of course, tell Camilo that he is gripped by fear, "O senhor tem um grande susto" [you, sir, are quite afraid], but that his fear is not warranted: "o terceiro ignorava tudo" [the third one is unaware] (482). The reassuring words of the cartomante resonate profoundly in Camilo's head as he makes his way to Rita's house, bringing him not only a sense of "peace" but also a "new, vibrant faith" in the future. Instead what he finds is destiny's terrible indifference. Rita lies dead, killed by her husband's revolver, and he is next. The abrupt ending of "A cartomante" reads like a slap in the face. Not only does it effectively satirize Camilo's naive decision to place his faith in the cards of the fortune-teller, it also exposes the fundamental vanity inherent in the desire of human beings to control their own destiny.

Machado's satirical portrayal of characters who are morally and philosophically adrift and, as a result, cling to belief systems involving the supernatural and place their faith, uncritically, in fortune-tellers and Spiritism, provides the reader with a window for understanding some of Machado's larger social concerns, namely the Brazilian elite's cultural, ideological, and artistic dependence on Europe, as well as the superficiality of Brazil's transition to a republican government without coming to terms with its colonial past. The prospect of Spiritists preparing the foundation for Brazil's future, Machado suggests, places Brazil on a path similar to Camilo's in "A cartomante," one where naïveté has tragic results. Machado's constant satirizing of the spirit world should be read, therefore, not so much as an atheist or merely materialist response to the supernatural but rather as a social criticism of those who have not bothered to fully scrutinize that which they profess to believe.

We have seen how, in his novels, chronicles, and short stories, Machado cast a skeptical eye on Spiritism and the Spiritist belief in reincarnation. At best he considered them to be examples of Brazil's cultural dependency on European positivism, and at worst, as a short step away from insanity. This is not to say, however, that Machado was unaware of the importance of the spirit world in Brazilian society. As Brazilian literary critic Raymundo Faoro proposes in *Machado de Assis: A pirâmide e o trapézio,* the satire embedded in Brás Cubas's posthumous narration was particularly effective because it was directed at a Brazilian readership that, "se não acreditava, sabia da possibilidade do espiritismo" [even if it didn't believe in it, was aware of the possibility of Spiritism] (465). Despite Machado's skepticism, his work is full of characters who, in one form or another, adhere to the supernatural and whose lives are swayed by the messages they receive from the spirit world. Furthermore, late-nineteenth-century Brazil's affinity for European and particularly French-derived forms of positivism did not mean that people had stopped listening to the spirits, whether they be of the dead, Catholic saints, Afro-Brazilian orixás, or those conjured up by fortune-tellers. The prevalence of the supernatural in Machado's work, even in the form of a parody, suggests that he was equally attentive to Brazil's "spirit idiom" as well as the manner in which the spirits spoke to his countrymen. In other words, Machado's parody of the spirits is effective because he was keenly aware of the extent to which the voices of the dead, for example, would resonate with his readers.

Linda Hutcheon, in her book *A Theory of Parody,* argues that parody is a form of imitation "characterized by ironic inversion" (6). She stresses that while parody implies a posture of critical distance in relation to the object or text that is imitated, its function extends beyond satire or mere ridicule. In other words, parody's ironic inversion does not necessarily subject its object to negative judgment.[10] I would argue, for example, that Machado's satirical treatment of Spiritism in "Uma visita de Alcibíades," where the doctrine is reduced to ridicule, differs in a subtle yet meaningful way from his parody of the dead in *Memórias póstumas.* While Machado's ironic portrayal of Brás Cubas as a kind of "inverted" spirit guide contains a clear criticism of Spiritism, I believe it also speaks to the larger issue of Brazil's relationship to its dead and to its past. As I have argued earlier, Machado was keenly aware of the dead's powerful hold over the Brazilian population's imagination, from the superstitious povo to the enlightened Carioca elite.

Death and the Dead as Tableau Mourant *in Machado's Fiction*

It is no coincidence then that dead figures and the rituals of death form a *tableau mourant* in Machado's fiction. This is particularly true for *Memórias póstumas* and his subsequent novels. In *Memórias* alone there are eight noteworthy deaths scattered through the narrative, starting with Brás Cubas himself; Leocádia, the captain's wife; Brás Cubas's mother and father; his fiancée, Nhã-loló; Dona Plácida; Quincas Borba; and Brás Cubas's first love, Marcela. It is no wonder that Brás Cubas describes the pages of his memoirs as the "miserable leaves of my cypress of death" (111). Most of these deaths are narrated in a tone that is either ironic or oddly detached. In Brás Cubas's own funeral, attended by only a handful of acquaintances and family, the narrator laughs ironically at his own fate and at the

> chuvinha miúda, triste e constante, tão constante e tão triste, que levou um daqueles fiéis da última hora a intercalar esta engenhosa idéia no discurso que proferiu à beira da minha cova:—"Vós, que o conhecestes, meus senhores, vós podeis dizer comigo que a natureza parece estar chorando a perda irreparável de um dos mais belos caracteres que têm honrado a humandidade." (31)

> [a thin, sad, constant rain, so constant and so sad that it led one of those last-minute faithful friends to insert this ingenious idea into the speech he was making at the edge of my grave: "You who knew him, gentlemen, can say with me that nature appears to be weeping over the irreparable loss of one of the finest characters humanity has been honored with."] (7)

Brás Cubas could not have flattered himself more.

When his father discovers that a large portion of the Cubas fortune is being squandered by his son on gifts for the lovely Spanish girl Marcela, the patriarch sends his love-struck boy packing to Coimbra to pursue a university degree. On the ship, the young Brás contemplates tossing himself overboard in protest over his separation from Marcela. However, when death comes to meet him, in the form of a terrible storm, Brás Cubas dares not look it in the eye. Rather, the storm is, in the narrator's words, "uma diversão excelente à tempestade do meu coração" (77) ["an excellent diversion from the tempest in my heart"] (43).

Death also comes to visit the young Brás Cubas in the form of the ship captain's dying wife, Leocádia. Upon her death, an aghast Brás Cubas flees from the sight of her dead body, as he did from the terror of the storm. The drama of her funeral at sea—"a cova que nunca mais se abre" (79) ["the grave that's never opened again"] (44)—is mitigated by the melodrama of the captain's lyrical verses in memory of his wife, composed on the day of her burial. After reading the elegy to Brás Cubas, the captain asks if it is worthy of the treasure he had lost, to which the young man politely responds, "acho os versos perfeitos" (80) ["I think it's a perfect poem"] (45). The captain concedes that it is the poetry of an old salt, "versos de marujo," but Brás Cubas pays the compliment even further by replying "de marujo poeta" ["a poetic old salt"]. The reader is never given examples of the captain's poetry and is therefore unable to judge its quality directly; however, the captain waxes poetic at one grief-stricken moment, noteworthy for its melodramatic clichés and hackneyed technique: "Pobre Leocádia! (. . .) um cadáver . . . o mar . . . o céu . . . o navio" (79) ["Poor Leocádia!" (. . .) "A corpse . . . the sea . . . the sky . . . the ship"] (45). Brás Cubas confesses that on one occasion, while the captain was reciting poetry, the old salt's gestures made the boy laugh out loud. We hear the simultaneous laughter of the deceased Brás Cubas, who laughs out loud at the banal eulogisms of the "marujo poeta," much as he had done while observing the melodramatic platitudes offered by the friend at his own funeral. In both cases the elegy and eulogy as rhetorical forms are subject to parody, as are the mourning rituals normally practiced on such sacred occasions as funerals and wakes.

Brás Cubas begins chapter 124 with the question, "Que há entre a vida e a morte? Uma curta ponte" (218) ["What is there between life and death? A short bridge"] (171). As if to prove his point, the next chapter contains only the epitaph of Nhã-loló, the girl Brás Cubas is set to marry: "Aqui Jaz Dona Eulalia Damascena de Brito, Morta aos Dezenove Anos de Idade, Orai por Ela!" (219) ["Here Lies Dona Eulália Damascena de Brito[,] Dead at the Age of Nineteen[,] Pray for Her!"]

(172). Brás Cubas provides scarce details concerning her death, save that she fell victim to the yellow fever epidemic and that he accompanied her body to her last resting place. According to Brás Cubas, "O epitáfio diz tudo" (219) ["The epitaph says everything"] (172). The parsimony with which he narrates his fiancée's death, however, reflects a more profound indifference to the conventions usually reserved for mourning the loss of a loved one. An epitaph, of course, is no substitute for an actual description of the circumstances surrounding her death, his feelings of loss, or the reaction of family and friends. That the narrator is undoubtedly aware of this only underscores his emotional detachment from the world of the living.

Like the elegy and the eulogy, the epitaph represents one more formality in the mourning process that is susceptible to ironic inversion through the narrator's deceased voice. Brás Cubas can break with such funerary conventions precisely because he too speaks to us from the other side of life. He also understands the weight of social formalities—"o bordão da vida, o bálsamo dos corações" (221) ["the staff of life, the balm of hearts"] (174)—in *this* life. Nhã-loló's father, Damasceno, for example, seems to lament the poor attendance at his daughter's funeral (only twelve people out of eighty accepted the invitation) more than his daughter's death itself. When Brás's brother-in-law, Cotrim, insists that the others would have come out of mere formality, Damasceno can only respond: "Mas viessem!" (220) ["But they would have come!"] (173). The father's preoccupation with a well-attended funeral was the norm during nineteenth-century Brazil, according to João José Reis: "Families worked hard to make members' burials a major social occasion, sending out dozens—sometimes hundreds—of invitations. . . . Throughout the nineteenth century, there persisted in Brazil the idea that families had to seek a large audience for funerals" (*Death,* 110). Reis adds that many of the brotherhoods charged with the proper burial of their members maintained a core group of *irmãos zeladores* (brotherhood caretakers) whose responsibility it was to round up brothers when there was a funeral (128). Brás Cubas's satirical treatment of both

Nhã-loló's funeral and his own underscores the importance of (and is a critique of) the value placed on funeral attendance as part of an appropriate social response to death in nineteenth-century Brazil.

Brás Cubas's callous description of Dona Plácida's death possesses the brevity and neutrality of an epitaph. For the woman who over the years concealed his affair with Virgília from the scrutiny of others, he says only,

> Depois do almoço fui à casa de Dona Plácida; achei um molho de ossos, envolto em molambos, estendido sobre um catre velho e nauseabundo; dei-lhe algum dinheiro. No dia seguinte fi-la transportar para a Misercórdia, onde ela morreu uma semana depois. (237)

> [After breakfast I went to Dona Plácida's place. I found a bundle of bones wrapped in rags lying on an old and revolting cot. I gave her some money. The next day I had her taken to Misericórdia, where she died a week later.] (188–89)

Brás Cubas's penurious obituary for Dona Plácida, however, turns out to be a counterfeit, as he admits in the next line: "Minto: amanheceu morta; saiu da vida às escondidas, tal qual entrara" (237) ["I'm lying. She was found dead in the morning. She'd sneaked out of life just the way she'd come into it"] (189). Brás Cubas's disingenuous account of Dona Plácida's death is motivated in part by his own necessity to appear philanthropic toward the former servant. In this respect his stingy use of language reflects his own tight-fisted attitude toward Dona Plácida.

Before discovering her body, Brás Cubas had, in fact, decided he would not heed Virgília's warning that he should visit Dona Plácida, because he was convinced that the old woman had squandered the five *contos* he had given her before. Whereas the living Brás Cubas would have trumped up the lie in his own favor, the deceased Brás Cubas seizes the opportunity to falsify his posthumous narrative and reveal his own hypocrisy. His word, like Dona Plácida's life, possesses only "relative utility." Meanwhile, common belief in the sanctity of death is also tarnished. Indeed, the small degree of dignity reserved for Dona Plácida on her deathbed is seriously compromised by Brás Cubas's narrative double-dealing. Even in death Dona Plácida is the portrait of misery. According to Brás Cubas, it is a portrait that completes a miserable cycle, for she departed as she entered this world. The result of "luxúrias vadias" [empty sensuality] between her poor mother and a lascivious church sexton, Dona Plácida's birth poses the question, "Aqui estou. Para que me chamastes?" [Here I am. Why did you call me?] Her parents' reply is merciless in its sarcasm:

> "Chamamos-te para queimar os dedos nos tachos, os olhos na costura, comer mal, ou não comer, andar de um lado para outro . . . até acabar um dia na lama ou no hosptial; foi para isso que te chamamos, num momento de simpatia." (159)
>
> ["We called you to burn your fingers on pots, your eyes in sewing, to eat poorly or not at all, to go from one place to another . . . until one day you end up in the mire or in the hospital."] (116)

The "moment of sympathy" from which Dona Plácida has randomly sprung and that has largely determined her fate represents the opening stanza in a pattern of abuse that ends only with Brás Cubas's insincere obituary.

Indeed, insincerity and abuse are the elements that give shape to her otherwise anonymous life. Brás Cubas tells us shortly after his fib, in a chapter entitled "Simples repetição" [A Simple Repetition] that the money he had given her was "invested away" by an opportunistic stonemason who pretended to be in love with her (237/189). Is the scenario a simple repetition of the disingenuousness and abuse that has plagued Dona Plácida's life? Or is it the simple repetition of Brás Cubas's own dissemblance, one more fabrication meant to imply that his generosity was more than sufficient for Dona Plácida to live off of? In either case, the old servant's life and death are entangled in deceit from the day she was born, through her role in Brás Cubas's and Virgília's adulterous affair, up to the confabulation of her death.

Dona Plácida's demise sets off a chain of deaths that swiftly brings Brás Cubas's own posthumous memoirs to an end. Following Dona Plácida's death comes Lobo Neves, who had "one foot on the ministerial step" when he died. Brás Cubas admits that he was filled with envy and that, upon hearing of Virgília's husband's death, he experienced "um ou dous minutos de prazer" (243) ["one or two minutes of pleasure"] (195). This pleasure dissipates quickly, however, at Neves's funeral, when Brás Cubas witnesses Virgília, in a foreshadowing of Capitu's mourning for Escobar in *Dom Casmurro,* shed legitimate tears over her cuckolded husband's coffin. Jealousy and guilt seem to mix with the spadefuls of lime that Brás Cubas heaps over the coffin of his betrayed childhood friend. Later, "a tarde tinha o peso e a cor do chumbo" (243) ["the afternoon had the weight and color of lead"] (195), much like the weight of his conscience. The death of Lobo Neves also coincides with the death of Brás Cubas's oppositional newspaper, which is, as the narrator describes, found dead in the morning (like Dona Plácida) after only six months of circulation.

Troubled by the apparent sincerity of Virgília's weeping for her husband, Brás Cubas eventually likens her grief to Vespasian's coin: "não cheira à origem, e tanto se colhe do mal como do bem" (244) ["it doesn't smell of its origins and can be collected just as well from evil as from good"] (196). Morality may condemn his concubine, however this is of no consequence "uma vez que lhe recebeste pontualmente as lágrimas" (244) ["once you have punctually received the tears"] (196). Therefore, it is the exterior of Virgília's emotions, particularly when in mourning, that matters. She must uphold the tradition of grieving outwardly and intensely, the tears must be "punctually received," regardless of their emotional origin. Brás Cubas's cynical assessment of Virgília's behavior at her husband's funeral (to that of a carpideira essentially) betrays a similar skepticism of the social conventions usually observed at burials. In this respect, Virgília's weeping runs parallel with Damasceno's desire for a well-attended funeral. Though on one level they represent the mourning sentiments of individuals, each is also a gesture of social formality, and as such, are subject to Machado de Assis's moral dissection.

A few pages later Brás Cubas tells of two encounters he has on the same day, each coinciding with a former love interest. First, while distributing alms in a slum, he comes across Eugênia, still as lame and sad as when he rejected her years before. Later that day, with the woeful impression of Eugênia still on his mind, he visits a hospital, where he is surprised to find the decrepit remains of a once beautiful Marcela, the girl over whom he had almost drowned himself. She dies one half hour after his arrival. The next chapter describes the bizarre death of a demented Quincas Borba, swearing repeatedly on his deathbed that pain is an illusion. At this point in the novel death strikes down characters at a dizzying rate. The reader does not have time to assimilate the death of one character before the next demise is announced. One obituary seems to bleed into the next. The quick succession of deaths also relativizes their significance for both Brás Cubas and the reader. The pain of loss becomes an illusion for the narrator as Brás's relationships fall to the wayside of his hollow existence. It is as if there is insufficient substance to Brás's life to support their implicated existences. The leaves of his miserable cypress tree fall swiftly at this juncture.

Indeed, the swiftness of the death scenes in the final chapter stands in contrast to the relatively involved descriptions of his father's, and particularly his mother's, deaths earlier in the novel. We know, for example, that his father dies disheartened by the defeat of his son's ministerial and marital candidacies. "A Cubas!" was the incredulous response he took to the grave with him, his family legacy having been struck a mortal blow (77). Brás Cubas's observations of the body's preparation for burial are presented in the form of notes, written with an economy of emotion but an abundance of cultural detail regarding death culture in nineteenth-century Brazil:

> Soluços, lágrimas, casa armada, veludo preto nos portais, um homem que veio vestir o cadáver, outro que tomou a medida do caixão, caixão,

> essa, tocheiros, convites, convidados que entravam, lentamente, a passo surdo, e apertavam a mão à família, alguns tristes, todos sérios e calados, padre e sacristão, rezas, aspersões d'água benta, o fechar do caixão, a prego e martelo, seis pessoas que o tomam da essa, e o levantam, e o descem a custo pela escada, não obstante os gritos, soluços e novas lágrimas da família, e vão até o coche fúnebre, e o colocam em cima e traspassam e apertam as correias, o rodar do coche, o rodar dos carros, um a um. . . . Isto que parece um simples inventário, eram notas que eu havia tomado para um capítulo triste e vulgar que não escrevo. (117)
>
> [Sobs, tears, the house all prepared, black velvet over the doorways, a man who came to dress the corpse, another who took measurements for the coffin, bier, candle holders, invitations, guests slowly entering, stepping softly, shaking hands with the family, some sad, all serious and silent, priest and sacristan, prayers, the sprinkling of holy water, nailing shut the coffin, six people lifting it and carrying it down the steps in spite of the cries, sobs, the new tears on the part of the family, and going up to the hearse, placing it on top and tying it down, the hearse rolling along, and the carriages, one by one . . . What looks like a simple inventory here are notes I'd taken for a sad and banal chapter that I won't write.] (77–78)

What he has written proves, however, to be a richly detailed account of funerary preparation and mourning customs in late-nineteenth-century Brazilian society. The narrator's impressionistic inventory creates a kind of ethnography of the well-rehearsed rituals surrounding death, from the draping of black velvet over the doorways to the type of hearse used to transport the cadaver.

The death of Brás Cubas's mother, on the other hand, stands out as the only death (and perhaps the only chapter) in the novel in which the narrator relinquishes his attitude of cynical observer. Entitled "Triste, mas curto" [Sad, but Short], the chapter is indeed sad but comparatively much longer (and deeper) than the subsequent death scenes in regard to its emotional content. For once the lyrical potential of the narrator's prose remains unchecked long enough to allow the reader to join him in his moment of grieving. Brás's description of his sick mother's reaction, when he arrives in Rio de Janeiro after a long absence, elicits true pathos:

> —"Meu Filho!"
>
> A dor suspendeu por um pouco as tenazes; um sorriso alumiou o rosto da enferma, sobre o qual a morte batia a asa eterna. Era menos um rosto do que uma caveira: a beleza passara, como um dia brilhante; restavam os ossos, que não emagrecem nunca. Mal poderia conhecê-la; havia oito ou nove anos que nos não víamos. Ajoelhado, ao pé da cama, com as mãos dela entre as minhas, fiquei mudo e quieto, sem ousar falar, porque cada palavra seria um soluço, e nós temíamos avisá-la do fim. (85–86)
>
> ["My son!"
>
> The pain held back its pincers for a moment. A smile lighted the face of the sick woman over whom death was beating its eternal wings. It was less a face than a skull. Its beauty had passed like a bright day. The bones, which never grow thin, were left. I could hardly recognize her. It had been eight or nine years since we'd seen each other. Kneeling by the foot of the bed with her hands in mine, I remained mute and still, not daring to speak because every word would have been a sob and we were afraid to tell her of the end.] (50)

When Brás Cubas asks "Why?" in this chapter, it is without his usual philosophical pontifications and cynical aloofness (51). In other words, Brás contemplates the death of his mother without the political or philosophical appurtenances that characterize the rest of his memoirs. Pain is no illusion to his mother, nor to Brás Cubas when he tries to understand why such a docile, loving person should die such a painful death.

Should we read Brás's account of his mother's death as simply a brief anomaly in an otherwise jaded book? A sad, but ultimately short exception to the rule? Or might the chapter serve some other function? Although Brás Cubas recognizes her limitations—"Minha mãe era uma senhora fraca, de pouco cérebro e muito coração" (55) ["My mother was a weak woman with not much brain and lots of heart"] (25)—his love for her is genuine: "Eu amava minha mãe" (84) ["I loved my mother very much"] (49). Brás's mother is exceptional precisely because she is the sole figure in the novel who appears to have had a nurturing effect on the narrator. Similarly, her death has the ability to elicit the narrator's compassion, a trait that is almost universally absent in Brás Cubas. The pathos is short-lived, however. Brás Cubas spends some time alone in a family house in Tijuca contemplating life and death, but he eventually finds that he has had enough of solitude and reflection. One senses that the opportunity for genuine self-reflection is buried along with Brás Cubas's mother.

With the exception of his mother's death, and to a lesser degree his father's, the novel's numerous death scenes are portrayed with both narrative sparseness and emotional detachment. Similarly there is a gradual intensification of these traits as the novel approaches its conclusion, which is characterized by an acceleration of minimized death scenes. While early on the reader is drawn into sharing the narrator's grief over his mother's death, by the end of the novel, Marcela's physical degeneration and Quincas Borba's dementia are too pitiful and swift in coming to evoke empathy. One might argue that, as did his life, Brás Cubas's posthumous memoirs gradually wither away, victim to their author's cynicism. Along with his observation that his narrative style is no longer as "*lesto*" [agile] as it was during the earlier chapters, Brás adds:

> O que eu quero dizer não é que esteja agora mais velho do que quando comecei o livro. A morte não envelhece. Quero dizer, sim, que em cada fase da narração da minha vida experimento a sensação correspondente. (231)
>
> [I don't mean I'm older now than when I began the book. Death doesn't age one. I do mean that in each phase of the narration of my life I experience the corresponding sensation.] (183)

Thus, narratively speaking, Brás Cubas dies again, or better yet, his narrative expresses both a "second life" and a "second death." Brás

Cubas's confession that he experiences the sensation of aging in the process of recounting his life partly explains the (de)evolution of his narrative approach to the novel's death scenes. The "defunto autor" admits that he too has begun to tire of his own memoirs: "o livro é enfadonho, cheira o sepulcro, traz certa contração cadavérica" (154) ["the book is tedious, it has the smell of the grave about it; it has a certain cadaveric contraction"] (111). It is not the first time that Brás Cubas refers to a book, and implicitly his memoirs, as a metaphor for his life. Earlier, during his "delirium" before death, he imagines that he has been transformed into a morocco-bound volume of St. Thomas Aquinas's *Summa theologica.*

Similarly, in his first description of a youthful Virgília, Brás Cubas anticipates his lover's (and the reader's) logical question, "Mas, dirás tu, como é que podes assim discernir a verdade daquele tempo, e exprimi-la depois de tantos anos?" (94) ["'But,' you're probably saying, 'how can you discern the truth of those times like that and express it after so many years?'"] (57). Brás responds that it is our power to restore and ameliorate the past that makes humans rulers of the earth: "Cada estação da vida é uma edição, que corrige a anterior, e que será corrigida também, até a edição definitiva, que o editor dá de graça aos vermes" (94) ["Every season of life is an edition that corrects the one before and which will also be corrected itself until the definitive edition, which the publisher gives to the worms gratis"] (57). This statement, of course, echoes his dedication and would thus seem to suggest that with his posthumous memoirs, Brás Cubas is submitting the perfected, definitive account of his life. If we view his otherworldly memoirs as the ultimate exercise in restoring the past we may then ask, to what degree do they represent a corrected version of his life? Similarly, if we regard text as a legitimate means for the expression and preservation of memory, to what extent do Brás's memoirs preserve its author's memories?

The manner with which the narrator hurries toward the conclusion of his memoirs, eager to dispose of the people and memories that gave shape to his life, suggests that Brás Cubas fails to come to terms with his past. Like the dead who are not given a proper "burial" in his narrative, due to the author's ridiculed eulogisms, heartless epitaphs, and falsified obituaries, Brás Cubas never convinces the reader that his own past has received a proper funeral. In this sense his memoirs constitute a spectacular but ultimately failed attempt at coming to terms with his past. The lack of resolution that characterizes Brás's postmortem existence would have been particularly unsettling for nineteenth-century readers in Brazil, accustomed to the belief that the dead are summoned to advocate on behalf of the living, and to act as harbingers of truth and wisdom. Brás's volubility, irreverence, and disdain, instead, instill the reader with a profound sense of distrust and uncertainty as to whether his wayward spirit will show us the truth.

Brás Cubas and the Carnivalesque

In *Rabelais and His World,* Mikhail Bakhtin describes carnival as "moments of death and revival, of change and renewal" leading to a "festive perception of the world" (9). During carnival, the social order is turned momentarily on its head, a reversal symbolized by the ritual decrowning of the king and the subsequent crowning of the pauper. It is, in short, the ritual trading of social places. During the Middle Ages the carnival spirit of folk culture was evoked as a nonofficial alternative to the official political and ecclesiastical order. According to Bakhtin vestiges of this carnival spirit remain embedded in the modern novel, with its traces of carnival "laughter" and the "grotesque."

Moreover, the concept of the revenant may be said to be inherently carnivalesque. In essence, ghosts trade social places with the living by pretending that they are alive. Neither entirely dead nor completely alive, the ghost transiently masquerades as the living by returning and assuming corporal form. In this respect, the revenant is an inversion of the living, who, by dressing as skeletons or death during carnival or the Day of the Dead, assume the form of the dead.[11] At the same time the revenant represents the past trading places with the present. As Jacques Derrida points out in *Specters of Marx,* the revenant belongs neither fully to the past nor the present. Rather, each time the specter returns it is making its apparitional debut, and consequently "one cannot control its comings and goings because it begins by coming back" (10–11). In a similar vein, Peter Buse and Andrew Stott in *Ghosts: Deconstruction, Psychoanalysis, History* argue that ghosts are intrinsically anachronistic: "Indeed, anachronism might well be the defining feature of ghosts, now and in the past, because haunting, by its very structure, implies a deformation of linear temporality: there may be no proper time for ghosts" (1). Fruitful parallels exist between the cyclical nature of the ghost, deforming "linear temporality" with its untimely apparitions, and Bakhtin's notion of a carnival time punctuated by temporary "moments of death and revival." Intrinsic to the cyclical mode of both ghosts and carnival is a subversion of linear or absolutist conceptualizations of human history.

Death and carnival are similarly grounded together by their mutual capacity to relativize. Death, of course, as the great social equalizer, has constituted a persistent literary and religious theme throughout the ages, from Lucian's *Dialogues of the Dead* to Catholic sermons in Brazil. Neither the emperor nor the slave escapes its inevitability, and both are thus, in the face of death, coequals. Carnival, if only temporarily and through ritualized forms (such as crowning/decrowning, public denouncements, and debasing, the juxtaposition of high and low cultures, and its subversion of hierarchical forms and arbitrary authority), functions in much the same way. In his discussion of Menippean satire, Bakhtin calls attention to the "consistent carnivalization of the nether world" in the literary realm of the seriocomic:

> The nether world equalizes representatives of all earthly positions in life; there the emperor and the slave, the rich man and the beggar come together on equal terms and enter into familiar contact; death decrowns all who have been crowned in life. Representation of the nether world

> often applied the carnivalistic logic of a "world upside down": an emperor in the nether world becomes a slave, a slave an emperor, and so forth. The carnivalized nether world of the menippea determined the medieval tradition of representations of *joyful hell,* a tradition which found its culmination in Rabelais. (*Problems,* 133; emphasis in original)

Instances in *Memórias póstumas* where characters are subject, as well as the narrator himself, to a "carnivalistic logic" are abundant. The transformation of Brás Cubas's childhood friend, Quincas Borba, is the embodiment of this logic. As a child, Brás Cubas admired this well-to-do classmate for his inventiveness, charisma, and mischievous pranks. Thirty years later, however, Brás encounters his friend in ragged clothes living a desolate life on the street. Quincas Borba comments on the irony of the situation:

> Não é preciso contar-lhe nada, disse ele enfim; o senhor adivinha tudo. Uma vida de misérias, de atribulações e de lutas. Lembra-se das nossas festas, em que eu figurava de rei? Que trambolhão! Acabo mendigo. (137)

> [I don't have to tell you a thing, you can guess it all. A life of misery, tribulation, and struggle. Remember our parties where I played the part of the king? What a fiasco! I end up a beggar.] (95)

Brás Cubas lends his former friend some money and bids him farewell, only realizing afterward that his pocket watch has been stolen by Quincas during their embrace. Curiously, Brás Cubas's thoughts, before he happened across his former classmate, were on another childhood friend, Lobo Neves, whose political position and marriage to Virgília he has come to envy. The sudden appearance, however, of his desolate friend serves to relativize Brás Cubas's own fate in life. The irony of the situation is underscored by Quincas stealing his watch, perhaps the ultimate symbol of linear progress on both a temporal and social level. Moreover, Quincas's theft (and life) relativizes the very idea of progress by showing just how easily it can be taken away. Some time later Brás Cubas encounters his friend again, this time in patent leather shoes and a stylish frock coat, the beneficiary of a rich uncle's inheritance. The carnivalesque crowning and decrowning of Quincas Borba is reinforced by the character's self-styled philosophical system, called Humanitas, which Machado presents as a satirical portrayal of both positivism and naturalism.

Although there exists an inherent carnivalesque quality, in the Bakhtinian sense, to Brás Cubas's death, resurrection, and "free-spirited" seriocomic narration, subversive irony, and relentless unmasking of social norms and psychological inconsistencies, Brás's narration belongs to the more modern *romantic* version of the grotesque genre, in contrast to the collective nature of medieval folk culture and its popular carnivals. Like Laurence Sterne's *Tristram Shandy,* Brás Cubas's carnival is an individual one, celebrated in the "private chamber" of the character's fundamental sense of isolation.

The "Bad" Death of Brás Cubas

Certainly, the afterlife enjoyed by Brás Cubas bears some resemblance to, if not a "joyful hell," a joyful purgatory. It was during the twelfth century that the idea of purgatory, as an intermediary place where the souls of the faithful were purged of their sins before ascending to heaven, took hold in Europe. Yet throughout the Middle Ages (and later) the official geography of the afterlife sanctioned by the church was offset by the popular belief that the dead remained with the living for some time following their death, haunting the places and people they had left behind. The unquiet dead were those souls who had suffered an unnatural, or "bad," death (by drowning, suicide, murder, or the absence of a proper burial attended by loved ones), and consequently wandered the earth seeking redemption.

Despite the Christian funeral given on his behalf, Brás Cubas's demise by no means constitutes a "good" death. Having neglected his health, he dies "possessed" by his quest for personal glory. Like his failed oppositional newspaper, his antimelancholy poultice never comes to fruition. Moreover, he dies companionless and his funeral is attended by only a handful of people. Perhaps the most visible sign of his bad death, however, is his failure to produce offspring. With his death, the Cubas lineage comes to a halt, a misfortune that Brás Cubas seems to relish when, at the novel's conclusion, he takes stock of his life:

> Somadas umas cousas e outras, qualquer pessoa imaginará que não houve míngua nem sobra, e conseguintemente que saí quite com a vida. E imaginará mal; porque ao chegar a este outro lado do mistério, achei-me com um pequeno saldo, que é a derradeira negativa deste capítulo de negativas:—Não tive filhos, não transmiti a nenhuma criatura o legado da nossa miséria. (251)

> [Putting one and another thing together, any person will probably imagine that there was neither a lack nor a surfeit and, consequently, that I went off squared with life. And he imagines wrong. Because on arriving at this other side of the mystery I found myself with a small balance, which is the final negative in this chapter of negatives—I had no children, I haven't transmitted the legacy of our misery to any creature.] (203)

Brás Cubas's cynical assessment of his life and death and the absence of descendants may, however, be read on a broader level. A good death, one recalls, ensures not only the possibility of personal salvation for the deceased but also the preservation of social coherence within the community. In this regard, to die is not a solitary activity. Rather, it involves the participation of the community at large in its rituals and symbolic gestures and lays the groundwork for reconciliation and solidarity among friends, family, and neighbors. Moreover, these factors are essential for sustaining a sense of continuity among diverse groups and generations.

Along these lines, it is perhaps not incidental that Brás Cubas leaves no children to inherit his legacy, particularly when we consider the allegorical connotations of *Brás* in terms of nationhood: Bras—Brasil.[12] Thus, Brás Cubas's bad death may also be read as the impending bad death of Brazil's empire, a system still haunted by the specter of its colonial past—an empire whose transition to republic was perceived by

Machado de Assis as lacking continuity or clear vision. A national allegorical reading of this kind leads one to believe that for Machado, Brás Cubas, with his restless narrative style and elusive sense of morality, represented the "wandering souls" of the Brazilian elite—a class he viewed as lost in an ideological purgatory.

Brás Cubas's soul wanders precisely because he has consistently ruptured the reciprocal ties that link him to the world of the living and, in the process, violated the sanctity of memory. In essence Brás has condemned himself to a purgatorial existence by estranging himself from his family, his friends, and his community. His smug assessment of his life's balance—childless, he came out slightly ahead in this reckoning because he didn't transmit the legacy of human misery—poses the question, who then is left to pray for Brás Cubas's soul? With neither wife nor children, and estranged from both his family and his social circle, Brás Cubas essentially alienates himself from those who would potentially advocate on his soul's behalf. The reader is similarly severed from any degree of reciprocity based on trust and philosophical or spiritual guidance. In other words, Brás Cubas's (and by extension, Brazil's) soul is lacking the requisites for salvation.

Moreover, Brás Cubas's spirit falls considerably short of the spirit guides with whom Spiritism professes to communicate. He is not an illustrious figure, but rather a failed writer and inventor who leaves no living legacy—aside, one might argue, from his memoirs—and adheres loosely to Humanitas, a perverse philosophical system that dies along with its demented founder.

The lack of continuity embodied by Brás Cubas's bad death and his ruptured ties to the living speaks to a segment of Brazilian society that was becoming estranged from its origins. Gilberto Freyre in his seminal work *Sobrados e mucambos* portrays the decline of the rural patriarchy in Brazil as a gradual process that took place throughout the nineteenth century. During this time period the locus of political power and social prestige shifted from the rural casa-grande to the urban sobrado, or aristocratic mansion. The curtailment of the plantation system's absolute rule and autonomy coincided with the emergence of stronger state, judicial, military, and ecclesiastical control in Brazil's urban centers. Freyre observes, however, that Brazil's modernizing trend during the monarchy and First Republic was incomplete. The development, for example, of a new liberal mentality and appreciation for more diversified commercial undertakings stood in stark contrast to the Brazilian economy's dependence on slave labor. For this reason industrialization arrived prematurely in Brazil, according to Freyre, resulting in the "severing of paternalistic links between master and slave" (184).[13]

The severing of paternalistic links, however, was not limited to the slaveholding class and their slaves. Rather, the same may be said for the tenuous paternalistic links of the elite—those, for example, that extend out from Brás Cubas's generation to both the past and the future generations of his family. Brás Cubas's father is morally and physically defeated when his son is unable to carry on the glorious legacy of the Brás Cubas family name. Moreover, in his failure to produce offspring, Brás perpetuates the disintegration of the family's patriarchal name by, in effect, taking it to the grave with him. Brás's only fleeting claim to a paternal legacy comes when Virgília discovers herself pregnant and allows Brás to believe he is the father. Brás's sudden enthusiasm for fatherhood reveals the hypocrisy of his last words about parenting in the chapter "Das negativas":

> Eu só pensava naquele embrião anônimo, de obscura paternidade, e uma voz secreta me dizia: é teu filho. Meu filho! E repetia estas duas palavras, com certa voluptuosidade indefinível, e não sei que assomos de orgulho. Sentia-me homem. O melhor é que conversávamos os dous, o embrião e eu, falávamos de cousas presentes e futuras. (180)

> [I only thought about that anonymous embryo of obscure paternity and a secret voice told me: "It's your child." My child! And I would repeat those two words with a certain indefinable voluptuous feeling and I don't know how many feelings of pride. I felt myself a man.
>
> The best thing was that we would both converse, the embryo and I, talking about present and future things.] (135)

Brás then imagines himself reflected in the unborn child and projects his own worldly ambitions upon it. It would grow up to become a lawyer and deliver a speech in the chamber of deputies. It assumes his eyes, his forms, and his gestures, becomes both baby and deputy, schoolboy and grown-up dandy. Brás Cubas's imagined dialogue with the embryo offers the possibility of a present organically linked to the future, despite the child's illegitimate conception. Brás Cubas's dreams of fatherhood, however, are shattered when Lobo Neves himself informs him that Virgília has suffered a miscarriage. Upon hearing the news, Brás Cubas's lament turns toward the past: "Onde estão elas, as flores de antanho? Uma tarde, após algumas semanas de gestação, esboroou-se todo o edifício das minhas quimeras paternais" (186) ["Where are they, the flowers of yesteryear? One afternoon, after a few weeks of gestation, the whole structure of my paternal dreams crumbled"] (140). Brás Cubas's paternal dreams were destined to crumble because they were built on an illusion and fostered by illegitimacy.[14] Moreover, Brás Cubas's delusory discussion of "cousas presentes e futuras" ["things present and future"] with the embryo suggests that any continuity between past, present, and future is predicated on the illusion of renewal. Like Brás Cubas's bad death, Virgília's miscarriage is laden with allegorical meaning on a national level. We need only draw parallels between Brás's unborn child and nineteenth-century Brazil's "miscarried" modernity, its unfulfilled paternalistic dreams, and illegitimate liberalism. In this regard, the death of Virgília's and Brás Cubas's unborn child is a concentrated version of the many untimely deaths (and unfilled lives) that occur in *Memórias póstumas de Brás Cubas.*

Deceased Narration and Otherworldly Voices

The dead constitute a powerful cultural symbol in Machado de Assis's fiction, and as such, speak to two distinct problems that the author conceived as necessary to confront, namely, the Brazilian elite's cultural and intellectual dependence on European value systems and ideological models (Spiritism being emblematic of this dependency) and Brazil's struggle to reconcile its past with its present during the critical juncture of its transition from a patriarchal monarchy to a modern nation. Moreover, I propose that deceased narration cannot be fully understood, either in its authorial context or in the impact it has had on Brazilian readers, without taking into consideration the sociohistorical realities of death culture in Brazil. Given that, traditionally, the dead were expected to intervene on behalf of the living in Brazilian society, Brás Cubas's relationship to both the novel's characters and his reader represents a series of highly problematic interventions from beyond the grave. These interventions have an unsettling and subversive effect upon the reader who expects some degree of moral guidance. Ultimately, Machado inverts the notion of an illustrious spirit guide and makes a parody of the intimate and sacred relationship that existed between the living and the dead. Rather, Brás is the exemplification of a wayward spirit tormented by a past that remains unresolved, and as such may be viewed metaphorically as the spectral voice of a nineteenth-century Brazilian elite that has lost its moral and ideological bearings.

Deceased narration, however, did not end with *Memórias póstumas,* and there is good reason to believe that Machado increasingly found the ironic voice of the *defunto autor* an ideal rhetorical position from which to view the world. In 1884 he published the short story "Galeria póstuma" [Posthumous Gallery] in the collection *Histórias sem data* [Stories without a Date]. Like *Memórias,* the story begins with the unexpected death of its central character, Joaquim Fidélis, a retired city deputy, who is described as "rico e letrado," "um profundo céptico" [rich and erudite/a profound skeptic] in the later years of his life, yet highly admired and loved by all who knew him (*Obra completa,* 2:396). His nephew, Benjamin, whom he lived with and treated like a son, happens to come across the old man's personal diary on the occasion of the seventh-day Mass, and takes the opportunity to share some of the first entries with his uncle's close circle of friends. For Benjamin and the group of friends, the "secret memories" contained in the diary serve to resurrect Joaquim, in effect, to bring back the finest qualities of his life:

> Com efeito, era um diário das impressões do finado, espécie de memórias secretas, confidências do homem a si mesmo. Grande foi a comoção dos amigos; lê-lo era ainda conservá-lo. Tão reto caráter! Tão discreto espírito!
>
> [In effect, it was a diary of the dead man's impressions, a kind of hidden memoir, containing secrets intended for only him. This caused great excitement among his friends; to read it was to keep him alive. Such an upright fellow! What a discreet spirit!] (398)

After agreeing to meet again the following day to finish the diary, the friends depart, leaving Benjamin alone to read the manuscript. He soon discovers that the entries read aloud had been for public consumption, while what follows constitutes the diary's pithy core, "o texto primitivo e interior, a lição exata e autêntica" [the primal and inner text, the exact and authentic lesson] (400). Inserted in the narration of this short story are Joaquim's posthumously read diary entries, brutal in their honesty, as the old man dissects the habits, faults, and inconsistencies of the very friends who had been listening in earlier, the very pallbearers of his coffin! He describes one close colleague as "estúpido e crédulo" [stupid and naive], another as engaging in conversation that is "vulgar, polida e chôcha," [vulgar, superficial, and dull] and of another he says simply: "mente com facilidade" [he lies with ease] (399–400). Incredulous about his dead uncle's relentless character assassinations Benjamin tries to invoke the gentler version of his deceased relative:

> Evocou a figura do tio, com o olhar espirituoso e meigo, e a pilhéria grave; em lugar dessa, tão cândida e simpática, a que lhe apareceu foi a do tio morto, estendido na cama, com os olhos abertos e o lábio arregaçado. Sacudiu-a do espírito, mas a imagem ficou. Não podendo rejeitá-la, Benjamin tentou mentalmente fechar-lhe os olhos e consertar-lhe

a bôca; mas não depressa o fazia, como a pálpebra tornava a levantar-se, a ironia arregaçava o beiço. Já não era o homem, era o autor do manuscrito.

[He invoked his uncle's previous persona, with his spiritual and gentle gaze, his good nature; in the place of this uncle, so candid and kind, the figure that appeared to him was that of the dead uncle, stretched out on his deathbed, with eyes wide open and lips turned up. He tried to shake this image from his head, to no avail. Unable to reject it, Benjamin mentally tried to close his dead uncle's eyes and fix the expression of his mouth; but no sooner had he done so, than the uncle's eyebrow lifted slightly and his lips began to pout with a look of irony. He was no longer the man, he was the author of the manuscript.] (401)

Joaquim's diaries do indeed prove to possess restorative powers, however, it is not the affable uncle, "o homem," who emerges, but rather the diary's ironic author. The distinction formed here between Joaquim's living person and his deceased authorial voice is reminiscent of Brás Cubas's narrative claim as a defunto autor. Although his diary entries were composed before his demise, they are read to us posthumously and therefore represent the voice of the dead. Furthermore, we cannot assume that the uncle's essential nature was any different in life than it is in death, the difference being that in death his irony is intensified and targeted unabashedly at the affectations and hypocrisies of others. In this sense, Joaquim shares some of the intrinsic properties of the carnivalesque defunto. "Galeria póstuma" also underscores the conflict that often exists between the idealized memory we construct of the deceased and the often unseemly traces of their lives that they leave behind.

The appearance of two additional stories in *Histórias sem data* in which deceased narration emerges, alongside "A segunda vida" with the "reincarnated" José Maria, suggests that Machado was fully appreciative of the impact of dead souls and their otherworldly narrations on his readers during the 1880s. In this vein, the story "Fulano" [So-and-So] begins with the narrator inviting the reader to attend the reading of his friend's will, which is also a form of posthumous narrative. This invitation is repeated several times throughout the story until the conclusion, when Fulano Beltrão's will is read and we learn of his wish to have thirty contos designated toward the building of a statue in honor of Pedro Álvares Cabral. Incidentally, we find a slightly earlier example of the reading of a will in the opening of Machado's short story "Verba testamentária" [Final Request], published as part of *Papéis avulsos* [Separate Papers] (1877–82).

Also included in *Histórias sem data* is "Último capítulo" [Final Chapter], in which deceased narration appears in the form of a suicide note written by a man named Matias Deodato de Castro e Melo. About his note, which he started writing an hour before taking his own life, Matias says,

> Costume excelente: em primeiro lugar, é um ato de cortesia, não sendo êste mundo um baile, de onde um homem possa esgueirar-se antes do cotilhão; em segundo lugar, a imprensa recolhe e divulga os bilhetes póstumos, e o morto vive ainda um dia ou dois, às vêzes uma semana mais. (*Obra completa,* 2:380–81)

> [It is an excellent idea: in the first place, it's an act of courtesy, as this world is not a ballroom from which a man can sneak away before the cotillion begins. In the second place, the press always gathers and divulges the posthumous letters, and the dead man lives on for a day or two, sometimes a week more.] (*Devil's Church,* 44)

Like Joaquim's diary, Matias's suicide note extends his life beyond physical death. As he explains, it is a recapitulation of his life, without which his accompanying will would make little sense. In a peculiar twist to Brás Cubas's "negative" legacy, Matias leaves his entire collection of boots to his fellow "caiporas" [unlucky people], convinced that no worldly or philosophical achievement is comparable to the realization that "a felicidade é um par de botas" (386) ["happiness is a pair of boots"] (51).

Another short story by Machado de Assis in which deceased narration appears in an interesting way is "O enfermeiro" [The Companion], published in his collection *Várias histórias* [Various Stories] (1896). Procópio, the story's narrator, recounts his unhappy days as a live-in nurse for a sickly yet tyrannical *coronel* who has a fondness for striking his servants with a cane: "Era homem insuportável, estúrdio, exigente, ninguém o aturava, nem os próprio amigos. Gastava mais enfermeiros que remédios" (529) ["He was an unbearable, strange, and demanding person, and even his friends found his behavior extremely difficult to tolerate for long. He used up more companions than medicine"] (*Devil's Church,* 78). As the colonel's suffering increases so does the physical and verbal abuse he inflicts on Procópio. This abuse continues until, in a particularly violent fit of rage, the colonel provokes Procópio to defend himself by snuffing out the old man's life with a grip around his neck. Overtaken by guilt and unsure of what to do next, the panic-stricken nurse begins to hear his victim's screams and other accusatory voices coming through the walls: "Assassino! Assassino!" (532) ["Murderer! Murderer!"] (80). He begins to see shadowy figures in the yard spying in on him and then disappearing. The colonel's threats while still alive, that he would return as a ghost and haunt the young man, seemingly come true:

> Procópio. . . . Há de ir, há de rezar ao pé da minha sepultura. Se não for, acresentou rindo, eu voltarei de noite para lhe puxar as pernas. Você crê em almas de outro mundo, Procópio?—Qual o quê!—E por que é que não há de crer, seu burro? redargüiu vivamente, arregalando os olhos. (530)
>
> ["Procópio. . . . You've got to go and pray over my grave. If you don't," he added laughing, "my ghost will come back at night and haunt you. Do you believe in spirits from the other world, Procópio?"—"Of course not!"—"And why shouldn't you believe, stupid?" he rejoined excitedly, his eyes bulging.] (79)

The colonel's question rings like a refrain in Machado's fiction, as if he were posing the same question to his reader.[15] Eventually, the nurse comes to his senses and spreads the word that the colonel has finally succumbed to his illness and died naturally. During the funeral his agitation is perceived as grief, a misconception that he himself begins to believe and that compels him to make additional "sincere" eulogies and masses on behalf of his secret victim. To his great surprise, however, Procópio discovers some time later that he has been named full heir to the colonel's estate. Morally conflicted, the nurse at first swears to himself that he will donate his newfound wealth to charity in a conscience-assuaging tactic not unlike Brás Cubas's theory regarding the "equivalência das janelas" [the equivalency of windows]. As times goes on, however, justifications for both why he should keep the money and why the coronel was nearly dead even before the incident have a dissipating effect on his original guilt-driven philanthropy.

What makes "O enfermeiro" precisely an example of deceased narration is the detail that Procópio, the narrator, states in the opening lines of the story:

> Parece-lhe então que o que se deu comigo em 1860, pode entrar numa página de livro? Vá que seja, com a condição única de que não há de divulgar nada antes da minha morte. Não esperará muito, pode ser que oito dias, se não fôr menos. (528)
>
> [So do you think what happened to me in 1860 could be put in a book? Very well, but on the sole condition that you publish nothing until after my death. You won't have to wait long—a week at the most.] (77)

Consequently, the story we are reading actually constitutes the words of a dead man. This subtle yet significant detail infuses Procópio's narration with an added spectral quality. In effect, it is a haunting within a haunting. Procópio's story of personal guilt and the wrath of an abusive old man's ghost comes to us from the afterworld, and in so doing, haunts us with its account of cruelty, violence, dissemblance, and false eulogies. Like the colonel, the narrator projects a restless soul that lingers and haunts the reader with his story of violent death and buried secrets.

The concept of deceased narration stimulates other germane questions, such as, can writing constitute a form of haunting? To what extent can text serve as the symbolic medium for spirit interventions? The examples of posthumous narration provided above suggest that

Machado de Assis entertained these questions with increasing poignancy in the years following the publication of *Memórias póstumas de Brás Cubas.* Machado had found in the defunto autor not only a voice remarkable for its unconstrained candidness but also a worldview that originated from beyond the gaze of public opinion and whose carnivalesque irony exposed the fundamental contradictions between the inner "self" and the social mask. At the same time, deceased narration enabled Machado to problematize the memorialist genre in new and unexpected ways. For example, the distinct irony employed by Machado's posthumous narrators challenges the reader's expectation that memorialist accounts provide a "true" portrayal of the author's life. Indeed, as these examples have demonstrated, restoring the past with fidelity is slippery business, particularly when that restoration originates from beyond the grave.

"Ah, come ye back once more, ye restless shades?"

Voices of the dead reverberate with similar consistency in the novels Machado published after *Memórias póstumas de Brás Cubas.* While the narration in *Dom Casmurro* is not posthumous, Bento does begin by describing how he will go about resurrecting his past by building a replica of his childhood home and writing his memoirs. Bento's line "Deste modo, viverei o que vivi" (13) ["In this way, I will relive what I lived then"] (7), suggests a kind of personal resurrection brought about through memorialist writing, much like Brás Cubas's claim to be a "defunto autor para quem a campa foi outro berço" (13) ["a dead man who is a writer, for whom the grave was a second cradle"] (7).[16] Bento's decision to write his life's story is similarly motivated by a desire to wile away the time:

> Foi então que os bustos pintados nas paredes entraram a falar-me e a dizer-me que, uma vez que eles não alcançavam reconstituir-me os tempos idos, pegasse da pena e contasse alguns. Talvez a narração me desse

a ilusão, e as sombras viessem perpassar ligeiras, como ao poeta, não o do trem, mas o do Fausto: "Aí vindes outra vez, inquietas sombras?" (13)

[Then it was that the busts painted on the walls started to talk to me, and to tell me that, since they couldn't bring back times past, I should take a pen and recount some of them. Perhaps the narration would beguile me, and the old shades would pass lightly over me, as they passed over the poet—not the one on the train, but the other of Faust: "Ah, come ye back once more, ye restless shades?"] (6)

Bento is initially urged on to write his memoirs by the replicated busts of Nero, Augustus, Massinissa, and Julius Caesar, whose voices emanate from the walls of his re-created home. The scene is not so different from the unanticipated Spiritist session in "Uma visita de Alcibíades," where the desembargador evokes the illustrious Roman statesman to discuss contemporary fashion. All important figures of antiquity, the busts in Bento's house, however, carry a somewhat more sinister tone from the afterworld. With the exception of Augustus, their lives were marked by tragedy and betrayal, which, as we know, are the twin pillars of Bento's obsession. If we are familiar with Machado's prior estimation of people who receive messages from the spirit world this scene should alert us to the state of Bento's mind. Since these spirits are unable to bring back his past, Bento turns to the *sombras,* or shades, of people with whom he lived and who now inhabit his memory. Bento's summoning of the shades to restore his past represents an inverted example of the necromancy practiced by Faust, who conjured the spirits of the dead in order to predict the future.

The act of conjuring the spirits of the dead as a metaphor for writing one's memoirs is expressed as a central narrative feature and conceptual link in both *Dom Casmurro* and *Memórias póstumas.* Just as Bento surrounds himself with the spectral relics of his past that speak to him and compel him to write his history, Brás Cubas performs a kind of inverted narrative necromancy with his posthumous memoirs. For both narrators, writing becomes the externalization of a process of haunting, where the past intrudes like a specter in the text.

Indeed, haunting is a central motif in *Dom Casmurro.* This becomes most apparent in the chapters following Escobar's death. Bento's first suspicion of his wife's infidelity is aroused by the way Capitu looks upon Escobar's dead body:

> Momento houve em que os olhos de Capitu fitaram o defunto, quais os da viúva, sem o pranto nem palavras desta, mas grandes e abertos, como a vaga do mar lá fora, como se quisesses tragar também o nadador da manhã. (134)
>
> [There was a moment when Capitu's eyes fixed on the body, like those of the widow though without her tears or cries, but large and wide open, like the waves on the sea out there, as if she too wanted to swallow up that morning's swimmer.] (212)

Chapter 123, in which this passage appears, is entitled "Olhos de ressaca" [Undertow Eyes], which is the second apparition of Capitu's enigmatic "undertow eyes" in the novel. The first takes place in chapter 32, also entitled "Olhos de ressaca," when Bento is young and thoroughly enamored with Capitu's mysterious vitality:

> Olhos de ressaca. Vá, de ressaca. É o que me dá idéia daquela feição nova. Traziam não sei que fluido misterioso e enérgico, uma força que arrastava para dentro, como a vaga que se retira da praia, nos dias de ressaca. Para não ser arrastado, agarrei-me às outras partes vizinhas, às orelhas, aos braços, aos cabelos espalhados pelos ombros; mas tão depressa buscava as pupilas, a onda que saía delas vinha crescendo, cava e escura, ameaçando envolver-me, puxar-me e tragar-me. (47)
>
> [Undertow eyes? Why not? Undertow. That's the notion that the new expression put in my head. They held some kind of mysterious, active fluid, a force that dragged one in, like the undertow of a wave retreating from the shore on stormy days. So as not to be dragged in, I held on to anything around them, her ears, her arms, her hair spread about her shoulders; but as soon as I returned to the pupils of her eyes again, the wave emerging from them grew towards me, deep and dark, threatening to envelop me, draw me in and swallow me up.] (63)

The recurrence of the powerful image of Capitu's undertow eyes suggests multiple hauntings. As a young man, Bento is haunted by Capitu's eyes, afraid he will be swallowed up by them. Then at his best friend's funeral, he is haunted by them once again, however this time they threaten to swallow up Escobar with their passion. The image of the ocean in the earlier chapter, dragging in its victim, also acts to foreshadow Escobar's later drowning in an angry sea. Haunting is thus interwoven into the narration itself. This becomes particularly apparent when we recall that Bento is narrating retrospectively throughout the entire story. Therefore, contained in his first description of Capitu's undertow eyes, is the specter of Escobar's drowning as well as the look Capitu bestowed on him at his funeral. Capitu's *olhos de ressaca* constitute an unforgettable motif for Bento in this endless cycle of haunting imagery. Like a ghost, Capitu's eyes pass through temporal and spatial boundaries in the narrative as they make what seem to be always their apparitional debut. In fact we never fully know where in Bento's life or memory the image originates.

Of all the characters in *Dom Casmurro,* however, it is Escobar who has the most haunting presence. His drowning is a textbook example of a bad death, both because it is sudden and because he is still in the prime of his life when he leaves his young family unexpectedly. It is no wonder then that, in Bento's mind, Escobar's ghost returns to possess Bento's son, Ezequiel. "Aí vindes outra vez, inquietas sombras?" Like Capitu's olhos de ressaca, Escobar's image haunts Bento's narration. This is particularly true near the end of the novel when Bento begins to see traces of his friend in his son's physical appearance. He first notices (by way of Capitu's observation) the resemblance in Ezequiel's eyes, "uma expressão esquisita" (139) ["an odd expression"] (220) that reminds him of Escobar. Soon the other parts of his son's body take on Escobar's presence in a kind of gradual ghostly possession: "Nem só os olhos, mas as restantes feições, a cara, o corpo, a pessoa inteira, iamse apurando com o tempo" (139) ["Not only the eyes, but the other features, the face, the body, the whole person, were gradually rounded out with time"] (221). As Bento's jealousy grows so does Escobar's specter:

> Escobar vinha assim surgindo da sepultura, do seminário e do Flamengo para se sentar comigo à mesa, receber-me na escada, beijar-me no gabinete de manhã, ou pedir-me à noite a benção do costume. Todos essas ações eram repulsivas. (140)
>
> [So Escobar began to rise from the tomb, from the seminary, and from Flamengo to sit beside me at table, greet me on the stairs, kiss me in my study in the morning, or ask for my customary blessing at night. All these actions were repulsive.] (222)

To a lesser degree Escobar's ghost commingles with Capitu in Bento's mind, as in this passage where he expresses his regret for having described his stormy relationship with Capitu using imagery from the ocean:

> Releva-me estas metáforas; cheiram ao mar e à maré que deram morte ao meu amigo e comborço Escobar. Cheiram também aos olhos de ressaca de Capitu. (140)
>
> [Excuse these metaphors; they smell of the sea and the tide, which brought death to my friend, my wife's lover, Escobar. They smell, too, of Capitu's undertow eyes.] (223)

Years later a grown Ezequiel returns from Europe to visit Bento shortly after Capitu's death. The chapter is appropriately entitled "Regresso" [The Return], signaling the return of both Escobar's ghost and Bento's now hardened conviction about his wife's guilt:

> A voz era a mesma de Escobar. . . . [O] meu colega do seminário ia ressurgindo cada vez mais do cemitério. (150)
>
> [His voice was the same as Escobar's. . . . [M]y seminary friend began to arise even more from the cemetery.] (240)

and then later,

não gostava da ressureição. Às vezes, fechava os olhos para não ver gestos nem nada, mas o diabrete falava e ria, e o defunto falava e ria por ele. (150)

[I took no pleasure in the ressurection. At times, I shut my eyes so as not to see gestures or anything, but the young devil talked and laughed, and the dead man laughed and talked through him.] (241)

The defunto that laughs through Ezequiel has predecessors in Brás Cubas, with his profound disdain for the living and Joaquim, the deceased uncle and derisive "autor do manuscrito" in "Galeria póstuma." The irony contained in each of these dead voices reveals both the parallels between haunting and memorialist writing, and the pitfalls of restoring one's past by conjuring up the spirits of the dead. Moreover, each narrative situation is characterized by a mourning process gone awry, where even the supposedly restorative powers of the memoir are unable to bring resolution or peace to the narrator and other characters. One way of reading Escobar's haunting figure and, subsequently, Bento's jealousy is from the point of view that Bento is unable to put his best friend to rest. The intimacy formed between the two during seminary school is broken only when Bento returns to Capitu and his family. The friends remain extremely close, even more so after each marries. That Bento's former intimacy with Escobar continues to haunt him even before Escobar dies is made apparent in the following scene from the chapter "A mão de Sancha" [Sancha's Hand], in which Bento's desire for Sancha is curiously transferred momentarily to Escobar:

—(Bento) Você entra no mar amanhã?
—(Escobar) Tenho entrado com mares maiores, muito maiores. Você não imagina o que é um bom mar em hora bravia, É preciso nadar bem, como eu, e ter este pulmões,—disse ele batendo no peito, e estes braços; apalpa.
Apalpei-lhe os braços, como se fossem os de Sancha. Custa-me esta confissão, mas não posso suprimi-la; era jarretar a verdade. Não só os apalpei com essa idéia, mas ainda senti outra coisa: achei-os mais grossos e fortes que os meus, e tive-lhes inveja; acresce que sabiam nadar. (131)

> [—(Bento) "Are you going in tomorrow?"
> —(Escobar) "I've gone in rougher seas, much rougher; you've no idea what a really good angry sea is like. You have to swim well, as I do, and have lungs like these"—he said, slapping his chest—"and these arms; feel them." I felt his arms, as if they were Sancha's. This is a painful confession to make, but I cannot suppress it; that would be to avoid the truth. Not only did I feel them with that idea in mind, but I felt something else as well; I thought they were thicker and stronger than mine, and I envied them; what's more, they knew how to swim.] (206)

Bento's somewhat ambiguous confession here and the frequency with which he conjures up Escobar's portrait in the subsequent scenes suggests that it is plausible to read Bento's ultimate inability to let go of his friend as a homoerotic impulse.[17] The possibility of this dynamic is further suggested by the fact that his mourning for Escobar (during the burial) coincides exactly with the germination of a jealousy that eventually consumes him.

Reading Bento's memoirs as an example of unresolved mourning (for his friend, for his wife and son, and, figuratively, for his own life) provides fertile ground for textual comparisons with *Memórias póstumas.* As in Brás Cubas's narration, mourning rituals are left unobserved. Of Capitu's death he says only, "creio que ainda não disse que estava morta e enterrada" (150) ["I don't think I've said that she was dead and buried"] (239), as if he had almost forgotten to include this detail in his narration. As in *Memórias* there is a simultaneous compression and acceleration of death scenes near the end of the novel. Within the span of five chapters, D. Glória, José Dias, Capitu, and Ezequiel all perish and their deaths are told in typically parsimonious terms. Paul B. Dixon in *Retired Dreams: Dom Casmurro, Myth and Modernity* proposes that much of the novel's movement is guided by a rebirth motif in which (quoting Maud Bodkin) "the tidal ebb towards death [is] followed by life renewal" (50). While Dixon argues that this is particularly true in the first half of the book, where narrating seems to restore life to Bento, by the end "he is every bit the 'casmurro' he was when he started" (115) (*casmurro*—sullen fellow). The restorative powers contained in his book, his "elixir of life," dry out by the novel's bitter conclusion, as they do in *Memórias póstumas de Brás Cubas.* Bento is possessed by Escobar, but he is equally haunted by the relics of his past, as symbolized by the recreation of his childhood house. Ultimately, the memoirs of Bento and Brás Cubas represent haunted narrations because they are, in the words of Kathleen Brogan, examples of "mourning gone awry [where] the possessed one is locked into repetition, doomed to reenact the past without relevance to present realities" (10).

Helen Caldwell suggests that Machado was well aware that his artistic innovations in *Memórias póstumas* were underappreciated by most of his contemporaries. As a result, she says, Machado "began, perhaps, to write more and more for posterity," that is, for an imagined reader in the distant future (125). This observation only lends support to the idea that Machado's fiction, beginning with *Memórias,* is characterized not only by memorialist writing, but also by his frequent adoption of a posthumous perspective. A brief examination of Machado's last two novels, *Esaú e Jacó* and *Memorial de Aires* reveals the author's consistent preoccupation with both deceased narration and the haunting presence of the dead. *Esaú e Jacó* begins with "Advertência" [A Note to the Reader] that explains the narrative situation of both this novel and the memoirs of Counselor Ayres:

> Quando o conselheiro Aires faleceu, acharam-se-lhe na secretária sete cadernos manuscritos, rijamente encapados em papelão. Cada um dos primeiros seis tinha o seu número de ordem, por algarismos romanos, I, II, III, IV, V, VI, escritos a tinta encarnada. O sétimo trazia este título: *Último.* (25)

> [When Counselor Aires died, seven notebooks in manuscript were found in his desk, firmly bound in cardboard. Each one of the first six was numbered in order, with roman numerals I, II, III, IV, V, VI penned in red ink. The seventh bore this title: "Last."] (*Esau and Jacob,* 1)[18]

The advertência's subsequent reference to the "desejo do finado" [desire of the deceased] only underscores the peculiar circumstances in which Counselor Ayres's works are published (25). Rather than publishing his memoirs (manuscripts 1–6) and the narrative (manuscript 7) during his lifetime, the counselor has carefully placed them in his desk, to be either published posthumously or kept for posterity's sake. Either way the words contained in both novels are those of a dead man. Perhaps more important, their narrations appear to be deliberately posthumous. Why else would Counselor Ayres guard them in his desk until his death? In so doing, the counselor transforms himself, like Joaquim in "Galeria póstuma," from the man to the author of the manuscript.

This is not the place to recount the numerous scenes in *Esaú e Jacó* in which the reciprocal relationship between the living and the dead is subjected to Counselor Ayres's refined sense of irony. Flora's death, however, merits a few words. Flora dies loving (and confusing) both Paulo, the republican, and Pedro, the monarchist. The twins' (and the nation's) eternal conflict takes place inside her, as it did when their mother, Nativity, was carrying them in her womb. It is a conflict, however, that Flora takes to the grave with her. Struck by this mutual tragedy, the twins initially see in her death the possibility for reconciliation. At her funeral they come to the realization together that "Talvez morrese para isso mesmo" (220) ["Perhaps she died for that very reason"] (231). Similarly, when Nativity is on her deathbed she makes her sons swear that they will end their conflict for their mother's sake: "Vocês vão ser amigos. Sua mãe padecerá no outro mundo, se os não vir amigos neste" (235) ["You will be friends. Your mother will suffer in the next world, if she cannot see you as friends in this one"] (249). The twins swear in unison.

The twins' ideological differences, however, prove to be irreconcilable and their resumed political discord leads Counselor Ayres to confirm "não mudaram nada, são os mesmos" (238) ["they haven't changed at all; they are the same"] (252). Both Flora's death and Nativity's death represent moments of collective mourning in which the family, the community, the nation have an opportunity to restore broken ties and find inroads for reconciliation. The gulf between Paulo's republican restlessness and Pedro's monarchist conservatism, the two poles of Brazil's political spectrum, is a reflection of the rancor that, in fact, originated in the womb. So too for Brazil, the political and ideological divide "vem desde o útero."

As in *Memórias póstumas* and *Dom Casmurro,* death in *Esaú e Jacó* ultimately fails to provide a sense of reconciliation or resolve. Consequently, Pedro and Paulo's conflicted past (and Brazil's divided past) continue to haunt the present and future. The opening scene of Machado's final novel, *Memorial de Aires,* takes place in a cemetery, with Counselor Ayres observing a beautiful woman praying before her deceased husband's tomb. Ayres's comment "parecia rezar" (33) ["appeared to be praying"] (11)[19] creates a level of ambiguity that poses one of the novel's fundamental questions: How true is Fidélia's devotion to her deceased husband, Eduardo Noronha? Fidélia's name suggests that she is the embodiment of faithfulness, not only to her husband, but also to the tradition of remaining close to the dead and preserving the dead's memory. Throughout the novel, Ayres's skepticism and emotional detachment gives way to a more trusting and accepting attitude, even when Fidélia begins to show interest in a new man, Tristão. When Fidélia brings flowers to her late husband's grave at the close of the novel, Ayres imagines her "diante da pessoa extinta, como se fôsse a pessoa futura, fazendo de ambas uma só criatura presente" (183) ["before the deceased person as if he were the future person, making of both a single present being"] (169). Indeed, Fidélia's placing flowers on Eduardo's grave is a powerful symbolic act of reconciliation. Unlike Flora, Ayres seems to be saying, the strong, capable Fidélia was able to reconcile the past with the future. In other words, her mourning was sincere and purposeful, in the sense that it simultaneously enabled her to come to terms with the past and embrace the future. Fidélia's "rebirth," in effect, teaches Ayres how to mourn purposefully and coincides in many ways with Ayres's own resurrection as a deceased narrator. The following diary entry, from April 8, 1889, suggests that, of all Machado's deceased narrators, Ayres is the only one who has learned this lesson well:

> Os mortos param no cemitério, e lá vai ter a afeição dos vivos, com as suas flôres e recordações. Tal sucederá à própria Fidélia, quando para lá fôr; tal sucede ao Noronha, que lá está. A questão é que virtualmente não se quebre êste laço, e que a lei da vida não destrua o que foi da vida e da morte. Creio nas afeições de Fidélia; chego a crer que as duas formam uma só, continuada. (192)

> [The dead stay in the cemetery, and there they have the love of the living, along with their flowers and remembrance. This will happen even to Fidelia when she goes there. This is what happened to Noronha, who is there. The question is, essentially, to preserve this bond unbroken and keep life's law from destroying what properly belongs to life *and* death. I believe in Fidelia's "two" loves; I have come to believe that they form one continuous, unbroken love.] (179; emphasis in original)

Machado's complex literary construction of the resurrected defunto, while frequently rendered in ironic and parodic terms, is a testimony to the tenacious bonds and symbolic force that have kept Brazilian society attuned to the voices of the dead. *Memórias póstumas,* published in 1880, introduced the postmortem voice of the deceased narrator to Machado de Assis's fiction. The echoes of this voice, of both the defunto autor and the autor defunto, in his subsequent short stories and novels form an enduring and salient leitmotif, cultivated until the final stages of Machado's literary production.

Chapter 4

Jorge Amado

Imagining a Good Death

To every thing there is a season, and a time to every
purpose under the heaven.
A time to be born, and a time to die; . . .
A time to weep, and a time to laugh;
a time to mourn, and a time to dance.

—Ecclesiastes 3:1–4

Me enterro como entender
Na hora que resolver.
Podem guardar seu caixão
Pra melhor ocasião.
Não vou deixar me prender
Em cova rasa no chão.

[I'll be buried when I please
In my own sweet way.
You can keep your coffin
For another time.
I ain't goin' down
In a hole in the ground.]

—Quincas Berro Dágua, according to
a ballad singer in the market

Death and the Dead According to Jorge Amado

Of all the twentieth-century Brazilian novelists it is perhaps Jorge Amado who is most responsible for bringing the topos of the resurrected dead to the attention of modern readers. Two of Amado's works of fiction give forceful account to the recurring presence of the carnivalesque defunto in modern Brazilian literature. The presence of a postmortem figure within the realm of the living assumes a different manifestation in each work, namely, as protagonist who returns from the dead for a final night of revelry in *A morte e a morte de Quincas Berro Dágua* [The Two Deaths of Quincas Wateryell] (1961) and as a primary character and participant, albeit deceased, in a love triangle that takes place somewhere between this world and the next in *Dona Flor e seus dois maridos* [Dona Flor and Her Two Husbands] (1966).[1]

This chapter is concerned with essentially the four overarching questions that guided my analysis of Machado de Assis's fiction in the previous chapter: (1) what does the topos of the resurrected defunto enable the author to accomplish? (2) how does the form and significance of this topos relate to both traditional and modern death rituals and customs in Brazil? (3) in what ways may the resurrected defuntos in Amado's fiction be described as carnivalesque in the sense proposed by Bakhtin? and (4) how is the author's use of this topos linked to the specific sociohistorical context of the 1950s and 1960s in Brazil?

The title *A morte e a morte de Quincas Berro Dágua* suggests multiple deaths, which is precisely the case for Quincas Berro Dágua, the protagonist in this novella. As the story opens, we learn of his physical death when his body is found in his apartment. Long before this, however, Joaquim Soares da Cunha, a mild public functionary, died a symbolic death when he forsook his middle-class existence, abandoned his oppressive family life, and was resurrected as Quincas Berro Dágua, King of the Vagabonds and local hero for the common folk in Salvador, Bahia. On the night of his wake, and in the company of his closest vagrant friends, Quincas is physically roused from his deathly slumber by a few generous swigs of cachaça. A night of drunken revelry culminates in Quincas's final, more personally spiritual death when he allegedly tosses himself off the bow of a boat during a storm, uttering these prophetic words: "Cada qual cuide de seu enterro, impossível não há" (ix) ["Everybody look out for his own funeral; Nothing's Impossible"] (n.p.). In keeping with the concept of multiple deaths, three episodes in particular give shape to the protagonist's fantastic demise, namely: his biological death, his resurrection, and his final death.

The narration begins on a speculative note: Which version of Quincas's death(s) should we believe? Indeed, Quincas's last words, presented as an epigraph, are in fact the result of secondhand knowledge: "Frase derradeira de Quincas Berro Dágua, segundo Quitéria que estava ao seu lado" (ix) ["Last words of Quincas Wateryell, according to Quitéria who was next to him"] (n.p.). This speculatory tone concerning Quincas's demise extends into the opening of the first paragraph:

> Até hoje permanece certa confusão em torno da morte de Quincas Berro Dágua. Dúvidas por explicar, detalhes absurdos, contradições no depoimento das testemunhas, lacunas diversas. Não há clareza sobre hora, local e frase derradeira. A família, apoiada por vizinhos e conhecidos, mantém-se intransigente na versão da tranqüila morte matinal, sem testemunhas, sem aparato, sem frase, acontecida quase vinte horas antes daquela outra propalada e comentada morte na agonia da noite, quando a lua se desfez sobre o mar e aconteceram mistérios na orla do cais da Bahia. (*Morte,* 1)

> [A certain amount of confusion about the death of Quincas Wateryell persists even today. There are doubts to be explained away, ridiculous details, contradictory testimony from witnesses, diverse gaps in the story. Time, place, and last words are uncertain. The family, backed up by neighbors and acquaintances, sticks to its version of a quiet death in the morning—with no witnesses, no fuss, and no last words—occurring almost twenty hours before that other, notorious death just before dawn, when the moon faded into the ocean and mysterious things took place on the docks of Bahia.] (*Two Deaths,* 3)

The level of doubt inserted at the outset proves to be an important element in Amado's narrative approach throughout the novella. As if part of a jury, readers are invited to hear conflicting accounts of Quincas's death from family and friends and then make a decision for themselves as to the veracity of each story.

It becomes apparent, however, that the truth does not necessarily lie in the story with the most probable explanation, but rather in the version that is most morally persuasive. For the narrator warns the reader at the conclusion of the first chapter that the whole truth of the matter may forever be shrouded in mystery:

> Não sei se esse mistério da morte (ou das sucessivas mortes) de Quincas Berro Dágua pode ser completamente decifrado. Mas eu o tentarei, como ele próprio aconselhava, pois o importante é tentar, mesmo o impossível. (4)

> [I honestly don't know whether the mystery of Quincas Wateryell's death (or deaths) can ever be cleared up. But I am going to try my best, for as Quincas said himself, the important thing is to attempt even the impossible.] (5)

With this statement, the narrator also reveals a certain degree of identification with Quincas's own outlook on life: one must try, even the seemingly impossible. The narrator's sympathy for Quincas and his bohemian lifestyle is further revealed in the frequent sarcasm and irony with which the family's point of view is depicted, as in this passage:

> Os patifes que contavam, pelas ruas e ladeiras, em frente ao Mercado a na feira de Água dos Meninos, os momentos finais de Quincas (até um folheto com versos de pé-quebrado foi composto pelo repentista Cuíca de Santo Amaro e vendido largamente), desrespeitavam assim a memória do morto, segundo a família. E memória de morto, como se sabe, é coisa sagrada, não é para estar na boca pouco limpa de cachaceiros, jogadores e contrabandistas de maconha. (5)

> [In the opinion of the family, the rapscallions who reported Quincas's last moments in the streets and alleys, in front of the Trade Mart and in the open-air market of Água dos Meninos, showed an appalling lack of respect for the dead. Furthermore, a leaflet containing doggerel verses composed by Cuica de Santo Amaro, the improviser, was enjoying a brisk sale. A dead man's memory is, as we all know, sacred and not meant to be bandied about in the dirty mouths of drunken sots, gamblers, and marijuana smugglers.] (6)

Thus, the ensuing narration chronicles not only conflicting reports surrounding Quincas's death but also the struggle over how Quincas (and the dead) should best be remembered. As the narrator tells us, "a dead man's memory is, as we all know, sacred" and, indeed, what constitutes a sacred burial, as well as the sanctity of memory, lies at the heart of the question here.

In turn, we may interpret the conflict over Quincas's burial and subsequent memory as a metaphor for the struggle over what constitutes a morally authentic existence. In other words, defining a good death runs parallel to defining a good life. After all, it is only in the aftermath of Quincas's mysterious death that the frequently contradictory components of his life are fleshed out. The intimate association of Quincas's demise, its quality and purpose, with Quincas's life explains, to a large degree, why there is so much at stake in defining Quincas's death. In the words of Octávio Paz from *The Labyrinth of Solitude* (1950): "Tell me how you die and I will tell you who you are" (46). Paz's discussion of Mexico's cult of the dead and the pervasive opposition between life and death in Mexican culture illuminates much of the symbolic value surrounding the nature of Quincas's death:

> Our deaths illuminate our lives. If our deaths lack meaning, our lives also lacked it. Therefore we are apt to say, when somebody has died a violent death, "He got what he was looking for." Each of us dies the death he is looking for, the death he has made for himself. A Christian death or a dog's death are ways of dying that reflect ways of living. If death betrays us and we die badly, everyone laments the fact, because we should die as we have lived. Death, like life, is not transferable. If we do not die as we lived, it is because the life we lived was not really ours: it did not belong to us, just as the bad death that kills us does not belong to us. (46)

In *Quincas Berro Dágua,* however, what constitutes a Christian death and what constitutes a dog's death is never clear-cut. What one character believes to be a dog's death, another sees as a morally proper death, and vice versa. For example, Quincas's daughter, Vanda, defends her derelict father's right to a proper burial, despite her relatives' reluctance: "Muito nos fez sofrer. . . . Mas nem por isso quero que seja enterrado como um cão sem dono" (26) ["He led my mother and me a hard life. . . . But even so, I won't have him buried like a stray dog"] (24). The implication here is that leaving her father's body in the hands of the povo, without at least the formality of a middle-class funeral, is comparable to the death of an ownerless dog.

Quincas's friends, on the other hand, are mortified by the tightfisted wake arranged for Quincas by his family, the indignity of a *velório* [wake] without, at the very least, *café* and cachaça. The underlying conflict, of course, revolves around opposing conceptualizations of morality. Amado keenly understood that death and its various accompanying rituals provided fertile ground for examining moral belief systems at odds with one another in Brazilian society.

While the social expectation, as Octávio Paz suggests, is that one should die as one lived, Quincas lives, to all intents and purposes, two lives and is thus allocated two deaths or, rather, one *official* death substantiated by the coroner's report, and a subsequent *unofficial* death affirmed by elements of Bahia's popular class. Indeed, Quincas did die as he lived in the last stage of his life, a product of Bahia's street culture, penniless but rich in personal relations. It is only when his biological family intervenes, in an effort to simultaneously expunge his bohemian identity and restore his former persona of respectable citizen and head of family, that Quincas's death is no longer fully his own.

In fact, from the standpoint of both his "families," Quincas's initial death is perceived as bad. In the eyes of his natural family, Quincas's demise in a hovel in the notorious Ladeira do Tabuão district represents the culmination of the shameless vagrancy that marked the later years of his life, away from his former home. The family's shame is simultaneously mixed with a sense of relief that scandalous reports of Quincas's derelict behavior will no longer surface.

For his street companions the news of his death, and more precisely the way he died, is received with equal dismay, although for different reasons. In an ironic inversion of the quintessentially bad death at sea, Quincas's solitary death on land is perceived by Salvador's mariners as both uncharacteristic and regrettable: "Velho marinheiro sem barco e sem mar" (42) ["an old sailor without a ship or an ocean to sail it on"] (38). Quincas's natural vocation and spiritual calling was to be a mariner and, as he had proclaimed on many occasions, the sea would be both his final resting spot and the place where he would carry out those journeys left unfinished in his own life. The sailors, therefore, give little credence to the news of Quincas's landlocked demise:

> Como fora então morrer de repente num quarto da ladeira do Tabuão? Era coisa de não se acreditar, os mestres de saveiro escutavam a notícia sem conceder-lhe completo crédito. Quincas Berro Dágua era dado a mistificações, mais de uma vez embrulhara meio mundo. (44)

> [How then, could Quincas have died in a room on Tabuão Street? Such a thing was beyond belief. The fishermen heard the news, but did not take it seriously. Wateryell was fond of playing mysterious practical jokes; this wouldn't be the first time he had bamboozled them all.] (42)

The sailors' sentiments about Quincas's connection to the ocean reflect the povo's general belief that Quincas's natural destiny is left unfulfilled by the circumstances of his first death. Moreover, the mariners' doubt suggests the possibility of an alternative version of his death, entirely different from the one promulgated by Quincas's relatives. The reader also begins to notice the extent to which the collective will of the povo is instrumental in reviving Quincas in order that his destiny be fulfilled. In other words, it is the povo's communal reaction to Quincas's bad death that paves the way for his subsequent resurrection and movement toward a good death. The concerned disbelief expressed by the sailors upon hearing word of their friend's death on land also suggests that Quincas will remain a restless soul until his final wish has been fulfilled.

Quincas's deviant lifestyle, of course, runs counter to that which his biological family understands to be his destiny as a reserved family man and upstanding citizen. Similarly, the family's reworking of his image, from Quincas back to Joaquim, indicates that they too seek to remedy a destiny truncated first by Quincas's earlier abandonment of his domestic life, then later left unrealized by his ignominious death. The confabulations surrounding Quincas's loss of life began, we discover, even before his physical death. Quincas's grandchildren, for example, have been led to believe that their grandfather Joaquim died in the distant past and that only the memory of this venerated patriarch lives on. Thus, the virtual embalming of Quincas's moral character occurs before the actual preparations performed on his cadaver by the funerary specialists.

Similarly, during the family's debate over Quincas's funeral, Tia Marocas proposes the arrival of a fictitious telegram announcing Joaquim's death occurring somewhere in the interior (*Morte,* 25). The family members finally agree to conduct the wake at Quincas's apartment, bury him discreetly the next day with the assistance of a priest, then invite friends and family to seventh-day Mass. While not directly falsifying Quincas's demise, the family's plan covers up the truth surrounding his life and death by excluding others from participating in his wake and funeral.

The Collective Nature of Quincas's Resurrection

Interestingly, it is not only the povo of Bahia who ultimately believe in Quincas's restorative powers. Indeed, the first person to be swayed by the possibility of Quincas's resurrection is Vanda, his cold-hearted daughter. Vanda is the first member of the family to look after Quincas's body and for some time finds herself alone with her deceased father. Her feeling is initially one of satisfaction over her father's transformation at the hands of the funerary specialists, and then one of triumph over Quincas's rebellious spirit. She closes the window and pulls the curtains to his room in order to create a more somber atmosphere and keep out the sounds of street life that had so characterized her father's bohemian lifestyle. Vanda's thoughts gradually turn to her childhood years spent with her father and to the moment he unexpectedly walked away from his family. Glancing back again at Quincas's body, Vanda is startled to see a smile on his face: "O sorriso não havia mudado, contra ele nada tinham obtido os especialistas da funerária" (36) ["The smile hadn't changed, and there was nothing the morticians had been able to do about it"] (33). Her disappointment grows as she realizes that her deceased father's new pair of shoes, black jacket, and shaven face are powerless against the irreverent cynicism of his smile. Then, with "insulting clarity," Vanda hears her dead father utter the word *jararaca* (36) [viper]. It is the first bit of concrete evidence we have in the novella that Quincas may be stirring from his deathly slumber.

Of course, *jararaca* was also the final word Quincas uttered as a summation of Vanda and his wife, Otacília, on the day he left them. The lasting impression of being called a viper suggests that Vanda, in her simultaneously nervous and reflective state, may well have imagined Quincas's insult. After all, the word was associated with a painful memory easily triggered by the trying circumstances of her father's death. Nevertheless, the reader has been gradually prepared for the possibility of Quincas's resurrection, both by the speculative tone of the novella's introduction and by the povo's general consensus that Quincas has yet to fulfill his natural destiny. The tension created at this narrative juncture between Quincas's "imagined" and "real" or, better, surreal resurrection is maintained until the novella's conclusion. Moreover, by leaving ample space for both interpretations, Amado encourages the reader to suspend disbelief of the fantastic events that unfold on the night of Quincas's wake. According to Earl Fitz, the narrative's "structural ambiguity" is a defining characteristic of the novella that "establishes for the reader a deeply satisfying compromise between what is 'realistically true' and what is 'poetically true' " ("Structural," 226). Moreover, the multitude of anecdotal evidence offered by eyewitnesses concerning Quincas's death has the added effect of relativizing an absolute understanding of the truth.

The second *jararaca* that Vanda hears escape from the smiling corpse of her father is accompanied by a teasing whistle and a thumb sticking defiantly in the air. Feeling suffocated by the confined quarters and beginning to question her own sanity, Vanda is then joined by Quincas's sister-in-law, Tia Marocas, who, noticing her stricken niece, opens the windows to allow fresh air into the room. Vanda wishes she could somehow plug her ears in anticipation of Quincas's favorite insult for his corpulent sister-in-law: "mas que adiantam mãos sobre as orelhas para conter voz de morto? Ouviu:—Saco de peidos!" (38–39) ["but you can't shut out a dead man's voice by putting your hands over your ears. She heard: 'Sackfull of shit!'"] (35). But only Vanda can hear her father's posthumous insults, lending weight to the interpretation that Quincas's "imagined resurrection" is a product of his daughter's overwrought psychological state and resurfaced memories. As Fitz points out, the supernatural elements of the scene are qualified by the "realistic" factors of an overly stuffy room and the exaggerated use of perfume by the undertakers on Quincas's body, both potentially contributing to Vanda's possible hallucinations (Fitz, 223–24).

Indeed, it is significant that, of all the characters, it is Vanda, a person who prides herself on rational decisions and responsible bourgeois values, who is first swayed by the possibility of Quincas's otherworldly return. The reader is undoubtedly less surprised by the willingness of Quincas's street companions—all products of a culture that views saints, orixás, and spirits as part of everyday reality—to accept the idea of his returning from the dead. Amado, however, provides us with an important detail concerning Vanda's susceptibility to Quincas's return. We discover early, in chapter 4, that Vanda's religious beliefs are, in typically Brazilian fashion, somewhat eclectic: "era pessoa religiosa, freqüentava a igreja do Bonfim, um pouco espírita também, acreditava na reencarnação" (18) ["she was a religious person, a regular worshipper at the Church of the Bonfim, and something of a spiritualist as well; she believed in reincarnation, for instance"] (19). Knowing that Vanda has Spiritist leanings and believes in reincarnation suggests that, despite her middle-class status and rational worldview, she is open to the idea of direct communication with the spirit world. Her identification with Spiritism and reincarnation appears to reside on an almost subconscious level, rather than as the manifestation of an association with any clear doctrine or principle.

Vanda's Spiritist sensibilities ultimately pave the way for her apperception of her father's postmortem utterances. Moreover, Vanda's receptivity to the voice of the dead breaks down any presumption that the supernatural in this story pertains exclusively to the "superstitious" povo. However, unlike Spiritist sessions in which a spirit guide is solicited for moral guidance, Vanda appears haunted by the specter of her father's anarchic voice and irrepressible smile. She tries to exorcise the ghost of her vagabond father through an elaborate ritual of transforming his identity and then propping up his hands as if in repentance for his sins. Quincas's ghost returns, however, to ridicule his former family and mischievously undermine their best-laid plans for laying his soul to rest once and for all.

Vanda, however, is not the only character who inadvertently breathes new life into Quincas Berro Dágua. Indeed, almost all the characters presented in the novella seek to revive Quincas, either through memory or by providing anecdotal evidence of his miraculous resurrection. In addition to her Spiritist leanings, Vanda expresses a desire to bring back the father who affectionately cared for her in her early youth. Tia Marocas, during the family's discussion regarding Quincas's burial, nostalgically makes reference to her brother's carefree approach to life. Upon hearing of his death, Leonardo's coworkers recount Quincas's exploits through anecdotes, using the *cachaceiro-mor de Salvador* [champion rum-drinker of Salvador] and his carefree existence not only as the butt of their jokes but also perhaps as a diversion from their own mundane lives as public functionaries. Quincas's four closest companions resuscitate "o pai da gente" [our father] in order to, above all, share one final drinking spree with their old companion. The sailors bring him back for a reunion at sea and to perform his predestined maritime burial. Quitéria vivifies Quincas long enough to share a romantic excursion at night before her lover throws himself into the waves. Even the narrator, whose speculative tone at the beginning of the story suggests neutrality, seems equally anxious to endow the novella's protagonist with new life, if only for sake of the story being told.

Acknowledging Quincas's resurrection as a collective endeavor, one that crosses over socioeconomic boundaries within Bahian society, opens the way for interpretations that move beyond a strict dichotomy of popular versus middle-class value systems and instead recognize the inherent overlapping and coexistence of such systems in Brazilian society. Vanda's receptivity to Quincas's deceased utterances works to dismantle the preconception of fantasy and the supernatural as elements pertaining exclusively to the povo and the stark facts as pertaining only to the family. Indeed, Quincas's biological death and miraculous resurrection are generally perceived by both his closest companions and the mariners as an elaborate prank, consistent with Quincas's malandro character, rather than as necessarily a supernatural occurrence. Quincas's return, in this sense, is firmly grounded in reality for those who believed that his *real* death occurs later at sea. Ultimately, each social group proves itself receptive to both a fantastic and a realistic reading of Quincas's death. In turn, the narrator cultivates the coexistence of multiple readings by preserving the necessary degree of ambiguity throughout the novel.

Conflicting Notions of Death in Brazilian Society

The situation of Quincas's "rebirth" during his wake is particularly illuminating because it reveals two conflicting approaches toward death at work in modern Brazilian society. Quincas's biological family, anxious to bury not only his body but also the memory of his bohemian lifestyle, dresses the corpse in new clothing to give him an air of respectability. As soon as his relatives leave, however, his clothes are promptly removed and divided up among Quincas's four closest companions, his "adopted family" from the street. A resurrected Quincas then proceeds to carouse through the streets in his usual shorts and T-shirt. This act amounts to a symbolic disrobing of the hypocrisies and materialism of middle-class values, while, in turn, constituting an affirmation of the personalized treatment traditionally given to the dead in Brazil.

In his essay "A morte nas sociedades relacionais: reflexões a partir do caso brasileiro" [Death in Relational Societies: Brazil as a Case Study], Roberto DaMatta points to some of the different ways in which modern societies (where individualism serves as the dominant ethic) and traditional or semitraditional societies (governed primarily by personal relations) view death. In doing so he makes an essential distinction between the modern society's preoccupation with death, in contrast to the traditional society's relatively greater concern for the dead. DaMatta argues that in modern societies, death in its abstract sense is referred to openly and often in scientific terms, whereas, a prolonged fixation on the actual deceased is viewed as overly sentimental and even pathological. He points to the relative absence of elaborate mourning practices in modern societies and their tendency to cremate the deceased as attempts to destroy or remove the dead as quickly as possible from the world of the living (*Casa,* 115). In contrast, traditional societies tend to extend their relations to the dead for much longer duration and with greater intensity. He adds, "I believe that an inverse attitude is found when we study tribal or traditional societies, societies where the social agent is not the individual but the *relations between individuals.* In these societies, one finds a highly developed relationship to the world of the dead, who are systematically invoked, wept for, remembered, revered, and commonly solicited. All this coincides with a profound silence regarding death as an isolated event or a philosophical problem" (116; emphasis in original). DaMatta's use of the word *systematically* should be highlighted here in light of his argument concerning social behavior in response to death. He points out, for example, that mourning rituals such as crying and wearing black are, to a large part, compelled by social norms, as opposed to some universal response to death. According to DaMatta, this is especially true in more traditional societies. On the other hand, in modern societies mourning behavior must always be legitimized by the mourner's "individual emotions" (118).

DaMatta also argues that contemporary Brazilian society, in reality, constitutes a synthesis of traditional and modern elements that are simultaneously at odds and complementary to one another. The parallels between DaMatta's theoretical framework for understanding death in contemporary Brazilian society and the social conflict surrounding death portrayed by Jorge Amado in *Quincas Berro Dágua* are numerous. Much of the family's response to Quincas's death, for example, revolves around money, doctors, and the logistical bureaucracy of having him buried. Similarly, they reject the notion of bringing the dead body into their home on the grounds that it would somehow corrupt the children or attract too much attention to Quincas's checkered past. Instead they decide to bury him as discreetly as possible and then invite friends and families to his seventh-day Mass. This plan ultimately reflects both modern and traditional approaches to dealing with the dead. While the family goes to great lengths to banish the body from their home, they also uphold the Catholic tradition of inviting family and friends to pray for his soul.

For the most part, however, Quincas's biological family and their behavior following Quincas's death is portrayed by Amado as quintessentially modern, in the sense proposed by DaMatta. When Vanda first arrives to see Quincas's body a group of residents from the squalid Ladeira district have already gathered in his apartment. The arrival of his daughter fills the room with the anticipation of intense mourning: "Afastavam-se para ela passar, curiosos de vê-la lançar-se sobre o cadáver, abraçá-lo, envolver-se em lágrimas, soluçar talvez" (13) ["They made way for Vanda to pass, waiting expectantly for her to fling herself on the corpse and embrace it, to dissolve into tears, or to burst out sobbing"] (12). Vanda, however, is incapable of expressing grief over her father's loss, nor even remorse over what she considers to be his unfortunate fate: "Vanda ficou imóvel. . . . Não tinha mais lágrimas para chorar nem soluços com que encher o quarto" (13–14) ["Vanda stood stock still. . . . She had no tears left to shed, no sobs to fill the room with"] (12). Similarly, her appraisal of Quincas's corpse (through the narrator) reflects a particularly modern and impersonal treatment of the dead, whereby the body is scientifically and anonymously disposed of: "Cadáver para necrotério, para ir no rabecão da polícia servir depois aos alunos da Faculdade de Medicina nas aulas práticas, ser finalmente enterrado em cova rasa, sem cruz e sem inscrição" (14) ["That corpse belonged in a morgue; it should have been dumped into a police wagon to be cut up by the medical students and buried in a shallow grave, with no cross and no inscription"] (13). Vanda's lack of compassion is admittedly motivated by bitterness over her father's abandonment of her and her mother years ago. Nevertheless, it was largely Vanda and Otacília's impersonal materialism that drove Quincas away in the first place.

Vanda's thoughts inevitably are focused on more practical matters: calling a physician to obtain a death certificate, acquiring decent clothes for the corpse and paying for his burial alongside Otacília. Moreover, she fails to understand why such a throng of people would gather in Quincas's apartment: "Que faziam ali? Não compreendiam que Quincas Berro Dágua terminara ao exalar o último suspiro?" (16) ["What on earth were they doing there? Didn't they realize that when Quincas Wateryell had breathed his last, that had been the end of him?"] (14). The notion that Bahia's street rabble would feel any connection to Quincas following his death is inconceivable to Vanda. She orders them to leave and, in typically individualistic fashion, opts to wait alone with Quincas until the doctor arrives.

The response of Quincas's street companions to their friend's death, on the other hand, is characterized by an outpouring of emotions and personal involvement. The news of Quincas's death sends a wave of grief through the streets of Salvador. The city's cheapest prostitutes are especially affected: "As mulheres choravam como se houvessem perdido parente próximo e sentiram-se de súbito desamparadas em sua miséria" (46) ["They wept as though they had lost a close relative, and felt suddenly unprotected in their misery"] (44). The intensity of their mourning is punctuated by that of Quincas's lover, Quitéria do Olho Arregalado, whose wailing echoes across the city: "seus gritos cruzavam a ladeira de São Miguel, morriam no largo do Pelourinho, eram de cortar o coração" (46) ["her heartbreaking cries crossed São Miguel Street and reached clear to the Square of the Pillory"] (44).

Similarly, the collective grief expressed by each of Quincas's four closest companions—Cúrio, Negro Pastinha, Cabo Martim, and Pé-de-Vento—is described in great detail by the narrator. We learn how each heard the news and to whom they passed it on. The scene involving Negro Pastinha and a crowd of well-wishers is particularly indicative of the collective, almost ritualistic response of the povo to Quincas's death. Crying profusely and clutching a nearly empty bottle of cachaça, Negro Pastinha expresses his grief openly to the crowd, exhorting them to mourn along with him:

> —Morreu o pai da gente . . .
> —. . . pai da gente . . .—gemiam os outros.
> Circulava a garrafa consoladora, cresciam lágrimas nos olhos do negro, crescia seu agudo sofrer:
> —Morreu o homem bom . . .
> —. . . o homem bom . . .
> . . .
> —Ele era bom . . .
> — . . . era bom . . .—repetiam os demais . . . (52–53)
>
> ["Our Daddy's dead!"
> "Daddy's dead!" the chorus wailed.
> The comforting bottle was passed around; tears welled up in the Negro's eyes and his suffering became more acute: "A good man's gone!"
> "Good man's gone!"

. . .

"He was a *good* man!"

"A *good* man!" would echo all the others.] (51–52; emphasis in translation)

The chorus of responses to Negro Pastinha's veneration of Quincas brings to mind church services in which the congregation echoes the blessings of the priest or minister. Similarly, as Earl Fitz points out, following his resurrection Quincas moves gradually through the streets of Salvador accompanied by his companions as if in a "funeral procession" ("Structural," 226). The religious undertones of the povo's response to Quincas's death are more explicitly expressed during the late hours of the wake when Curió leads Negro Pastinha, Cabo Martim, and Pé-de-Vento through an indecorous rendition of the Lord's Prayer. Soon after, Negro Pastinha also proposes a Candomblé chant as a means of summoning their old friend.

With the last relative gone, Quincas's companions also feel free to express their indignation, between shots of cachaça, over the family's penurious handling of Quincas's wake: "Aquela família de Quincas, tão metida a sebo, revelara-se mesquinha e avarenta. Fizera tudo pela metade" (73) ["You'd have to go a mighty long way to find a stingier bunch than those stuck-up folks of Quincas who thought so much of themselves. They had done everything by halves"] (71). From their perspective, several elements essential to any decent wake are conspicuously missing. There are no chairs placed in the room for visitors to sit. No food or drink is being served. Even the obligatory *cafezinho* and cachaça, served at the poorest of wakes, are blatantly absent. The family had forgotten to adorn the corpse with flowers. Perhaps most troubling to the friends, however, is the wake's lifelessness, particularly in view of Quincas's own festive lifestyle: "Cabo Martim comparecera a muita sentinela de defunto, nunca vira uma tão vazia de animação" (74) ["Private Martim had been to a good many death vigils, but he had never seen one as dead as this"] (71). The moral obligation felt by Quincas's companions to address some of his family's omissions and give the wake "a minimum of decency" is ironically juxtaposed with the family's own sense of moral righteousness (72). In the process the very notion of decency is put to question. Indeed, the scene of the family and Quincas's friends jostling for space around the coffin reflects the clash of two distinct moral codes, one based on modern and impersonal values and the other on a traditional value system.

Quincas's Final Death and the Carnivalesque Spirit

As DaMatta also points out in his essay on death, one essential difference between Protestant and Catholic doctrine lies in the Protestant belief that the individual is wholly responsible for his or her own salvation, while Catholicism considers the soul's salvation to be a collective effort (*Casa,* 114). Metaphorically speaking, Quincas's brief resurrection is, in many respects, purgatorial in the sense that his soul (or essential force) restlessly seeks salvation through the fulfillment of a personal destiny. His salvation, however, ultimately depends on the intervention of both key characters who bring him to the sea, as well as the narrator who brings him to life through a largely sympathetic narrative. The collective nature of Quincas's salvation represents an affirmation of those social ties that link the living and the dead in traditionally oriented, relational societies.

Aside from the relevance of certain religious attitudes in *Quincas Berro Dágua,* there is a basis within social anthropology for discussing Quincas's multiple deaths. Robert Hertz, in his seminal study "A Contribution to the Study of the Collective Representation of Death," examined the custom of "double burials" practiced by the Dayak in Indonesia in the early 1900s. He then extrapolated his findings to develop a model of more universal forms of mourning behavior. He noted that the Dayak first gave their deceased a provisional burial and then waited for the body to decompose completely before transferring the bones to a sacred space where a final burial was performed. The intermediary period between burials could last anywhere from a year to ten years, however the average was approximately two years. Inherent to the practice of a double burial was the connection made between the condition of the deceased person's corpse and the state of his or her soul. Only after the corpse has been rid of its physical impurities could the soul be admitted into the land of the dead. Second, physical death for the Dayak did not represent ultimate destruction of the individual, but rather a period of transition from one society to another. Similarly, for the living, this transitional period was a time of mourning and disconnection from the rest of society. Reintegration occurred only when the final burial had been completed. As the deceased person re-created him- or herself in the land of the dead, so did the living. Anthropologists have widely recognized the applicability of Hertz's theories on "second burial" to other societies, such as Brazil, where death is not seen as instantaneous but rather as the beginning of an intermediary period for the soul of the departed.[2]

Hertz's observations on "double burials" shed light on the period between Quincas's physical death at the beginning of the novella and the spiritual death he obtains at the end. Before he can be admitted into the afterlife, he must be stripped of any impurities. These include the artificial trappings that his family imposes on him, such as the new suit, dress shoes, and well-manicured appearance. Furthermore, the *peixada* [fish stew] feast at the end of the novella and the ordeal of the storm reaffirms the social ties that bind the povo together. Quincas's final burial at sea, then, is an affirmation of both his personal destiny and the povo's collective will. Various segments of Bahian society, both popular and middle class, are united in the collective retelling of the story of Quincas's death, its bizarre circumstances, and the potential fulfillment of his final wishes.

The struggle over Quincas's posthumous identity may equally be explained in Bakhtinian terms, that is, both families are playing out the carnivalesque ritual of "crowning" and "decrowning" Quincas and his legacy on earth.[3] Indeed, during the course of the wake he is metamorphosed from "the King of Vagabonds" to "head of the family" and back again. Robert Stam's *Subversive Pleasures* is a provocative inquiry into the application of Bakhtinian theory in film, literature, and Brazilian culture. In a defense of carnival's subversive potentiality and current vitality, against those detractors who view carnival as merely fleeting moments of licensed transgression, Stam makes a distinction between "authentic" carnivals and ones that have become "degraded" or coopted.[4] Truly carnivalesque festivities and strategies are above all, he adds, "participatory, joyfully critical, and potentially subversive" (92).

To what extent, then, may we attribute a carnivalesque vitality to Quincas's return from the dead? While by no means revolutionary in the political sense of the word, Quincas's return would seem to fulfill each of the requirements proposed by Stam. As I have argued, Quincas's resurrection is not a solitary affair but rather brought about through the collective amalgamation of eyewitness accounts, personal anecdotes, expectations, jokes, rumor, prophecy, occultist belief, memory, and narrative bias, involving nearly every character in the book as well as the narrator. His resurrection is, in this sense, fundamentally participatory and stems, to a large degree, from the act of storytelling itself. The collective narrative of this novella also brings to mind another theoretical cornerstone of Bakhtin's views on the relationship of language to literature: dialogism. According to Bakhtin, every human utterance is intrinsically relational and in dialogue with other discourses: "Utterances are not indifferent to one another, and are not self-sufficient; they are aware of and mutually reflect one another. . . . Each utterance is filled with echoes and reverberations of other utterances to which it is related by the communality of the sphere of speech communication. . . . Each utterance refutes, affirms, supplements, and relies on the others, presupposes them to be known, and somehow takes them into account" (*Speech Genres,* 91). The cycle of Quincas's death and resurrection is inherently dialogical in the sense that it takes its meaning principally from the "communality of the sphere of speech communication." Concurrently, the magic events that presumably occur on the night of Quincas's wake are balanced not only by the coexistence of certain judgment-impairing "realistic factors" (Quincas's stuffy apartment, the bottle of cachaça brought in by Cabo Martim, and the storm) but by the realistically dialogical process by which the news surrounding Quincas's death unfolds.

One other communicative feature that Bakhtin argues lies at the core of a carnivalesque spirit is laughter. Laughter's function during carnival, as Bakhtin sees it, extends far beyond mere amusement. Rather, it represents a unique perspective on human existence and, through its universal and relativizing gaiety, permits a radical rethinking of the world. In this sense it is no less philosophical than serious or tragic forms of representing existence. Intrinsic to medieval folk culture, laughter received its most radical expression, according to Bakhtin, during the European Renaissance in the works of Rabelais and Cervantes, Boccaccio's *Decameron,* and Shakespeare's plays. Bakhtin often stresses the regenerative powers of carnivalesque laughter. With laughter, "the world is seen anew, no less (and perhaps more) profoundly than when seen from the serious standpoint. . . . Certain essential aspects of the world are accessible only to laughter" (*Rabelais,* 66). Moreover, it is during carnivalesque moments that all forms of seriousness, dogmatism, and hierarchy are mocked through particularly corrosive laughter.

The image of the smiling defunto with which Amado portrays Quincas Berro Dágua is emblematic of the carnivalesque laughter proposed by Bakhtin. It is precisely his irrepressible and irreverent *sorriso* [smile] that undermines Vanda's self-righteous dominion over her deceased father. Quincas's laughter is directed especially at those symbolic elements of Vanda's attempted bourgeois transformation of her father's cadaver: the black clothes, new shoes, and shaven face: "Quincas ria daquilo tudo, um riso que se ia ampliando, alargando, que aos poucos, ressoava na pocilga imunda. Ria com os lábios e com os olhos" (36) ["Quincas was making fun of it all, and his laughter was growing; in another minute it would echo through the sordid room. He laughed with his lips and his eyes"] (34). The novella abounds with expressions of Quincas's "joyfully critical" attitude toward the petty materialism and soulless impersonalism of his biological family, in particular, and Bahia's urban bourgeois in general.

The critical posture assumed by Quincas's smiling defunto undoubtedly differs from the more overtly revolutionary stance frequently taken by the protagonists portrayed in Amado's earlier novels. Quincas is neither the proletarian leader of workers' strikes and cultural voice of black empowerment personified by Antônio Balduíno in *Jubiabá* (1935), nor the revolutionary leader embodied by Pedro Bala in *Capitães da areia* [Captains of the Sands] (1937). To what extent then can we characterize his actions as subversive? While Quincas's revolution is primarily personal (at no point does he position himself, for example, as a defender of the povo's socioeconomic interests), his rejection of a conventional bourgeois existence has subversive undertones. Furthermore, Quincas's malandragem and corrosive laughter represent a form of opposition and an alternative to the status quo of Bahian middle-class society.

Beginning with his novel *Gabriela, cravo e canela* (1958), Amado increasingly opted for humor over overtly socialist rhetoric as a weapon against middle class prejudices and crass materialism. Roger Bastide identifies this emerging form of Amado's social criticism:

> A crítica à burguesia vai então assumir uma forma inédita, será a caricatura da pequena classe média saída das grandes famílias decadentes, mas conservando todos os preconceitos de origem, cristalizando-se, contra o povo no qual se acotovela e do qual não pode separar-se a não ser pondo entre ela e êste povo o muro de seu puritanismo hipócrita, "convenções" a respeitar e "aparências" a salvar.

> [Amado's criticism of the middle class would become particularly poignant, as it caricatured the petty bourgeois whose lineage may be traced back to the once powerful, but now diminished, families of Bahia. Despite this fall, this class would preserve and intensify all of its former prejudices against a class that it now rubbed elbows with and

was unable to separate itself from, except by way of constructing a wall, between itself and the masses, made of hypocritical puritanism, conventions to respect, and appearances to uphold.] (*Romancista,* 51)[5]

Although Quincas's earlier rejection of his family and adoption of a deviant lifestyle are undoubtedly oppositional, it is only in death that Quincas assumes his most subversive form. In life, Quincas enjoyed a near-mythic status within, and beyond the parameters of Bahia's popular culture. In death, and in light of his magical "second death," Quincas becomes a martyr for the povo. Ultimately, it is not so much Quincas himself who is subversive but rather the collective stories that surface regarding his mythical death. Quincas's death (and resurrection) allows the underprivileged and marginalized to adopt a carnivalesque spirit and make their own claim on reality, in opposition to a middle-class worldview. As Bakhtin suggests, "Carnival is the place for working out, in a concretely sensuous, half-real and half-play-acted form, *a new mode of interrelationship between individuals,* counterpoised to the all-powerful socio-hierarchical relationships of noncarnival life" (*Dostoevsky's Poetics,* 123; italics added). Indeed, Quincas's eternally smiling defunto presents an irrepressible alternative to the modus operandi of modern, impersonal relationships, rational laws, and omnipotent social institutions.

Quincas Berro Dágua: Biblical Parody and Martyrdom for a New Collective Order

Bobby Chamberlain makes a compelling case for reading *Quincas Berro Dágua* not only as social satire but also as biblical parody (*Jorge Amado,* 55–60). He calls the reader's attention to the more obvious parallels between Quincas's resurrection and the resurrection of Jesus Christ. Many of the events surrounding Quincas's death lend weight to this theory, such as his mysterious appearance before his four "disciples" at the wake, the symbolism of the peixada as Quincas's "last supper," his relatives' discovery of his empty coffin, and the parallels between the inverted epithets used to describe Quincas (King of the Vagabonds, Grand Drunkard of Salvador, Our Father) and those used in the Bible to describe Christ (King of Kings, Light of the World, etc.).

Although Chamberlain makes a strong case for the existence of these parallels, he does not delve deeply into the implications of reading *Quincas Berro Dágua* as a biblical parody. The novella's overriding message, according to Chamberlain, may be found in its "celebration of the freedom of the individual" (60). This is undoubtedly a common reading of Amado's novella, but one that ultimately ignores how Quincas's resurrection and self-made burial represent not only the celebration of the individual's will but also the affirmation of the community's collective will and its control over important rites of passage. To this degree, Quincas acts as a kind of savior because his life and death serve to reinstate important social ties. Because his resurrection is also a parody of the Gospels, he dies not for our sins but for the very forms of popular culture that are perceived by the middle class as sinful. Albeit in a parodied and carnivalized form, Quincas's death and resurrection, like Christ's, represents the possibility of redemption for the greater community, and particularly for those social outcasts to whom he had shown sympathy.

The relevance of carnivalesque theory to Quincas Berro Dágua's life/lives and death(s) has been demonstrated by several critics. Besides the article by Affonso Sant'Anna, Dorine Cerqueira explores the many uses of irony, the tragicomic, as well as the carnivalesque in Amado's novella. Ultimately, Cerqueira's existentialist reading of the story's underlying message does not differ greatly from Chamberlain's. She compares Quincas to Gregor Samsa from Kafka's *Metamorphosis* (1915) on the basis that these two protagonists are engaged in both an internal conflict with themselves as well as the world that surrounds them. She affirms that for both, the absolute ideal is to be authentic to oneself, "faithful to one's own inner Law" in opposition to the ideals and norms of society (*Ironia,* 123).

Certainly one of Amado's preoccupations in writing *Quincas Berro Dágua* was to portray Quincas's quest for an authentic life outside the constrictions of an oppressive middle-class existence. Reading this novella as, above all, an "affirmation of the individual," however, has obscured other coexisting and, in my estimation, equally important moral and philosophical purposes contained within the text. For Quincas does not so much reject society per se but rather substitutes one society for another. Moreover, the street community to which he adheres maintains its own laws, expectations, and values, as becomes evident from his companions' mutual indignation over what they perceive to be his family's penurious and indecent handling of Quincas's wake. Thus, Quincas's resurrection constitutes less the *individual* rising out of the ashes of an existential crisis than the martyr of an alternative *collective* order, embodied by Salvador's povo and based on a code that prioritizes personal relations over individual ambitions and relational laws over impersonal laws. The concept of an inner law stems primarily from an individualist worldview, one that precludes, even rejects, the notion of reciprocity so cherished in personalistic societies. In the end, Quincas's actions are guided as much by the "external law" of communal relations as the internal law of his own individual quest for authentication. Even Quincas's seemingly individualistic last utterance—"Cada qual quide de seu enterro, impossível não há"—is presented as dialogic, intrinsically relational, because it is told to us through an eyewitness.

It has often been noted by Amado's critics that, with the publication of *Gabriela, cravo e canela* [Gabriela, Clove and Cinnamon] in 1958 and *Os velhos marinheiros* [The Old Sailors] in 1961 (which included *Quincas Berro Dágua*), the elements of fantasy and humor began to take precedence over Amado's former socialist position as a writer. The reasons for Amado's rupture with the Communist Party in Brazil appear to have been both ideological and personal. Itazil Benício dos Santos, in his semibiographical sketch of Amado and his work, points out that events in Eastern Europe during the mid-1950s drove a wedge between Amado and the more Stalinist-oriented members of Brazil's Communist Party. Soviet suppression in 1956 of the anticommunist revolution in Hungary led by Imre Nagy, is described by Amado himself as the turning point:

> "Quando as tomadas de posição liberais foram sufocadas pela União Soviética, assumimos uma posição que não coincidia com as do Partido, de um sectarismo estreito, que eram as de sufocar todas as tentativas de democratização da Hungria."
>
> [When the adoption of liberal positions were suppressed by the Soviet Union, I took a position that did not coincide with the party's own narrow sectarianism, which, in effect, stifled all attempts to democratize Hungary.] (Santos, 161)

Amado's break from the party was viewed by many leftists and critics at the time as disloyal to the revolutionary cause. In a speech given at the Brazilian Academy of Letters in 1991, Amado reflected on his reasons for leaving and the criticism he received for doing so:

> Socialismo sem democracia significa ditadura, e nenhuma ditadura presta, seja de direita ou de esquerda. Atrevo-me a dizer que as de esquerda são as piores, pois contra as de direita pode-se lutar de peito aberto; quem o fizer contra as de esquerda acaba patrulhado, acusado de reacionário, vendido, traidor. . . . Eu próprio me vi sujeito a tais acusações quando, em fins de 1955, mantendo intactas minhas convicções socialistas, deixei de militar no Partido Comunista e passei a denunciar o stalinismo. . . . Pensei, muito tempo, pela cabeça do PC. Para sair disso, o processo é longo, doloroso e cruel. No dia em que resolvi pensar pela minha cabeça, comecei a levar pau por todos os lados.
>
> [Socialism without democracy means dictatorship, and no dictatorship is worthwhile, whether it be from the right or the left. I dare say that the leftist dictatorships are the worst, because against those on the right one can fight openly; one who does so against those on the left ends up being scrutinized and labeled a reactionary, a sell-out, a traitor. . . . I

> found myself the target of such accusations when, at the end of 1955, while maintaining my socialist convictions, I broke ranks with the Communist Party and began to denounce Stalinism. . . . For a long time my thinking was the product of the Communist Party. To break away from this is a long, painful, and cruel process. And the day that I started to think for myself was the day that I started to get it from all sides.] (Santos, 163–64)

Following his fall from grace with the Brazilian Communist Party, Amado's subsequent novels reflected their author's rebellious stance against any form of thought that compromised either the individual's freedom or the freedom of the common people. Just as Gabriela did not want to be tied down by the gender expectations and social institution of marriage, Quincas rejects his bourgeois family and the impersonal materialism that characterized his middle-class existence.

Amado's social criticism, however, is directed as much at the dogmatism of the Communist Party as it is at the capitalistic immorality of the bourgeoisie. Quincas's abandonment of his oppressive family is, in this sense, very much Amado's abandonment of a political party that, he believed, constrained his ideological, artistic, and personal freedom. Amado's comment that he had learned to think through the party suggests that members of this political family were conforming to a certain mold, much like Vanda's replication of her mother's rigidity and status-oriented values. Also implicit in Amado's description of Quincas's family and its disdain for Quincas's street friends, is the notion that the Brazilian Communist Party had lost touch with the most marginalized segments of Brazilian society. Furthermore, Quincas's resurrection speaks to Amado's own artistic resurrection after certain critics had tried to bury his literary voice prematurely.

Similarly, Quincas's contested wake and return from the dead poses a broader question: what constitutes the Brazilian family? This question, of course, can be interpreted on both a national and a local level. In *Quincas Berro Dágua,* Amado portrays bourgeois culture as petty and soulless, in contrast to the life-affirming posture of Bahia's popular culture. The two social stereotypes are, nevertheless, closely linked to DaMatta's dichotomy of impersonal and personal relations, respectively. The vitality with which the povo's collective voice contributes to Quincas's resurrection, together with the narrator's own identification with Quincas's adventurous spirit, tip the balance heavily in favor of a social model based primarily on personal relations and reciprocity. At the same time, the carnivalesque undertones of Quincas's martyrdom are ultimately an affirmation of the particular folk culture that exists in the urban centers of Bahia.

Dona Flor e seus dois maridos

Jorge Amado brings another carnivalesque character back from the dead in his novel *Dona Flor e seus dois maridos* [Dona Flor and Her Two Husbands] (1966). In fact, Vadinho's sudden death in the novel's opening pages occurs during carnival as he is dancing through the streets of Salvador dressed as a woman. The parallels between the two rogues, Vadinho and Quincas, are numerous, although Vadinho is still quite young when he dies and very much in love with his wife, Dona Flor, despite his infidelity to her. After an intense period of mourning during which Dona Flor separates herself from her family and friends, she reemerges and eventually marries again, this time to a pharmacist who is as restrained as Vadinho was uninhibited. Over time, however, the emotional and physical connection between Dona Flor and her memory of her former husband elicits Vadinho's resurrection and subsequent presence, alongside the subdued Teodoro, in Flor's natural/supernatural love triangle. As in *Quincas Berro Dágua,* we do not know if the ghost has actually returned or if it is just a figment of Flor's imagination, a phantasm created by her need for companionship. To Amado's credit, this ambiguity is preserved throughout the novel, lending the reader's response to the narrative a dramatic suspension of disbelief.

Jorge Amado: Imagining a Good Death

Dona Flor and the Supernatural

In his extensive interview with Alice Raillard, published as *Conversations avec Alice Raillard,* Amado describes how he became inspired to write *Dona Flor e seus dois maridos.* The supernatural premise of the story stemmed from a conversation Amado had with poet Álvaro Moreyra in the early 1930s concerning the sister of one of the poet's friends. According to Moreyra the woman had once been married to a journalist who lived like a "bohème terrible" and ended up dying young (283). She married again, this time to a Portuguese merchant. The woman, who also happened to be a Spiritist and thus receptive to otherworldly visitations, was visited by none other than her former husband, who appeared every night anxious to sleep with her again. This supposedly caused her great distress because she was an honest woman and did not want to betray her second husband.

The story stayed with Amado until, roughly thirty years later, he came across a person lying in the street who reminded him of an old gambling friend from his youth, nicknamed Vadinho [vagrant, idler]. Further up the street he came upon a plaque reading Escola de Culinária Sabor e Arte [School of Culinary Flavor and Art] next to a window, and inside a pretty young woman. These experiences, says Amado, formed a series of images in his mind that resonated with the story Álvaro Moreyra had told him years before, images that eventually were transformed into words in *Dona Flor.*

The presence of Spiritism as one facet of Bahia's spiritual and social milieu is confirmed by the number of references Amado makes to the movement in his writings. In his speech upon being admitted to the Brazilian Academy of Letters in 1961, Amado confesses that in his youth he, along with several other idealistic and rebellious young writers, had formed the so-called Academia dos Rebeldes [Academy of Rebels] with the expressed purpose of plotting the venerated academy's demise. The first meeting of the rebels was held in one of the rooms of a Spiritist center in Salvador, where, he adds with tongue-in-cheek bravado, "vossa sentença de morte fôra ditada e confirmada" [your death sentence was written down and confirmed] (*Jorge Amado,* 6). He informs the members of the academy that, in fact, they were "saved by the spirits," for upon arriving at the center for their next meeting the rebels were greeted by the center's director, a medium, who informed them they could no longer use the space. The director added that it was the custom of the center to call upon purified and virtuous spirits. However, ever since the rebels' sinister first meeting, only infernal spirits carrying obscene messages had visited the center, much to the scandal of the other members. Satisfied that the significance of their literary rebellion had reached even the realm of the spirit world, Amado and his cohorts were, however, without a headquarters and ultimately thwarted. As Amado quips in his speech to his fellow members of the academy: "É evidente que não podíamos lutar com êxito ao mesmo tempo contra vossa imortalidade e contra a imensa legião dos espíritos" [It was obvious that we could not fight effectively against both your immortality and against the immense legion of the spirits] (7).

The satire with which Amado treats Spiritism in his speech finds a similar, ultimately more elaborate expression in *Dona Flor e seus dois maridos.* Below the Bahian Association of Pharmacy, where Teodoro meets with his colleagues to debate the fate of pharmaceutical medicine, is a Spiritist center. The narrator adds, in a lightly satirical tone, that the center's mediums competed fiercely with the druggists through the promotion of their own distinctly "metaphysical" prescriptions. The contest between the two centers over the well-being of Bahian society functions also as a metaphor for the two husbands' rivalry over Dona Flor and her emotional well-being. Teodoro, the pharmacist, prescribes well-measured portions of faithfulness and order as antidotes to the solitude and confusion Dona Flor experiences as a young widow. Vadinho's spirit, on the other hand, injects her with a "metaphysical" dose of passion and spontaneity, the two elements so conspicuously missing in her life with Teodoro. Vadinho is more of a drug pusher than a druggist, as his "medicine" brings both ecstasy and anguish, a potent combination that Flor ultimately becomes addicted to. By juxtaposing the two "medicinal" centers, Amado also seems to be suggesting that the well-being of the social body is predicated on two distinct but mutually dependent forms of therapy, one grounded in the empiricism of Western medicine, the other in the metaphysics of both Western and non-Western supernatural forces.

The juxtaposition of these two cultural approaches within Bahian society occurs frequently in *Dona Flor,* and with varying degrees of narrative intention. Very often this difference manifests itself in the distinction between erudite and popular culture. Teodoro's disciplined practice of the bassoon and his rehearsals with the mostly elitist music group Filhos de Orfeu [Sons of Orpheus] certainly do not strike the same chords of intense pathos as Vadinho's moonlight serenade to Flor while his friends accompanied him with a *modinha* [popular love song]. Albeit in a decidedly more structured way, Teodoro also performs a serenade for Flor during his solo in her honor at a concert put on by the Sons of Orpheus. Though in a more measured way, Flor is moved by her second husband's devotion to her:

> Tanto lhe dera, tanto: paz e segurança, tranquilidade, ordem e confôrto, quanto ela desejou e ele pôde adivinhar, projeção e nem um só desgôsto, nem um sobressalto. Agora ia buscar no ventre magro do fagote a grave nota de seu amor, de sua devoção. Ninguém poderia desejar melhor marido. (404–5)

> [He had given her so much: peace and security, tranquility, order and comfort, everything she wanted and he could think of, protection, and never a bad moment, never a worry. Now he was seeking in the lean belly of the bassoon the deep note of his love, his devotion. Nobody could ask for a better husband.] (415)

While its members consist primarily of Salvador's upper class, the Sons of Orpheus see themselves as, above all, "brothers in art" during the Saturday rehearsals, free from professional obligations and social distinctions:

> Aquêles grão-senhores transformavam-se nos sábados à tarde em crianças alegres e desprocupadas.... Punham de lado as distâncias sociais, confraternizando ... o meritíssimo juiz ... com o caixeiro da pequena loja. (368)
>
> [On Saturdays those important figures became gay, carefree children.... They laid aside all social differences, the wholesale fraternizing with ... the brilliant judge ... with the clerk of a little store.] (375–76)

By portraying the Sons of Orpheus as a space where fraternity and the love of music transcend social differences, Amado seems to suggest that the world of artistic and creative endeavors can bridge social gaps. Both Vadinho and Teodoro are amateur serenaders, but their respective songs resonate in different, though equally important, spaces in Flor's heart.

The reader is introduced to the entire Bahian spectrum of occultists and advocates of the supernatural, when the *don* of Salvador's gambling casinos and crime world, Pelancchi Moulas, seeks spiritual assistance. Unbeknown to him, Vadinho's spirit has rigged all the roulette wheels, cards, and dice in his casinos to the benefit of his former gambling companions. Previously down on their luck, his companions hear Vadinho's voice from the afterworld telling them which card or number to play. The results are disastrous for Pelancchi: he not only suffers financial loss, he is terrified that some sort of malevolent force from the spirit world is at work.

The gangster first employs the services of a mystic named Cardoso e Silva, who is famous in Bahia for his spiritual wisdom and powers of reincarnation. Over the centuries his mummy had been discovered in the Great Pyramid and under the snows of the Alps; he had sold dates in the souks of Egypt and been burned in the Spanish Inquisition. After examining the evidence in the gambling halls (as well as the breasts and buttocks of Pelancchi's girlfriend, Zulmira, where Vadinho had pinched her) the mystic concludes definitively that it is the mischievous work of Martians. Amado's satirical portrayal of Cardoso e Silva, "o capitão dos cosmos" [the captain of the cosmos], and his supposed links to extraterrestrials pokes fun at the highly imaginative, though often dubious, figures in Bahian society that claim to be in communication with the spirit world. It is in the name of science, of course, that Cardoso e Silva must study the mulatta Zulmira's anatomy:

> Foi-lhe então mostrado o amplo local, e êle demorou-se (a pressa é inimiga da ciência) a estudá-lo: a côr, a solidez, a arquitetura, tudo em verdade de primeira. Zulmira ia deixando, risonha e encabulada: não era Cardosinho quase um puro espírito, liberto da vileza da matéria? Quase.—Igual às montanhas de Marte, na conformação e nos abismos—revelou o Geógrafo dos Planetas. (522)

> [So she showed him the extensive locale, and he took his time (haste is the enemy of science) studying it: the color, the firmness, the architecture, all really first-class. Zulmira let him get his fill, smiling and shy: wasn't Cardosinho practically a pure spirit, free of the baseness of matter? Almost. "Like the mountains of Mars, in its promontories and abysses," commented the Geographer of the Planets.] (538)

Even the satiric title attributed to this "elevated" sage—Geographer of the Planets—reveals just how terrestrial the sage's motives actually are.

Pelancchi is inclined, however, to not deposit all his spiritual eggs in one basket; he therefore visits a colorful array of "specialists," which include a clairvoyant named Aspásia, who, following an eye-popping trance into the beyond, corroborates Pelancchi's suspicions that his enemies, the Strambi family, have sabotaged his gambling ring. After snuffing out the Strambis (with no turn of luck in the casinos), Pelancchi and a few of his henchmen visit Josete Marcos, a pretty Spiritist medium who, while the mobsters hold hands to establish a "current of thought," summons the illustrious spirit of Brother Li U, a Chinese sage from the Ming dynasty, amid an elaborate display of mysterious lights and catlike squeals. Speaking through Josete, the Chinese sage informs Pelancchi in a strange tongue, resembling Portuguese from Macau, that his ill fortune has been caused by a spiteful Italian woman he had known in his youth. Not surprisingly Pelancchi identifies who the culprit must certainly be. Before his pilgrimage of spiritual healing is over, Pelancchi visits a turban-wearing archangel; a surgeon who graduated, with honors, from the University of Jupiter (who manages to cure the gangster of an ulcer but not his bad luck); a fortune-teller who reeks of rum and whose chronic stomach pains are due to the fact that she was about to give birth to the Apocalypse; and another doomsayer called the Prince of Baghdad, who informs Pelancchi rather enigmatically: "Só o mestre do Absurdo pode lhe salvar" (518) ["Only the Master of the Absurd can save you"] (532).

In times of crisis and uncertainty Flor also makes use of specialists in healing, in her case generally the priests and *mãe-de-santos* [female priests] of Candomblé. As Flor makes her way to Vadinho's grave with flowers, it is the *negro* soothsayer, Didi from the Amoreira *terreiro* [sacred space], who instructs Flor on how to quiet Vadinho's restless *egun,* or spirit of the dead. Tying her flower bouquet with a braid of African straw, he tells her to untie the knotted straw over Vadinho's grave. Later in the novel Flor calls upon Didi's magic again (through her friend Dionísia de Oxóssi) when, at her wit's end and powerless to resist the sexual advances of Vadinho's ghost, she fears that her deceased husband will ultimately steal her away. Flor is speaking figuratively here, for her deepest fear is actually that Vadinho may once again be stealing her heart, to the detriment of her second marriage. Dionísia takes her message literally and rushes to tell Pai Didi of the return of Vadinho's restless spirit. Didi has powers that surpass that of even other priests and mãe-de-santos in Salvador's Candomblé terreiros, especially in the realm of the egun. As Dionísia says, "Essas coisas de egun não é para qualquer" (494) ["This business of the spirits of the dead is not for just anyone"] (507). Father Didi possesses a special role in the Candomblé sect, that of Korikoê Ulukótum in the "Amoreira terreiro dos eguns," or House of the Dead (446). In a clearing in the woods, Didi manipulates the *búzios,* or sacred shells, to summon each of the orixás in an effort to quell Vadinho's rebellious spirit. To the scene of crackling thunder and a swept-up sea, all the orixás respond, with the exception of Exu, Vadinho's patron saint in Candomblé.

The fantastic events that occur during Didi's ceremony, where the very forces of nature are transformed, are depicted by the narrator with a degree of credibility that is missing, in both tone and poetic force, from the bogus seances and fortune-teller sessions attended by Pelancchi and his thugs. Unlike the lights flashed onto a curtain at Josete's Spiritist session, we believe the narrator when he says that the orixás responded to Didi's call "cavalgando raios e coriscos" (495) ["mounted on lightning and flashes"] (508). By modulating the level of satire inserted into scenes involving the supernatural, Amado creates a hierarchy of spirit world belief systems. While he largely satirizes the Spiritists and fortune-tellers, exposing them through humor as essentially charlatans, the practitioners of Candomblé, and the orixás themselves, are woven into the narrative as a given, as just more characters in the story. The orixás' battle over the fate of Vadinho's restless egun is inextricably linked to Dona Flor's internal struggle over how best to incorporate her memory of Vadinho into her present life. While the intervention of the orixás in the narrative may indeed be interpreted as projections of Flor's psychological state, there is no indication from the narrator that discredits the actual existence of the orixás. In this regard they are as much a part of the Bahian landscape as the cliffs around the *elevador* and the churches in Pelourinho.

The credibility attributed to the pantheon of Afro-Brazilian deities and the rituals associated with Candomblé also spills over onto Vadinho's character. In both life and death Exu acts as Vadinho's patron orixá. Of all the orixás, Exu is most often associated with the Christian Lucifer, the fallen angel. Like Vadinho, he is mischievous and brings disorder as well as vitality to the world. He is the one who waits at the crossroads at night for life's unsuspecting travelers. The novel's third section begins with a humorous description of the orixás' culinary idiosyncrasies, where we learn that Dr. Teodoro's orixá, Oxalá (associated with Jesus Christ), eats only *ojojo,* a porridge with yam, corn, and snails. Moreover, his diet includes nothing spicy. He even refuses to use salt or oil. Exu, on the other hand, eats "tudo quanto a bôca prova e come" (421) ["anything in the way of food"] (432). Exu drinks only one beverage, however: straight cachaça. This detail, of course, provides strong evidence that Exu is also the orixá of another exclusive cachaça consumer, Quincas Berro Dágua. Exu's gluttony is, at the same time, clearly a metaphor for Vadinho's own voracious sexual appetite.

Vadinho: Egun and Sensual Defunto

After his physical death, Vadinho is generally referred to as *o finado* [the deceased]. However, when reference is made specifically to his restless spirit, particularly by Dionísia and other practitioners of Candomblé, he is called *egun.* In his study concerning death and the dead in Afro-Brazilian culture, entitled *Os vivos e a morte* [The Living and Death], French sociologist Jean Ziegler examines the House of the Dead in the village of Amoreira on the island of Itaparica in Bahia. After studying the egun ceremonies practiced there, Ziegler found that the egun perform three essential functions within the community of the living (67). First they assist in the transmission of messages between the community's deceased ancestors and their descendants. Second, the egun assist in the ongoing governance of the community, providing guidance in the event of any unresolved conflicts. Third, they serve a therapeutic function. For example, when a Candomblé priest is unable to cure an individual who is ill, an egun is summoned and enlisted to help remedy the person's suffering. The egun's presence in the Amoreira community, however, is not entirely benevolent, as Ziegler points out:

> Um profundo equívoco domina assim a Casa dos Mortos. Assassinos e mediadores, protetores dos vivos e assaltantes de estradas, os Egun simbolizam numa só figura as características aterrorizantes e contraditórias de um morto, que mesmo o admirável sistema nagô não consegue dominar totalmente.
>
> [Thus, a profound ambiguity pervades the House of the Dead. Assassins and mediators, protectors of the living and highway assailants, the

> Egun symbolize in one entity the terrifying and contradictory characteristics of the deceased, whom not even the admirable system of the Nagô is able to dominate completely.] (70)

Vadinho's restless and mischievous egun certainly embodies many of the traits that Ziegler attributes to the Candomblé spirit of the dead. While he does not actively serve as a spokesperson for Bahia's ancestors, he does dialogue directly with his former wife and friends. Furthermore, his interventions on behalf of the decrepit French prostitute (putting a gambling chip into her brassiere, for instance) and his former gambling companions who are down on their luck, serve to reinstate a sense of universal justice and equilibrium in the face of a gambling ring that preys on the destitute. Moreover, by reawakening Dona Flor's sensuality and passion for life, Vadinho's egun also serves an important therapeutic function.

However, as Ziegler makes clear, the egun is both assassin and mediator, a protector of life and a highway bandit. Indeed, for certain characters Vadinho's otherworldly presence takes the form of haunting. Pelancchi, the mobster, is terrified of the malign supernatural forces that he is convinced are haunting his gambling operation. Vadinho's closest companion and partner in "crime," Mirandão, is goaded by the voice of his deceased friend to head to the casinos and place his bet on seventeen, Vadinho's lucky number. After repeatedly breaking the bank Mirandão goes home, but he still hears Vadinho's haunting voice:

> Abrindo os olhos, Mirandão viu-se sózinho com as sombras da noite e aquela voz. Encolhido entre os lençóis, morto de mêdo, tapou os ouvidos com o travesseiro, não queria ouvir. (487)
>
> [Opening his eyes, Mirandão found himself alone with the shades of night and that voice. Cowering under the sheets, scared to death, he covered his ears with the pillow, he did not want to hear.] (498–99)

Frightened out of his wits, Mirandão swears never to gamble again. Dona Rozilda, Flor's ill-natured and meddling mother, is also haunted by Vadinho, when she decides that she is going to move into Dona Flor's house. After twenty-four hours of having her hair yanked and obscene words and insults whispered into her ear, Dona Rozilda packs her bags, swearing never again to set foot in the house, clearly haunted by her demonic former son-in-law. Vadinho's verbal abuse of his insufferable mother-in-law is of course reminiscent of Quincas Berro Dágua's burlesque derision of Vanda and her family.

Most important, Vadinho's return throws Dona Flor's life into disarray and her emotions become increasingly conflicted as she struggles to preserve her womanly virtue and fidelity to Teodoro, while simultaneously opening the door to Vadinho's temptations little by little. Dona Flor senses that she is losing control over her body at the same time that her moral defenses are weakening: "Não era mais dona de seu corpo, a matéria indócil não mais obedecia a seu espírito, e, sim, ao desejo de Vadinho" (482) ["She was no longer the mistress of her body; the rebellious matter no longer obeyed her spirit, but the desire of Vadinho"] (494). In this respect, Flor's fall contains echoes of Eve's temptation and subsequent fall from Paradise, as we can see in the following passage:

> As portas do inferno se abriram e o anjo revel transpôs a entrada do quarto de dormir (e amar) de dona Flor, aceso o olhar em frente, a bôca num convite e todo inteiro nu. . . . [A]manhã o bom nome de dona Flor, símbolo de virtudes, vai estar na bôca do mundo, na lama, no desprêzo. Amanhã outra mulher, apontada a dedo, coberta de remorso e de vergonha. (501)
>
> [The gates of hell swung open and the rebellious angel crossed the threshold of Dona Flor's bedroom (and love room), his lustful eyes gleaming, his mouth inviting, and completely naked. . . . Tomorrow the name of Dona Flor, the symbol of virtues, will be a laughingstock, dragged through the mud, an object of contempt. Tomorrow she will be a different woman, pointed out, covered with remorse and shame.] (514)

Vadinho's infernal presence is nevertheless complemented by his bewitching sensuality. Indeed, Vadinho is nude each time he makes his spectral appearances with Dona Flor. On one occasion he wears a shirt that had been given to Teodoro as a joke, for it is decorated with images of nude women. In this case the sexually explicit shirt only enhances the immodesty of Vadinho's own exposed sexuality underneath.

Interestingly, the seduction of Dona Flor by Vadinho's ghost shares some characteristic features with the image of Death as seducer, a motif that emerged particularly in the art and literature of the European Renaissance and Baroque periods. The image of Death as a "crassly sensual lover" conjoins the two irrevocable consequences of Adam and Eve's fall: death and sexuality (Guthke, 96). Often entitled Death and the Maiden, paintings of the period depicted a grotesquely formed skeleton or cadaver crudely seizing a woman's half-naked body. In some images the woman appears to actually invite Death's sexual advances.

Though Vadinho is by no means equated here with the figure of Death itself, he is certainly a highly seductive morto whose eroticism is intertwined with his death. Shortly after his death at the beginning of the novel, Vadinho's body is brought back to Dona Flor's house and laid down nude on their conjugal bed. For the first time since the news of his sudden death, Flor is able to contemplate her new status as widow, and her thoughts reflect a combination of grief and sexual longing:

> Só quando trouxeram Vadinho do necrotério e o deixaram nu no leito do casal onde tantas e tantas vezes tinham feito o amor, então, e sòmente então, encontrou-se sózinha com a morte do marido e se sentiu viúva. Jamais voltaria êle a derrubá-la na cama de ferro, arrancando-lhe vestido e combinação, e as peças mais íntimas, atirando com o lençol para cima da penteadeira, tomando de cada detalhe de seu corpo, fazendo-a delirar. (31)

> [Only when they brought Vadinho back from the morgue and left him naked on the bed where they had made love so many times, then and only then did she find herself face to face with the death of her husband and feel herself a widow. Never again would he tumble her in that iron bed, pulling off her dress, slip, and more intimate pieces of attire, throwing the sheet over the dressing table, and then storm her entire being, making her frenzied with pleasure.] (13)

The quasi-necrophilic desire that Flor feels for her dead husband at this moment is realized, at least in her imagination, later in the novel when Vadinho's ghost succeeds in sexually possessing her again. The intensity of Flor's longing for Vadinho amplifies her erotic encounter with his spirit, "Nunca se dera assim; tão sôlta, tão fogosa, tão de gula acesa, tão em delírio" ["never had they found such pleasure in one another: so free, so fiery, so gluttonous, so delirious"], provoking her to shed her modesty, along with her clothes, "sou tua cadela, tua égua, tua puta" (504) ["I am your bitch, your mare, your whore"] (517).

The lighter side of Vadinho's eroticism is generally expressed through his mischievous and carnivalized spirit. Picking up where he left off during his lifetime, Vadinho's spirit ogles Dona Flor's culinary students, at times floating overhead to gain a better vantage point. He goes so far as to put his spectral hand down the shirt of one particularly well-endowed student, Zulmira, much to Dona Flor's chagrin. He also takes the voyeuristic liberty of watching Dona Flor and Teodoro make love, pointing out what he sees as deficiencies in Teodoro's technique:

> Dona Flor ouvia sua voz dentro do peito, seu riso libertino, de troça e de debique:—É isso que você chama de vadiação? . . . Nunca vi coisa mais insípida. . . . Se eu fosse tu, pedia a êle, em vez disso, um frasco de xarope: cura tosse e é mais gostoso. . . . Porque o que êle está fazendo, meu bem, é a coisa mais triste que eu já vi. (469)

> [Dona Flor could hear his voice within her breast, his debauched, bantering laugh: "And you call that screwing? . . . I never saw anything more insipid! If I were you, I would ask him to bring me a bottle of cough syrup instead of this; it's good for a cold and is pleasanter. Because what he is doing, my pet, is the sorriest thing I have ever seen."] (480)

The mocking, sarcastic tone of Vadinho's libertine laugh, poking fun at Teodoro's restrained sexual habits, exhibits much of the same carnivalesque functions that were characteristic of Quincas Berro Dágua's own posthumous laughter. Vadinho mocks the pharmacist's seriousness and the dogmatism of a lifestyle in which "everything is in its proper place" and sex is performed routinely on Wednesdays and Saturdays. In doing so, he also undermines the notion that Flor's heart should belong exclusively to her second husband.

For the most part, however, Vadinho's laugh is less acerbic than Quincas's and carries a more playful tone than, for example, Quincas's acrimonious and insulting "Jararaca." To some degree, this difference in tone may be attributed to who is listening in each case. Like Vanda, Flor is initially the only person who can hear the defunto's laughter. Yet, whereas Vanda's recollections of her father are largely negative, Flor remembers Vadinho in both a positive and negative light. Therefore, the level of sarcasm expressed through the carnivalesque laughter of each defunto is very much a product of the specific expectations of the respective women who are mourning their loss.

The image of the sensual defunto vividly presented by Vadinho, particularly in his sexual interactions with Dona Flor, condense many of the elements that Bakhtin suggests make up the "grotesque body" so prevalent in carnival. According to Bakhtin, the three primary acts in the life of the grotesque body are: sexual intercourse, death throes, and the act of giving birth (*Rabelais,* 353). In this sense Vadinho's death, supernatural rebirth, and sexual energy are an expression of Bakhtin's emphasis on a constant metamorphoses of death and renewal as fundamental to the human experience. Furthermore, the key features of the grotesque body are those that extend the body's limits to the outside world, that bring the body and the world into relation with one another. These include bodily protrusions such as the genitals and breasts and other permeable sites such as orifices, where bodily fluids are excreted and food is either consumed or expelled. Significantly, upon being seduced by Vadinho's spirit, Flor is drawn to his "boca ardida" (504) ["burning mouth"] (517) and the smell of pepper, ginger, and raw onion on his breath (536), while Vadinho remarks that Flor tastes of honey, pepper, and ginger (518). The image of Vadinho's consuming mouth, even in death, reflects both Dona Flor's (who is herself a culinary expert) association of her former husband with food, as well as

Vadinho's inherent carnivalesque spirit. The gluttony and indefatigable sexuality of Vadinho's ghost ultimately link his metaphysical state in death to the carnal materiality of this world. In Dona Flor's "battle between the spirit and matter" it is Vadinho's spirit that tempts her material desires, whereas it is Teodoro, her husband of flesh and blood, who represents her spiritual and moral intentions.

Vadinho embodies the carnivalesque spirit because: (1) before his death he led a life of Dionysian abandon; (2) he dies during carnival itself, dressed as a Bahian; (3) as a revenant he subverts the order of things in both Dona Flor's home and psychological state; (4) his activity as a sensual defunto calls attention to the body's functions, such as eating and sex; (5) he exerts a relativizing effect on the living, as when he transforms his destitute friends into kings for a day at the gambling halls and humbles the gambling lord through haunting; and (6) his return sparks a battle between the orixás, an event that, in turn, subverts the natural and social order of things.

Dona Flor *in Its Sociohistorical Context*

The passages in which the narrator describes the people's reaction to these supernatural disturbances are significant in that they constitute the few moments in the novel where Amado directly raises the question of sociopolitical change:

> Foi naqueles dias que o povo, em lucidez e raiva, atacou a sede do monopólio estrangeiro da energia elétrica, exigiu a nacionalização das minas e do petróleo, pós a polícia em fuga e cantou a Marselhesa sem saber francês. Tudo teve princípio naquela ocasião. (446–47)

> [It was during those days that the people, lucidly and furiously, attacked the headquarters of the foreign monopoly of electric power, demanded the nationalization of the mines and oil wells, routed the police, and sang the *Marseillaise* without knowing French. It all started on that occasion.] (457)

Then later during the orixás' climatic battle when Dona Flor intervenes to save Vadinho's egun:

> Vinha o povo correndo nas ladeiras, com lanças de petróleo e um calendário de greves e revoltas. Ao chegar na praça, queimou a ditadura como um papel sujo e acendeu a liberdade de cada esquina. Quem comandou a revolta foi o Cão e às vinte e duas horas e trinta e seis minutos ruíram a ordem e a tradição feudal. Da moral vigente só restavam cacos, logo recolhidos ao Museu. (532)
>
> [The people came running down the hillsides with javelins of kerosene, and a long list of strikes and uprisings. When they arrived in the square, they set fire to the dictatorship as though it were a piece of dirty paper, and lighted the torch of freedom on each corner.
>
> The commander of the uprising was the Devil, and at thirty-six minutes past ten, order and feudal tradition crashed to the ground. Only the shards of what had once been accepted as morality remained, and these were later gathered up and guarded in the Museum.] (548)

These scenes suggest that the povo's sudden zeal for revolution is galvanized by both the rebellious spirit of Vadinho's egun, as well as the general disorder of things caused by the warring orixás. It would seem unlikely that, less than two years after the military coup of 1964, Amado would not make some reference to the dramatic sociopolitical changes that had occurred in Brazil, especially considering the author's history of social criticism.

Notwithstanding the fleeting passages mentioned above, it is evident that Amado deliberately chose not to tackle these issues head on but rather address them with a more circuitous narrative approach, one that employed fantasy and the supernatural as symptoms of the changing times. As Bobby Chamberlain points out, some critics have read *Dona Flor* as a political allegory of the ideological struggle waged in Brazil during the 1950s and '60s between leftist populism (Vadinho being a man of the people) and the positivist, technocratic stance of the military government (Teodoro being a man who maintains order) (63). Considering that Amado, beginning with *Gabriela, cravo e canela* in 1958, had turned away from making overt political statements of the kind that marked the social realism of his earlier novels, and recognizing the limitations of making a strict parallel between a pacifist Teodoro and the military regime, one might be more inclined instead to accept Roberto DaMatta's reading of the novel as an example of Brazil's systematic depolarization of opposing ethical systems (house/street, personal/impersonal, heaven/hell) and the subsequent creation of a third relational element (*Casa,* 83). Dona Flor is, according to DaMatta, the embodiment of this third element, and her decision to keep both Vadinho and Teodoro is emblematic of Brazilian society's tendency to build bridges between diametrically opposed ideological spaces. As for *Quincas Berro Dágua,* DaMatta's theoretical framework is useful for understanding the essential struggle that takes place in *Dona Flor* (between personal relations and impersonal relations), and why the intervention of the dead is so important for bringing resolution to this particular social dilemma.

Several elements in *Dona Flor* point to why Amado once again uses the topos of the resurrected defunto in this novel. First, Vadinho must return from the dead in order to demonstrate the irrepressible nature of passion. He represents the life-affirming force that brings creative disorder in counterposition to the monotony of Teodoro's orderly life. Alive, he had brought Flor great suffering along with joy. Dead, he is able to awaken her passion without compromising her integrity as a married woman. Furthermore, his miraculous return and supernatural presence strike a balance with the rational order of things.

By the mid-1960s, when Amado was writing *Dona Flor,* the optimism of the Kubitschek era and the idealism of João Goulart's reform-minded populism had given way to a military dictatorship. The leaders of the 1964 coup believed that military intervention was necessary to restore a sense of order, common sense, and honesty to Brazil, after fifteen years of "irresponsible" and "wheeling-and-dealing" populist governments, beginning with Getúlio Vargas's return in 1951 (Skidmore, 160). President Castelo Branco's policy for economic development was determined largely by a group of technocrats who pushed for economic stabilization and other measures that would not only curb inflation but also bring Brazil in line with the demands of the International Monetary Fund. From the standpoint of the political left in Brazil, Goulart's brief time in power represented an opportunity foregone, where badly needed sociopolitical reforms such as the nationalization of public services and petroleum, the extension of suffrage to illiterates, and agrarian reform were left unrealized.

Symbolically, the 1964 military coup also represented an attempt by the right to exorcise the ghost of Getúlio Vargas, who had leaned increasingly to the left during the early 1950s and whose dramatic suicide in August 1954 subsequently breathed new life into the populist cause (Skidmore, 138). An astute political observer, Jorge Amado may have had the charismatic former president in mind when he created Vadinho, who, like Vargas, saw himself as a man of the common people and whose sudden death was seen by some as tragic and by others as a blessing. And like Vadinho's spirit, Vargas's influence extended well beyond his physical death. One also finds parallels between Vadinho's premature death and the political demise of João Goulart, whose promising yet tumultuous years in office marked the end of Brazil's experiment with democracy, at least until the mid-1980s.

In light of the dramatic sociocultural changes that were occurring in Brazil during the 1950s and '60s it is perhaps not necessary to attribute such literal political analogies to *Dona Flor e seus dois maridos.* Within the span of roughly fifteen years Brazil had gone from an underdeveloped, third world country to an expanding, industrialized nation whose per capita economic growth was three times that of the rest of Latin America (Fausto, 256). Brazil's economic importance as well as its growing cultural influence abroad (particularly with the international appeal of bossa nova and the success of its national soccer team) suddenly thrust the giant South American country onto the world stage. Indeed, many of the components of Kubitschek's dream of "fifty years of progress in five years" had come true, including the construction of a new capital,

Brasília, in the deserted highlands of the state of Goiás. An expanding middle class in Brazil found itself with a greater disposable income and a wider variety of consumer goods from which to choose.

At the same time, this general trend toward modernization was mitigated by a consistently high level of social stratification, not only between the traditional landowning and financial elite and the largely illiterate or semiliterate popular class, but also geographically between the south and the north of Brazil. Thus, during these early years of Brazil's economic "miracle" a large percentage of Brazil's population, both urban and rural, never experienced the benefits of modernization and, in fact, found themselves victims of a system that was progressing rapidly while at the same time clinging to traditional forms of social hierarchy (Skidmore, 143).

Mourning as Metaphor in Quincas Berro Dágua *and* Dona Flor

It is within this incongruous set of historical circumstances that Jorge Amado wrote both *Quincas Berro Dágua* and *Dona Flor e seus dois maridos.* While no longer assuming an overtly proletarian stance, Amado clearly continued to sympathize with the plight of the most disenfranchised segments of Brazilian society, those who, in the country's zeal to modernize, had been largely forgotten. Whereas Quincas voluntarily leaves behind his middle-class existence as a bureaucrat, Vadinho is clearly the product of a former era wherein a strong network of family and friends was highly valued and personalistic politics routinely practiced. Moreover, the death of both protagonists sparks a battle between two distinct social ethoi, one based on traditional, personalistic relations and the other on modern, impersonal relations. It is not incidental that their deaths bring this pivotal social conflict to the surface for, as Peter Metcalf and Richard Huntington argue, "the issue of death throws into relief the most important cultural values by which people live their lives and evaluate their experiences. Life becomes transparent against the background of death, and fundamental social and cultural issues are revealed" (25).

One cultural element of life in Brazil that certainly becomes transparent in these two novels is the significance of mourning as a response to death, as well as the specific way in which the memory of the dead is to be preserved. In other words, the question of how Quincas and Vadinho are to be mourned, the quality of their deaths, and the specific rituals intended to extend social ties into the afterlife are all fundamental to an understanding of the broader social and cultural implications of *Quincas Berro Dágua* and *Dona Flor*.

Frequently, the process of mourning portrayed in these novels functions on a metaphorical level. The conflicting opinions over what constitutes a decent wake for Quincas reflect opposing social ethoi (personal vs. impersonal, traditional vs. modern). Though Amado clearly identifies, through his narrator, with the life-affirming virtues of the personalistic ethos, he does allow for the coexistence of these value systems by way of the narrative's ambiguity concerning Quincas's death. Both attitudes are present in Brazilian society, and in fact are necessary to the construction of an authentic profile of Brazil in the 1950s and early 1960s. With Quincas, Amado has not let go of his idealistic view that hope for Brazil rests in the vitality of its povo, however his message is coupled with an underlying uncertainty regarding Brazil's future in the face of such rapid changes. Thus, one might argue that the intense mourning expressed by Quincas's companions speaks to Amado's own mourning over those cultural traditions and values that he sees as endangered by Brazil's often dehumanizing quest for order, progress, and modernization.

While the dehumanizing effects of modernization are clearly evident in *Dona Flor* as well, Amado's emphasis on mourning in this novel is more precisely directed at the process of healing. As Robert Hertz points out the death of a loved one temporarily places relatives and other mourners outside the realm of normal social interactions. This new estranged status is often characterized by specific taboos and cultural prescriptions to which mourners must conform. The end of the mourning period also marks their reintegration into normal society:

> For the collective consciousness death is in normal circumstances a temporary exclusion of the individual from human society. This exclusion effects his passage from the visible society of the living into the invisible society of the dead. Mourning, at its origin, is the necessary participation of the living in the mortuary state of their relative, and lasts as long as this state itself. In the final analysis, death as a social phenomenon consists in a dual and painful process of mental disintegration and synthesis. It is only when this process is completed that society, its peace recovered, can triumph over death. (86)

Hertz's description of mourning as a period of social exclusion during which the mourner participates in the "mortuary state" of the deceased is particularly applicable to Dona Flor's reaction to Vadinho's death. Indeed, the different stages of Dona Flor's mourning give structure to the first half of the book. The first section, entitled "Da morte de Vadinho, primeiro marido de Dona Flor, do velório e do entêrro de seu corpo" ["The Death of Vadinho the First Husband of Dona Flor, His Wake and Burial"] is followed by "Do tempo inicial da viuvez, tempo do nojo, do luto fechado . . ." ["Of Her Early Widowhood, a Period of Trial, of Deep Mourning"]. Flor's deep mourning during this stage is expressed both externally by her black dress and internally by her deadened spirit. For a full month she never leaves her home except to attend Mass on two occasions on behalf of Vadinho's soul. As the narrator says, only desire and memory (for Vadinho) kept her living and, in fact, much of this section consists of flashbacks to her life with Vadinho. Otherwise, she is more dead than living during this stage. Her vicarious participation in Vadinho's "mortuary state" is noticed by her friends and family, including Dona Norma, who comments,

> Vai completar um mês e você vive como uma alma penada, rodando dentro de casa. E sua casa que era um brinco está se enchendo de bolor; mais parece, Deus me perdoe, uma sepultura onde você se encerrou. Reaja, acabe com isso, alivie êsse luto. (192)

> [Almost a month has passed, and you live like a soul in purgatory, shut up here in the house. And your home, which used to shine, is getting all mildewed. God forgive me, it's more like a tomb where you've shut yourself up. You must get yourself in hand, stop living like this, not give way to your grief.] (192)

When Flor's *comadre* Dionísia de Oxóssi, from the Candomblé terreiro, pays her a visit, she too is alarmed by Flor's exanimate state: "Enterre o xará de uma vez, comadre. . . . Senão êle começa a feder e a consumir tudo por aqui, até vosmicê" (193) ["Bury the man once and for all, comadre. Otherwise he will begin to rot and do away with everything here, including you"] (193). Flor must, therefore, perform a second burial (in the sense theorized by Hertz) of Vadinho before she can begin to reintegrate herself back into society. Her visit to his grave with the feiticeiro's charm serves this purpose.

In the third section, "Do tempo do luto aliviado, da intimidade da viúva em seu recato e em sua vigília de mulher moça e carente" ["Of the Period of Half-mourning, of the Private Life of the Widow in her Retirement, and the Sleeplessness of a Young and Bereaved Woman"], Flor enters a period of half-mourning in which, after six months of wearing only black high-necked dresses, she begins to also wear white and faint traces of makeup. It is a full year before she would add green, pink, blue, red, or other brighter colors. Even so she maintains the tradition of not saying the name of her deceased husband: "Cerrou a bôca ao nome do finado, parecendo tê-lo esquecido por completo" (223) ["She had closed her lips over the dead man's name, seeming to have forgotten him altogether"] (223), thereby avoiding his unwanted return. However, like her guardian orixá, Oxun, Flor is serene waters on the outside, but a squall on the inside, as her desire begins to break down the modesty of widowhood, marking a prelude to the ensuing battle between spirit and matter.

One might argue that from the very first line of the novel, when we learn of Vadinho's death on Carnival Sunday, until the book's final chapter, the narrative is galvanized by the overarching question of Dona Flor's mourning process and those forces that facilitate her return to normal life. Like the Spiritist center located below the Bahian Association of Pharmacy, Vadinho and Teodoro offer two contrasting, yet ultimately complementary paths toward healing. Similarly, if we accept Dona Flor as a metaphor for Brazil, then her mourning may be seen as a national response to those traumatic losses that Brazil had experienced in the years leading up to the novel's publication. The suicide of the "wheeling-and-dealing" Vargas and the failure of João Goulart's government were both causes for mourning for large segments of the population, particularly on the left. The loss of democracy under the military dictatorship was another. Published, however, only a few years after the 1964 coup, when a measure of free speech was still possible and the full extent of the regime's brutality still years away, *Dona Flor* is, on the political front, written with a tone of reconciliation, healing, and guarded optimism.

Nevertheless, such an allegorical reading far from exhausts the meaning of Amado's novel. The relatively greater emphasis that Amado places on cultural over political struggles in *Dona Flor,* however, suggests that, above all, the author was mourning the loss of humanity brought on by the dehumanizing effects of accelerated modernization. The role of the supernatural in Amado's novels, as both a sign of the times and a healing agent, takes center stage during the first half of the 1960s, beginning with *A morte e a morte de Quincas Berro Dágua* (1961), continuing with the Candomblé rituals and intervention of the orixás in *Pastores da noite* (1964) [Shepherds of the Night], and culminating in the beneficial (and indeed sensual) intervention of the dead in *Dona Flor e seus dois maridos* (1966).[6] In light of the story that inspired Amado to write *Dona Flor,* in which the troubled woman is a Spiritist, it is significant that Dona Flor shows no inclination toward Spiritism, and that her involvement in Candomblé is only peripheral. By omitting this original detail from his fictitious story, Amado seems to be saying that Dona Flor (and Brazilians in general) do not need to be Spiritists in order to believe in and communicate with the dead on some level. Dona Flor's immediate acceptance of Vadinho's otherworldly presence in her life is, therefore, a commentary on Brazilian society's reluctance to sever its reciprocal ties with the dead, even in modern times. Flor's lack of surprise upon seeing Vadinho's ghost for the first time ("'You?' she asked in an ardent voice . . . as though she had been expecting him"), therefore may be interpreted as both a psychological projection of her longing onto Vadinho's ghost and an indication of how, as a Brazilian, she is accustomed to maintaining close connections with the dead (425).

The supernatural forces summoned by Amado in his fiction during the first half of the 1960s serve to counteract the dehumanizing rationality and materialism of Brazil's rush toward modernization. The figure of the carnivalesque defunto, in particular, emerges as an important protagonist in this struggle to preserve people's fundamental humanity. In contrast to Brás Cubas's bad death, the relatively good deaths of Quincas and Vadinho bring a sense of rebirth and continuity to the communities whose social ethoi they have helped shape. Indeed, Quincas and Vadinho use their malandragem as a way to negate the status quo, whereas for Brás Cubas malandragem is a sign of his social unaccountability. Ultimately, the realization of a good death in both *Quincas Berro Dágua* and *Dona Flor,* however, comes about only through the intervention of the living, who see to it that the final wishes of the dead are fulfilled and that the necessary communal links remain unsevered. It is particularly in times of sociopolitical and cultural transformation, Amado seems to suggest, that Brazilians turn to the supernatural as a means of preserving these very links. In this sense, the enigmatic figure of the sensual, carnivalesque defunto portrayed by Amado stems from both a centuries-old tradition of proximity to the dead as well as the unprecedented challenges of a uniquely modern sociohistorical context.

Chapter 5

Voices of the Unburied Dead

Call for the robin-redbreast and the wren,
Since o'er shady groves they hover
And with leaves and flowers do cover
The friendless bodies of unburied men.

—John Webster, *The White Devil*

É preciso enterrar os nossos mortos.
[It's necessary to bury our dead.]

—Autran Dourado, *Uma poética de romance*

The Hour of the Seventh Angel

In an interview with *Veja* magazine in 1971,[1] Brazilian author Érico Veríssimo reveals how the idea for his final novel, *Incidente em Antares* [Incident in Antares] (1971), came to light:

> Por mais estranho que pareça, a idéia me foi inspirada por uma foto que vi numa revista estrangeira: um cemitério, tendo à frente uns dez ou doze caixões enfileirados, por ocasião de uma greve de coveiros. Pensei assim: "E se esses mortos resolvessem erguer-se e fazer greve contra os vivos?" Achei que era um bom ponto de partida para um conto ou uma novelinha.
>
> [As strange as it appears, the idea was inspired by a photo I saw in a foreign magazine, of a cemetery with ten or twelve coffins lined up during a gravediggers' strike. I thought to myself: "What if these corpses decided to rise up and go on strike against the living?" I thought it was a good starting point for a short story or novella.] (Veríssimo, *Liberdade,* 51)

When he saw that macabre and provocative photograph, Veríssimo was engrossed, however, in the preparation of a different novel, tentatively entitled "Hora do sétimo anjo" [The Hour of the Seventh Angel], a project that he never completed.[2] Nevertheless, Veríssimo does provide some general ideas regarding the premise of this unfinished book, by way of several comments made during a series of interviews he gave between 1971 and 1975, the year of his death. Of particular relevance to this study is Veríssimo's intention to incorporate, as he does in the second part of *Incidente em Antares,* the motif of the living-dead as a central narrative feature in "Hora do sétimo anjo." In the *Veja* interview, Veríssimo describes the narrative structure of "Sétimo anjo" to Paulo Totti:

> Era uma versão sofisticada do *Incidente,* embora com técnica narrativa diferente. Passava-se em Porto Alegre. A figura central vive apenas durante alguns dias da ação do livro. Depois que morre, a narrativa passa a ser feita, ou melhor, a estória passa a ser vista do ângulo privilegiado onipresente e onisciente do morto. Fantástico, não?"
>
> [It was a sophisticated version of *Incidente,* but with a different narrative technique. It takes place in Porto Alegre. The central figure lives for only a few days during the story. After his death, the narrative is told, or better yet, the story is seen from the privileged, omnipresent, and omniscient point of view of the dead man. Fantastic, don't you think?] (*Liberdade,* 54–55)

Moreover, according to Veríssimo, many of *Incidente*'s salient themes, notably the perception of society as a "baile de máscaras" [masked ball], featured in the plan for "Hora do sétimo anjo." Veríssimo's preliminary notes and outlines for "Hora do Sétimo Anjo" make reference to "baile de máscaras" as the initial working title for this book. Later, in 1973, in an interview with the newspaper *Correio do povo* from Porto Alegre, Veríssimo affirms that *Incidente* and "Sétimo Anjo" were linked by a common idea: "Uma foi ponto de partida da outra" [One was a starting point for the other] (118). This link is strengthened by the title of his unfinished work. It is the seventh angel, of course, in the

Apocalypse who sounds the trumpet announcing the second coming of Christ, and the subsequent resurrection of the dead to face the Hour of Judgment. Both the Apocalypse and the resurrection of the dead are presented as central themes in *Incidente.*

Veríssimo's plan to structure the greater portion of the narrative for "Hora do sétimo anjo" from the "omnipresent and omniscient" point of view of a deceased character, coupled with the protests levied by the dead against the living in *Incidente,* suggests that, in the final stages of his literary career, Veríssimo found the unburied dead to be a useful metaphorical tool for addressing sociopolitical reality in Brazil following the 1964 military coup. This chapter explores the emergence of the unburied dead as a literary metaphor within, and in response to, the historical context of the social turmoil that characterized the Brazilian military dictatorship in the latter half of the 1960s, and as a central narrative feature in two significant works of fiction produced during this period, namely, Veríssimo's *Incidente em Antares* and Autran Dourado's *Ópera dos mortos* [The Voices of the Dead].

Critical Interpretations of the Living-Dead in Incidente em Antares

Incidente em Antares (1971), Veríssimo's last novel before his death in 1975, has two main parts. The first provides a historical backdrop of Antares, an imaginary frontier town in the state of Rio Grande do Sul, and traces the long-standing rivalry between two warring clans who, by the time of the "incident" on December 13, 1963, represent the old power structure of the *coronéis* [local patriarchal chiefs] and their latifundia. It is in the second part of the novel that we learn of the incident. A general strike led by workers in the city sets in motion a series of bizarre events, culminating in the resurrection of seven corpses that, during the confusion, have been left in their coffins at the entrance of the town's municipal cemetery. Representing diverse socioeconomic and ideological positions, the cadavers find solidarity in their indignation for having been left unburied. They agree to stage their own demonstration in the town square and remain there until their grievances are heard and they are given a proper burial.

While the imagery of defuntos and *velórios* [wakes] was hardly a new element in Veríssimo's fiction, the fantastic description of the unburied corpses reentering the city square and interacting with the living has led some critics to interpret the second part of *Incidente* as a Brazilian example of magical realism, a narrative style that had become a trademark of the Latin American literary boom during the 1950s and '60s. Veríssimo denied any direct influence by Spanish America's so-called magical realists on *Incidente,* citing several short stories from his first publication, *Fantoches* (1932), in which fantastic or gothic elements appear, and that were written, Veríssimo points out, before many of these Latin-American writers were even born (*Liberdade,* 56). Nevertheless, critics have called attention to the predominant role that fantasy plays in *Incidente,* which, they argue, differentiates this novel from its predecessors.[3] The creation of a fictitious town, much like Macondo in Gabriel García Márquez's *Cien años de soledad* (1967), in conjunction with the first part's sweeping narration of Antares' history, from its prehistorical origins to the present day, contributes to the story's mythical atmosphere that, to some degree, sets the stage for the fantastic events that follow.

Still, it is the resurrection of the dead that propels *Incidente* decisively outside the aesthetic parameters of the social realism that had characterized Veríssimo's prior novels, which, like *Incidente,* frequently explore the sociohistorical reality of Rio Grande do Sul, Veríssimo's home state. While ostensibly there exists some consensus among Veríssimo's critics concerning the symbolic meaning of the defuntos' return in *Incidente*—the rotting corpses of the dead are emblematic of the moral decay and deteriorating personal freedom that Veríssimo views as contaminating not only *gaúcho* [born in Rio Grande do Sul state] society, but all of bourgeois society in Brazil during the military dictatorship—

relatively little critical attention has been given to some of the broader socio-political and cultural implications that emerge from Veríssimo's preoccupation with the image of the unburied dead.

One of the first comprehensive studies concerning Veríssimo's work to be published after his death is *Érico Veríssimo: Realismo e sociedade* [Realism and Society] by Flávio Loureiro Chaves. Although the scope of Chaves's study is limited by the absence of concrete sociopolitical analysis and historical contextualization, he does provide some insight into the relationship between Veríssimo's fiction and the ideological stance of its author, which Chaves describes as a nonpartisan, liberal humanism (59). Similarly, Chaves argues that the development of Veríssimo's fiction, from an admittedly idealistic work such as *Saga* (1940) (which the author subsequently described as naive) to his later, more pessimistic works, such as *O senhor embaixador* [His Excellency, the Ambassador] (1964), *O prisioneiro* [The Prisoner] (1967), and *Incidente em Antares,* reflects within Veríssimo "a crise duma consciência liberal no mundo contemporâneo degradado" [the crisis of a liberal conscience in a defiled contemporary world] (55). Unlike many of his contemporaries writing during the height of the Brazilian regionalist movement, Veríssimo turned neither to political radicalism (a position assumed by Jorge Amado for many years), nor to nostalgia (as, for example, José Lins do Rego), as solutions to the many forms of social injustice and political corruption existing in both Brazil and abroad. The nucleus of Veríssimo's social criticism lies, according to Chaves, in the humanist search for the freedom of the individual, and in the denouncement of those political, socioeconomic, and philosophical systems that act as obstacles to the realization of personal freedom (67).

According to Chaves, *Incidente em Antares* functions as a synthesis of the many ideological and aesthetic directions taken by Veríssimo during his long literary career. Moreover, Antares may be seen as a microcosmic expression of places, either real or fictitious, that provided sociohistorical contexts for Veríssimo's earlier novels (114). On the other hand, Chaves argues, *Incidente em Antares* introduces something entirely new to Veríssimo's fiction:

> At the same time, an entirely new element appears whose ideological and structural implications are profound and fundamental to an interpretation of *Incidente em Antares.* The ethical judgment that denounces and condemns this corrupt society does not stem directly from the narrator —who maintains the third person perspective—nor from the kind of "alter-ego" standpoint that possesses such a predominant function in his other novels, but that is missing in this work. The *point of view* by which public judgment in Antares is rendered belongs specifically to the unburied dead; invested with a moral authority that death alone can grant, only they are able to see and reveal the community's rotten core. (115; emphasis in original)

Needless to say, the narrative shift of point of view from the living to the dead, as the principal voice of public denouncement in *Incidente em Antares,* echoes the posthumous narrative position assumed by Brás Cubas in *Memórias póstumas.* In contrast to Veríssimo's two previous works, *O senhor embaixador* and *O prisioneiro,* in which it becomes tragically clear to the respective protagonists that liberalism has failed as a viable political solution to social injustice in the modern world, the privileged moral position of the resurrected dead in *Incidente em Antares* provides an unexpected outlet for Veríssimo's ethical concerns. As Chaves argues, "It is left to the dead in Antares to fulfill the humanist aspirations of Tônio Santiago, the moralistic intentions of Floriano Cambará upon rewriting the History of Rio Grande, in short, the ethical-literary endeavor that Érico Veríssimo had outlined as early as 1934" (115–16). Furthermore, the capacity of the "morto insepulto" [unburied dead] to lend continuity to Veríssimo's humanistic and literary vision in the final stages of his career, as suggested by Chaves, is reconfirmed by the author's posthumous narrative approach for the unfinished "Hora do sétimo anjo."

One other critic who has interpreted the unburied dead as a measure of the decaying moral fiber of the living is Wilson Chagas in *Mundo velho sem porteira.* Indeed, Chagas argues that the theme of decay and rotting in *Incidente em Antares* is intimately related to Veríssimo's characterization of Brazilian society as a "mundo velho sem porteira," a chaotic world unable to renew itself or move in a direction that would ensure some degree of salvation for the most alienated segment of its population. He adds: "Daí que a realidade maior, na obra de Érico Veríssimo, não seja a Vida, mas a Morte" [Thus, the underlying reality, in Érico Veríssimo's work, is not Life, but rather Death] (138). Decay is also a fundamental manifestation of the human condition, since it represents the inevitable trajectory of our physical existence. Therefore, *Incidente em Antares,* according to Chagas, represents the culmination of one of Veríssimo's consistent themes: death's ultimate triumph over life, especially in a world where renewal is impossible (140). Chagas poses the question, do the collective voices of the seven unburied corpses, who are endowed with an uncommon degree of impudence and satirical irreverence, express all that Veríssimo had refrained from saying in his earlier novels? Should we read *Incidente* not only as the hour of truth for the population of Antares, but also for its author (110)?

While such line of questioning, in which the author's personal intentions are presumed to coincide with those of his characters is, I suspect, less productive than allowing the novel and its characters to speak for themselves, Chagas does highlight some biographical details that, I believe, bear some relevance to Veríssimo's apparent preoccupation with the unburied dead. In May 1955, Érico and his wife, Mafalda, traveled together by train from El Paso, Texas, to Ciudad Juárez, Mexico. During their stay in Mexico, Érico visited a cemetery in Guanajuato in which he encountered the mummified remains of dead bodies propped up along the walls of the catacomb, as if in a receiving line for a "macabre and silent fiesta" (Chagas, 122). Chagas observes that this scene, depicting the skeletal hosts of a Mexican catacomb, included in Veríssimo's *México: História duma viagem* [Mexico: History of a Journey] (1957), brings to mind the unburied corpses in *Incidente em Antares.* He goes on to note "que se reencontra, aqui, um tema persistente, obsessivo do romancista" [that here we find once again this persistent, obsessive theme of death in the novelist's work] (122).

The ritual importance of burying the deceased as a means of ensuring some degree of resolution for the living is elicited in a highly personal way by Veríssimo in the second volume of his memoirs, *Solo de clarineta* [Clarinet Solo].[4] In the chapter entitled "Granada: Em Busca do Menino Federico" [Granada: In Search of the Young Federico], Veríssimo tells how, during his stay in Granada, Spain, he became obsessed with finding the tombstone of Federico García Lorca, the Spanish poet who, following his death by a firing squad in the chaotic outbreak of the Spanish Civil War in 1936, was buried in an undisclosed place (281–95). It is said that García Lorca was forced at gunpoint to dig his own grave somewhere in the villa of Viznar in the early morning of August 19, before being gunned down by Falange militia. After searching in vain for the poet's burial spot, Veríssimo has a dream in which he goes searching for a friend's tomb, spade in hand, and is momentarily joined by his own father, who helps him in his quest.

Upon reflection the next day, Veríssimo realizes that his desire to locate García Lorca's tombstone has evoked an unresolved issue in his own past. Érico explains that, when his father died in 1935, he did not have the means to purchase a proper tomb for him, so he had a friend acquire a provisional one. However, when this friend passed away, the records concerning the whereabouts of his father's burial spot were lost. Érico, subsequently, was unable to locate his father's remains in the countless possible cemeteries in the city of São Paulo. Érico describes in his memoirs how he was stricken with guilt for many years as a result of not knowing where his father's body lay (291). Although his remorse gradually faded, his later search for García Lorca's burial spot in Granada apparently elicited memories of his father's death, a loss compounded by the subsequent loss of his father's body: "Eis que em Granada o desejo que ainda sinto de descobrir onde estão os seus restos mortais se me revela num sonho" [In Granada the need I felt, and which I still feel, to discover where my father's mortal remains are located, was revealed to me in a dream] (291). Both García Lorca and Érico's father remain, in his mind, unburied, not because their bodies were prevented from being placed in the ground but because the ritual of marking and recognizing their burial spots has been neglected.

Chagas confirms, in several instances, Veríssimo's own assertion regarding the presence of fantasy and, particularly the macabre, early on in his work. Embryonic expressions of *Incidente*'s full-blown grotesquerie are evident, according to Chagas, in Veríssimo's first published work, a collection of short stories and minidramas entitled *Fantoches* [Puppets] (1932). A facsimile edition of *Fantoches* was published in 1972 to commemorate the author's forty years of literary activity. Included in this edition are handwritten commentaries and drawings by Veríssimo in the page margins. Looking back on the stories he created nearly half a century earlier, Veríssimo's commentaries provide an informative and often humorous retrospective of his life's work. As Chagas points out, Veríssimo is quite explicit about the relationship that exists between *Fantoches* and his final novel, *Incidente em Antares.* For example, in the midst of a scene entitled "As duas mulheres e o defunto" [The Two Women and a Defunto], from the short drama "Quasi 1830" [Almost 1830], Veríssimo writes in the margin: "Clima do *Incidente em Antares*" [The mood of *Incident in Antares*] (148). Alongside the dialogue of one farcical short story entitled "Nanquinóte" (in which fictional characters come to life, including a stick figure named Nanquinóte, whose answer to Hamlet's existential struggle with life and death is to kick the famous skull carried by the Danish prince), Veríssimo writes: "Não estará aqui uma das sementes de *Incidente em Antares*?" [Isn't it here that we find one of the seeds of *Incident in Antares*?] (191). Veríssimo also mentions several short stories that were left out of the collection, including "Quarteto sem sol" [A Quartet without Sun] and "Noé" [Noah] (a biblical farce), whose "irreverent and sarcastic tone" reminds him of *Incidente.* In regard to another earlier short story, Veríssimo writes: "Quanto ao espírito macabro deste romance de 1971 [*Incidente em Antares*], ele já se encontra em 'O Professor dos Cadáveres,' escrito em 1929" [One already finds the macabre spirit of this 1971 novel, in the story "A Professor of Cadavers," written in 1929] (79).

In addition to highlighting the parallels that Veríssimo himself draws between the satirical irreverence and macabre elements woven into *Fantoches* and the supernatural events portrayed in *Incidente,* Chagas proposes that the "unburied dead," in particular, constitutes a rich thematic vein throughout Veríssimo's work: "Macabre is really the adjective that best describes the extraordinary events narrated in the novel (*Incidente in Antares*). However, we see that the theme of the unburied dead was already in gestation early on in the work of Érico Veríssimo" (110). Furthermore, Chagas asserts that "Érico é um escritor que nunca pôde esquecer os seus mortos" [Éric is a writer who is unable to forget his dead] (25). While Chagas does not point to any particular novel or short story in which this gestation occurs precisely, several possibilities exist aside from *Fantoches.* For example, the protagonist in Veríssimo's fourth novel, *Um lugar ao sol* [A Place in the Sun] (1936), written almost forty years earlier, is a young man named Vasco who leaves the interior of Rio Grande do Sul for Porto Alegre, in an effort to escape from the ghosts of his family's past. Nevertheless, despite these references, and aside from the allusions that Chagas makes to certain intriguing biographical details in which the theme of the unburied dead recurs in Veríssimo's own life, the critic provides no further explanation for the repeated appearance of this particular motif in Veríssimo's literature.

Gary M. Vessels places Veríssimo's incorporation of fantasy in *Incidente em Antares* and *Caminhos cruzados* [Crossed Paths] (1935) within the genre of Menippean satire. Vessels points to the "experimental fantasticality" and multiplicity of narrative genres employed in *Incidente em Antares,* as well as the obvious similarities that exist between Veríssimo's resurrection of the dead and Lucian of Samosata's *Dialogues of the Dead* (149–50). Vessels's analysis of Veríssimo's work is, in many respects, similar in its approach to Enylton de Sá Rego's study of Menippean satire in Machado de Assis's work. Rego, however, is able to demonstrate a considerably more direct influence of Lucian on the nineteenth-century Brazilian writer. One could also argue that the jocular side of Lucian's mocking laughter is lost in the more embittered and stern tones of the accusations made by Veríssimo's defuntos in *Incidente.* Unlike Menippus's implacable sarcasm, the defuntos in *Incidente* use sarcasm, at least initially, as a means of forging some reconciliation with the living inhabitants of Antares. As Rego does with Machado's fiction, Vessels traces the motif of the ironic, resurrected defunto in Veríssimo's work to a literary genre that has its origins in ancient Greek and Roman literature. By displacing attention away from the salience of the dead in *Brazilian* culture, however, both Rego and Vessels ignore the diverse ways in which images of the spirit world, and particularly the dead, in Brazilian literature interact with and illuminate concrete sociohistorical and cultural problems raised within each narrative that are especially pertinent within a Brazilian context.

13 de Dezembro—A Marcha dos Mortos

Márcia Ivana de Lima e Silva, in *A gênese de* Incidente em Antares (2000), traces the creation of Veríssimo's last novel to his precursory work on "Hora do sétimo anjo." Silva's methodology closely follows a critical approach known in French as *critique génétique* and in Portuguese as *crítica genética.* Her research therefore focuses specifically on the trail of annotated manuscripts and preliminary drafts contained within the surviving Veríssimo archives, in search of clues that may shed light, first and foremost, on the author's creative process. Silva proposes that the many additions, omissions, and modifications contained in Veríssimo's manuscripts reveal the author's underlying aesthetic and ideological intentions. She calls attention to the novel's diverse and often parodic narrative voices, its "mosaico de discursos," as an example of the text's heteroglossic relationship with sociohistorical reality in Brazil at the time of its production (166).

Included in Veríssimo's archives is a hand-drawn map sketched by Érico himself at the outset of his work on *Incidente.* The map illustrates in vivid colors the layout of the city streets, houses and central square in Antares and includes, in its margins, notes that give a chronology of the events that occur in the city during the incident. Silva points out that, originally, Veríssimo planned for the deaths to occur between December 14 and 16, 1963, and for the corpses to march on Antares on the seventeenth. In later outlines, according to Silva, the protest by the defuntos is changed to December 13, which is, of course, a significant date in modern Brazilian history, for it was on December 13, 1968, that the infamous Ato Institucional no. 5 was promulgated by the Costa e Silva government, essentially closing down Congress and suspending all political rights indefinitely. Márcia Silva suggests that, by altering the date in his novel, Veríssimo sought to call attention to the arbitrariness of the military's abuse of power on this day (120). According to Silva, the idea to begin working full-time on *Incidente em Antares* came to Veríssimo on May 8, 1970. The writing for the first part of the novel occurred between June and December 1970, while Érico was in the United States visiting his daughter. He began writing the second part in January 1971 and had finished the manuscript in October of the same year. Thus, Veríssimo was planning and writing *Incidente em Antares* during arguably the most turbulent and repressive period of the military dictatorship in Brazil. It is not surprising, then, that his novel incorporates elements of that oppression.

For example, the fictitious torture and murder of the syndicalist João Paz by the chief of police Inocêncio Pigarço in *Incidente em Antares* evokes both the actual killing of a student by military police during a 1968 demonstration in Rio de Janeiro as well as the many mysterious deaths that were occurring in the government's torture centers operated first by the Centro de Informações da Marinha [Naval Intelligence Center] and later by the Destacamento de Operações e Informações de Defesa Interna [Department of Operations and Intelligence for Internal Defense]. Opposition movements that formed in response to the military's hard-line stance, including university students and professors, certain left-leaning sectors of the church, and labor unions are also represented in the novel, respectively, by Professor Martim Terra Francisco, Padre Pedro-Paulo, and the striking workers in Antares. And like the strike in Veríssimo's novel, two worker strikes —one in Contagem, Minas Gerais, and the other in Osasco, São Paulo— heightened tensions in Brazil during 1968 and led to more repressive measures by the military. Furthermore, the kidnapping of U.S. ambassador Charles Burke Elbrick in September 1969 by radical leftists in exchange for the release of fifteen political prisoners only resulted in more torture and a tightening of military control. Another detail surely not lost on Veríssimo was the background of Brazil's military leaders during the *anos de chumbo* [dark years]. Both General Costa e Silva and General Médici were from Rio Grande do Sul.

Other interesting questions pertaining to Veríssimo's creative process while composing *Incidente* emerge through Silva's close examination of his notes and manuscripts. Why did Érico heed his wife's advice and remove the child character, Angelito, from the group of defuntos (121)? To what extent was his writing influenced by his extensive use of English during the planning and editing of the book? And perhaps more significant, what are some of the conceptual and philosophical linkages that exist between Veríssimo's unfinished novel "Hora do sétimo anjo" and the completed *Incidente em Antares* (70)? While Lima e Silva's mapping of *Incidente* as a work in progress does elicit some interesting observations about the direction Veríssimo ultimately wanted his novel to take, it fails to specify at which precise sociohistorical junctures the text overlaps with the complex and often contradictory nature of Brazilian reality during the most oppressive years of the military dictatorship.

Antares—Povinho da Caveira

One critic whose analysis extends beyond the level of sociopolitical generalizations, in an effort to identify specific historical correlations between Veríssimo's work and modern Brazilian history, is Joaquín Rodríguez Suro. Suro finds, for example, a direct correlation between the feeling of dread that envelops the city of Antares in December 1963 during the general strike, an unease that is compounded by the sudden death of seven of its citizens, and the actual sociopolitical climate of Brazil in late 1963, as tensions mounted in the final months of João Goulart's government (233). The apocalyptic mood set by the narrator before the incident—"Pesava sobre a cidade uma atmosfera de princípio de fim de mundo" [There weighed over the city a mood of impending apocalypse] (*Incidente,* 196)—simulates the growing sense of national anarchy in Brazil during the early 1960s, precipitated by President Jânio Quadro's unexpected resignation in 1961, and culminating in late 1963 as reactionary forces became increasingly threatened by João Goulart's populism. Suro, however, traces the origins of the political atmosphere suggested in *Incidente* back to the Vargas era and the enduring legacy left by Getúlio Vargas following his suicide. Simultaneously defeating his more conservative enemies and breathing new life into the populist movement, Vargas's death momentarily initiated the possibility of change: "triumph comes after death, as it does in the mythic-poetic part of *Incidente em Antares,* when the dead come back to life and momentarily transform the city" (Suro, 231).

Vargas's legacy, however, extends much further than his final left-leaning, populist persona, as Suro suggests: "In fact, the history of contemporary Brazil, as is manifested implicitly by Veríssimo, can be summed up by Getulismo and his legacy" (236). In this sense, the technocratic positivism of the post-1964 military regime is as much a continuation of Getúlio's positivist legacy as Goulart's populism was a continuation of Vargas's populist legacy. For Suro, Vargas's "return from the dead" is emblematic of a larger, more endemic phenomenon in Brazilian political history, which he describes as the country's inevitable cyclical-mythical regression to a basic patrimonial structure. Vargas's return to power in 1951, despite the considerable political fluctuations that had occurred in Brazil since the authoritarian Estado Novo [New State], is indicative of this regression as well as the enduring mythical status of Getulismo. As Suro observes, the coronel

Tibério Vacariano in *Incidente em Antares* manages to benefit more from corruption during Vargas's democratic period (1951–54) than during the Estado Novo (1930–45) (230). The important point here is that, despite modifications in the political style of the younger generation of gaúchos exposed to a broader world during the 1920s and '30s, socioeconomic stratification and resulting social injustices in Rio Grande do Sul (and in Brazil as a whole) were never significantly altered following the Revolution of 1930, nor in any subsequent political movement.

Vargas's ability, in *Incidente em Antares,* to unify the previously warring Campolargo and Vacariano clans in 1925 is symbolic of the consolidation of patrimonial power inherent to a cyclical-mythical interpretation of Brazilian political history. Intrinsic to the determinism of an essential continuation of patrimonial politics, especially in Rio Grande do Sul, is an unwritten code of violence and machismo. This sentiment is expressed most succinctly by Tibério, coronel of the Vacariano clan, when he tells Professor Martim Francisco Terra how the world works, in Antares and beyond: "Ora, professor, que cada qual cuide da sua vida. Quem for mais capaz e mais macho vence. É a lei do mundo. Sempre foi" [Well, Professor, may each man look out for himself. He who is most capable and macho wins. It's the law of the universe. Always has been] (471). It is both the finality and veracity of Tibério's patriarchal worldview, Suro believes, that is behind the pessimism one encounters in Veríssimo's novels concerning the long-term viability of liberal democracy in Brazil.

The prominence of death and the dead as well as the concurrent impossibility of renewal emerge as constant narrative references in *Incidente em Antares.* Significantly, the village later known as Antares is referred to, in early-nineteenth-century "historical" documents, as Povinho da Caveira, the Village of the Skull (3). We discover that indeed the community's origins are steeped in violence when the local patriarch, Francisco Vacariano, tells how through intimidation, thievery, and murder he was able to expand his cattle operation and meanwhile thwart any interventions by the central government: "Sabe o que fiz com o último lotador de impostos que apareceu nestas terras? Mandei matá-lo e atirei seu corpo no rio" [Do you know what I did with the last tax appraiser who appeared in these parts? I had him killed and his body thrown in the river] (5). The French naturalist interviewing Francisco is, needless to say, relieved to know that he would not be meeting the same fate.

Notably, during the Guerra dos Farrapos, the 1835 regional uprising in southern Brazil against the imperial government, Francisco Vacariano never takes a definitive ideological stance, seeking instead to profit from the presence of both the revolutionaries and the *legalistas:* "jogar com pau de dois bicos" [to hunt with the hounds and run with the hare], as one of his enemies would later comment (8). Opportunism would prove to be the primary motivating factor for political positions adopted by the landowning class in Antares, up through the twentieth century. The other consistent trait of this class is its underlying affiliation with patriarchal systems. Hence, Francisco's reservations about abandoning the empire during the Guerra dos Farrapos: "Um imperador é uma espécie de pai que a gente tem. Numa república me parece que todo o mundo fica meio órfão" [An emperor is a kind of father for the people. In a republic it seems to me that everyone becomes orphaned] (8).

Two mechanisms permit patriarchal opportunism to flourish in Antares over such an extended historical period: a dogmatic reverence for the past and a brazen willingness to employ violence as a means of acquiring, consolidating, and preserving power in the present and for the future. The arrival of the competing Campolargo clan in Antares sets in motion an intense and often violent rivalry with the Vacariano family that lasts nearly seven decades. Even the war with Paraguay, during which both families send sons to fight under the same imperial banner, fails to bring peace to Antares. And as the old patriarchs die, the new heads of each family express their allegiance to the past through a kind of ancestral cult: "Ambos haviam jurado em silêncio, junto aos cadáveres paternos, continuar aquela luta de família até ao fim do Tempo" [Both had sworn in silence, next to their fathers' dead bodies, to continue this family feud until the end of Time] (14). This passage is the first of many instances in the novel in which the vicious circle of violence and retribution sustaining Antares' patriarchal system is articulated in terms of the living being ruled by the dead.

The beginning of the twentieth century brings with it the promise of a new era filled with "Luz" [Light] and "Progresso" [Progress]. The festivities in Antares ushering in the New Year, however, end in a knife fight between two young members of each clan. The most poignant symbol of death's dominion over change comes in 1912 when, in protest against the newly installed electric street lamps, the old man who had lit the city's oil lamps for more than twenty-five years hangs himself to death on one of the new lampposts. The old lamplighter's protest, literally against a new kind of light, and figuratively against progress, represents an auspicious declaration of Antares' resistance to change, even as dramatic changes are taking place in the world around this gaúcho city.

By 1960, however, the aging patriarchs of the Vacariano and Campolargo families have put aside their long-standing rivalry, with the realization that together they represent a bygone era and therefore must consolidate the resources of their social class, as rural landowners, for the purpose of self-preservation. It is a past, however, that Coronel Tibério Vacariano continues to venerate. When the dying Zózimo Campolargo, now Tibério's friend, asserts on his hospital bed that "our time has passed," Tibério responds, "Nunca na vida caí de cavalo. E sou domador" [Never in my life have I fallen off my horse. I can tame any beast] (102). As the two men discuss the upcoming presidential election between General Teixeira Lott and Jânio Quadros, Zózimo whispers to his former rival:

> Nós . . . nós lá no Rio Grande não iremos . . . iremos nunca para diante . . . sem primerio enterrar definitivamente certos cadáveres simbólicos . . . Gaspar Martins, Júlio de Castilhos, Borges de Medeiros . . . Getúlio Vargas . . . e outros, outros . . .

> . . .
> Você quer então matar as nossas tradições?
> Não. Eu quero que os homens da nossa . . . da nossa geração compreendam que seu tempo passou . . . que não podemos continuar olhando para trás . . . recordando as nossas cargas de cavalaria . . . Sepé Tiaraju . . . As "califórnias" do Chico Pedro . . . Bento Gonçalves . . . Tempos novos chegaram, estão sempre chegando . . . Pedem outra espécie de gente . . . gente capaz de ousar . . . de olhar para a frente, enxergar longe . . . homens com um pé no presente e outro no futuro.
>
> [—Those . . . those of us from Rio Grande do Sul will not . . . will never move forward . . . without first burying once and for all certain symbolic cadavers . . . Gaspar Martins, Júlio de Castilhos, Borges de Medeiros . . . Getúlio Vargas . . . and others, others . . .
> . . .
> —So you want to eradicate our traditions then?
> —No. I want the men of our . . . of our generation to understand that their time has passed . . . that we can't keep looking back . . . remembering our cavalry charges . . . Sepé Tiaraju . . . The "Californias" of Chico Pedro . . . Bento Gonçalves . . . A new era has arrived, is always arriving . . . that calls for another type of person . . . bold enough . . . to look ahead, into the distance . . . men with one foot in the present and the other in the future.] (102)

On his own deathbed Zózimo realizes that certain political figures, such as Getúlio Vargas, and social institutions, like gaúcho machismo, persist as symbolic cadavers in Rio Grande do Sul and must be psychologically buried before change can occur. Zózimo's surprising words carry the tone of a last confession, made in the liminal state between life and death. Several references to Zózimo's own near-cadaverous state appear in this chapter: "Tibério, confrangido, teve uma antevisão da caveira de seu amigo" [an afflicted Tibério foresaw his friend's skull] (101); "Zózimo tornou a sorrir um sorriso que já parecia ter algo de além-túmulo" [Zózimo gave a smile that seemed already to be coming from beyond the grave] (103). In this respect, Zózimo Campolargo's words emanate, at least partially, from the beyond, and therefore possess some of the irony, candor, and perspicacity of the resurrected defuntos in the second part of the novel. Moreover, knowing that numerous blood transfusions in the hospital have taken the place of his "old blood," the Campolargo patriarch senses that the voices of hundreds of donors are speaking through him, thus radically altering his perspective on life.

The central question in this provocative dialogue is precisely what to do with society's unburied dead, or more broadly speaking, with a past that keeps reinstating itself into the present. Should the old blood be transfused out by newer blood or should it be guarded as the life essence of a particular tradition or way of life? By evoking the voices of the unburied dead, in the form of mythical-political figures, outdated socioeconomic institutions, and anachronistic codes of behavior, *Incidente em Antares* problematizes not only "traditional" gaúcho cultural norms but also Brazilian society's relationship to its own past. This is a theme that is manifested at both the micro and the macro level of the novel's narrative and therefore deserves in-depth attention.

Cultural Haunting

In previous chapters we have considered the importance of real and symbolic second burials in different social contexts, as well as certain anthropological theories that link the intermediary state of mourners with the liminal existence of the deceased, whose souls are believed to be suspended temporarily between the moment of physical death and their admittance into the land of the dead. This theoretical framework is also an important underpinning to the ideas put forth by literary critic Kathleen Brogan in *Cultural Haunting: Ghosts and Ethnicity in Recent American Literature* (1998), particularly in her analysis of Toni Morrison's novel *Beloved:*

> Haunting in *Beloved* signals the return of a past that can neither be properly remembered nor entirely forgotten. The novel records a battle

> between anamnesis and amnesia, the desire to account for the dead struggling against the need to obliterate them. At issue is the relation between historical consciousness and traumatic memory, the problem of how to represent what is experienced as "unspeakable." *Beloved* plots the movement from trauma to history as a story of possession and exorcism in which traumatic memory—or the eruption of a denied history—is figured as a dangerous form of haunting. (63)

Moreover, Brogan observes that the main action of *Beloved,* as well as in other narratives of "cultural haunting," occurs during the intermediary period between first and second burial rituals, in which mourners are bound to the liminal existence of the deceased, that is, until the final funeral when the dead can be safely incorporated into the realm of the living through memory (68).

Stories of cultural haunting differ from the more familiar Victorian and gothic genres of ghost stories in that they portray the collective struggle of a haunted community, rather than the psychological turmoil of the haunted self. Though Sethe, in *Beloved,* is haunted by her own personal history, her suffering speaks for the larger community of former slaves and African Americans still trying to come to terms with the horrors of slavery. Whereas the ghosts evoked by turn-of-the-century "psychological" authors, such as Henry James and Edith Wharton, bring into sharp relief the anguished psyche of an individual (as well as later authors influenced by Freud's theories of the repressed unconscious), the story of cultural haunting "brings to the foreground the communal nature of its ghosts," thereby exploring the unspoken elements of "a people's historical consciousness" (5).

Thus, the particular ghost stories analyzed by Brogan are also modern American tales of exploration and identification for historically disenfranchised ethnic communities, in which the ghost serves as both "an emblem of historical loss as well as a vehicle of historical recovery" (29). Tracing the emergence of contemporary haunted narratives across diverse ethnic groups represented in American literature, Brogan examines most closely, in addition to *Beloved,* Louise Erdrich's novel

Tracks (1988), in which cultural continuity in an American Indian community is negotiated through a Windigo possession and a ritual Ghost Dance, and Cristina García's *Dreaming in Cuban* (1992), in which a Cuban family's ghostly relative assists in the definition of a new Cuban American identity. Other examples of cultural haunting found by Brogan in contemporary American literature include Sandra Cisneros's *Woman Hollering Creek* (1991), William Kennedy's *Ironweed* (1983), Maxine Hong Kingston's *The Woman Warrior* (1976), Carole Maso's *Ghost Dance* (1986), Gloria Naylor's *Mama Day* (1988), Leslie Marmon Silko's *The Almanac of the Dead* (1991), Amy Tan's *The Hundred Secret Senses* (1995), and August Wilson's *The Piano Lesson* (1987).

Narratives of cultural haunting, Brogan suggests, are conveyed within the framework of two fundamental elements: mourning and possession. More precisely, ghostly haunting occurs when at some point mourning has gone awry and "the possessed one is locked into repetition, doomed to reenact the past without relevance to present realities" (10). The danger of repetition lies in both its indifference to present realities and its ability to forcefully reinstate the past. Only by exorcising the ghost and assimilating the past into the present in a meaningful way can onerous haunting be transformed into a more constructive historical consciousness.

The Ghost in the Brazilian National Machine

Brogan's definition of cultural haunting provides a valuable theoretical framework for understanding, in part, the function of the unburied dead and subsequent acts of collective mourning in Érico Veríssimo's *Incidente em Antares.* For example, the criticism that a dying Zózimo Campolargo directs at his generation's patriarchal ways, followed by Tibério's idolizing response (see above) reveals a case in which mourning for a now defunct past has gone awry for an entire community and therefore symbolic cadavers continue to haunt both those in power and those who have been historically oppressed by social and economic inequalities in the region. In a later passage, in which parts of Professor Martim Francisco's report on Antares are being read, this view is expressed by a young student who comes from one of Antares' traditional families:

> O Rio Grande do Sul é o Estado mais reacionário do Brasil, e Ribeira (Antares) a cidade mais reacionária do Rio Grande do Sul. . . . Reacionarismo em tudo. Veneramos morbidamente um passado e uma tradição já mortos, se é que de fato um dia existiram mesmo, e somos incapazes de sair dos trilhos da rotina e erguer a cara para o sol do futuro.
>
> [Rio Grande do Sul is the most reactionary state in Brazil, and Antares is the most reactionary city in the state. . . . Reactionary in every way. We morbidly venerate a past and a tradition that are already dead, if they ever even existed at all; we are incapable of straying off this beaten path and lifting our face toward the light of the future.] (140)

To morbidly venerate a past that is essentially dead is to be effectively held prisoner by a cycle of perpetual mourning. Although *Incidente em Antares* does not unearth the deeply buried, unspeakable past of a particular ethnic group that has been historically marginalized, in the same way that, for example, Morrison's *Beloved* does (as do many of the Spanish American works whose haunting revolves around an "ancestral impulse," as identified by Lois Parkinson Zamora), Veríssimo's novel does evoke certain institutions that have historically acted as impediments to real socioeconomic transformation in Brazil.

While Sethe's daughter, Beloved, can be read as an emblem of America's troubled racial history—what Morrison describes as the "ghost in the national machine"—the many defuntos resurrected by Veríssimo speak to the damaging effects of a ghostly patriarchal order in Brazil's own national machine, with its kindred expressions of *coronelismo* and machismo. It is this very order that stands to be severely threatened by the unusual occurrences in Antares, beginning with the general strike organized by its city workers. The apocalyptic mood that falls over the city before the incident suggests that the strike itself is viewed as a kind of death. In the eyes of the landowners and the bourgeoisie accustomed to a position of uncontested authority in Antares, the workers' sudden civil disobedience and demands for better wages and working conditions represent the end of the world as they know it, the death of a social order they believe to be everlasting.

This unexpected assault on the patriarchs' value system reaches its culmination when the striking gravediggers refuse to bury the bodies of Antares' recently deceased citizens. Among the dead are two of Antares' most esteemed citizens, Dona Quitéria, matriarch of the Campolargo family, and Dr. Cícero Branco, lawyer for the wealthiest and most corrupt segment of Antares' population. The remaining defuntos, lying in their coffins at the gates of the cemetery, represent a wide cross-section of Antares society and include José Ruiz, an anarchist cobbler and supporter of the strike; Professor Menandro Olinda, a piano teacher who committed suicide; Erotildes, a former prostitute; João Paz, a young radical whose murder by city officials was covered up; and Pudim de Cachaça, the city drunk slain by his own wife, whom he had abused. When D. Quitéria's family arrives with her lavish coffin at the cemetery, accompanied by Coronel Tibério Vacariano, the mayor, a judge, a priest, and twenty or so city police, they are met by roughly four hundred strikers, led by the syndicalist Geminiano Ramos, who have formed a human wall in front of the cemetery.

The confrontation between the city officials and the strikers at the entrance of the municipal cemetery resembles, in some respects, the 1836 Cemiterada in Salvador, Bahia, in which a popular revolt led by the local irmandades erupted at the scene of a cemetery owned by a company that had been granted a monopoly to bury the city's dead. As in the Cemiterada, the immediate struggle in Antares revolves around who has control over when, where, and how the dead are to be buried. Although the specific circumstances behind the revolt in Antares differ from those of the Cemiterada, in both cases the cemetery becomes an important social space where communal conflicts are negotiated. In

Incidente em Antares, more specifically, the struggle over the burial of the seven cadavers becomes a metaphor for the larger social struggle over how best to commemorate the past: through veneration or reintegration of the past?

The period between physical death and the actual burial of a loved one is, as anthropologists have pointed out, a particularly disquieting and precarious time, when the long-held values of a community are called into question and subsequently reaffirmed or transformed. Despite obvious circumstantial differences, the confrontation at the gates of the cemetery in Antares also shares much in common with the wake scene in *A morte e a morte de Quincas Berro Dágua,* when Quincas's biological family and his street companions, his adopted family, jostle for position around Quincas's body. As in *Quincas Berro Dágua,* the dead in Antares become the focal point for dissonant socioeconomic groups and opposing worldviews. Whereas in *Quincas Berro Dágua* the underlying conflict lies in the difference between personal and impersonal social ethos, the standoff between the proletariat and the patrões in *Incidente* revolves around the troubled dismantling of an obsolete patriarchal order. In both cases the burial of the dead becomes a prime site for negotiating how best to usher in a new world while discarding with the old.

Carnival or Judgment Day?

It quickly becomes evident to the reader that the return of the dead in *Incidente em Antares* is portrayed by Veríssimo in a satirical way. Unable to forge an agreement, the strikers decide to stand guard at the cemetery until their grievances are addressed. During the night, a professional thief, who has heard that one of the deceased is wealthy and may be wearing precious jewels, makes his way to D. Quitéria's coffin and quietly opens the lid. Surprised to find that there are no jewels, the thief pauses to view the old woman's face:

> Numa relutância supersticiosa focou o rosto do cadáver da dama e estremeceu. Os olhos dela estavam abertos, seus lábios começaram a mover-se e deles saiu primeiro um ronco e depois estas palavras, nítidas: *Senhor, em vossas mãos entrego a minha alma*. O ladrão soltou um grito abafado, ergueu-se rápido, deixou cair a lanterna acesa e o pé-de-cabra, e rompeu a correr na direção dos campos desertos.
>
> [With a kind of superstitious reluctance the thief peered at the face of D. Quitéria's cadaver and then started to shake. Her eyes were open and her lips began to move, forming first a grunt and then these clearly enunciated words: "Lord, I deliver my soul into thy hands." The thief let out a stifled cry, lifted himself up quickly, dropped his burning lantern and crowbar, and took off running into the countryside.] (229–30)

Thus begin the fantastic events—"tão insólitos, lúridos e tétricos" [so extraordinary, lurid, and macabre]—of the infamous incident in Antares (2). One by one, the remaining defuntos rise from their coffins and marvel at their misfortune of having been left unburied. They also speak to each other with unprecedented candor. Dr. Cícero Branco confesses to D. Quitéria that he attended her wake only because he had an eye on her fortune and wanted to ingratiate himself with her family. D. Quitéria, in turn, responds, "Bom, já que estamos no jogo de verdade . . . nunca simpatizei com o senhor" [Well, since we are showing all our cards . . . I never took much of a liking to you, Sir] (233). Cícero's ironic frankness—"Já que estamos mortos e não somos mais personagens da comédia humana, posso ser absolutamente franco" [Now that we are dead and no longer characters in the human comedy of life, I can be absolutely candid]—along with his denouncement of society's hypocrisy and the vanity of the living, strikes a chord similar to Brás Cubas's posthumous sarcasm (233).

The motivation behind the protest raised by the defuntos is succinctly articulated by their spokesperson, Cícero, shortly after their resurrection: "Qual é o nosso objetivo? O de sermos sepultados dignamente, como é de nosso direito e de hábito, numa sociedade cristã" [What is our goal? To be buried in a dignified fashion, as is our right, and customary in a Christian society] (249). They agree that if their demand for a dignified burial is not met within twenty-four hours they will remain in Antares' central square, Praça da República, and expose the city to the hygienic, aesthetic, and moral impurity of their rotting corpses (250). Like Quincas Berro Dágua, they are motivated in the afterlife by a desire to take control of their own burial by reshaping the rituals surrounding their death. The defuntos realize that the first step toward a proper burial is to pressure Antares' city officials, and the various multinational companies located in the city, to address the concerns of the strikers. Symbolically speaking, social change must occur before the past can be properly buried in Antares. In this sense, as they wait for the sun to rise before setting out into the city, the defuntos embody the hope of a new socioeconomic order in Antares: "E os sete mortos voltam a deitar-se nos seus esquifes e ali ficam, de olhos abertos, à espera dum novo dia" [And the seven cadavers laid back down in their coffins to wait, eyes wide open, for the dawning of a new day] (251). Similarly, when they "awake" that morning, Cícero describes their coffins as "sete úteros abertos" [seven open uteruses], and his dead companions as "criancinhas recém-nascidas" [newborn babies] (253).

The reaction in Antares to the appearance of the cadavers, as they stroll casually from the cemetery into the city, is one of general panic, confusion, and foreboding. Several people suffer from panic attacks upon seeing the defuntos: a striker suffers a cardiac arrest, one woman gives birth prematurely, a sharpshooter fires several shots at the defuntos with no effect, one man believes D. Quitéria to be his long-deceased mother returning to him, and the local priest, after seeing the cadavers march through the street, announces to his congregation that Judgment Day is upon them. The sudden presence of the defuntos in the city is described by the local journalist in both visual as well as olfactory terms:

> O sinistro bando, a todas essas, caminhava implacavelmente, em marmóreo silêncio tumular, para o centro da cidade, deixando para trás uma fétida esteira pestilencial, que em breve inundou todas as ruas

> adjacentes, de tal maneira ativa e nauseante que este homem de imprensa teve, a ainda hoje tem, a impressão de que, como diria Lady Macbeth, no drama do imortal Shakespeare, nem todos os perfumes da Arábia conseguirão jamais limpar nossa cidade dessa fedentina cadavérica.
>
> [This sinister assemblage continued their inexorable march in deadly, marmoreal silence toward the city center, leaving behind a pestilent smell that soon inundated all the adjacent streets and left this reporter with the lasting impression that, as Lady Macbeth, from Shakespeare's immortal drama, might say, "All the perfumes of Arabia will not sweeten our city from this cadaverous stench."] (259)

Another initial reaction shared by several eyewitnesses is to mistakenly take the macabre bunch for a group of carnival revelers. One woman responds, upon seeing the corpses outside her window, "Ué? bloco de carnaval em dezembro?" [Huh? A carnival parade in December?] (256). Similarly, a driver, whose way is obstructed by the cadavers, yells out his car window, "Saiam da frente, seus palhaços! O carnaval ainda não chegou!" [Get out of the way, you clowns! Carnival hasn't started yet!] (257). If the ghoulish appearance of the defuntos, and the general disruption they cause in the city, elicits a carnival-like atmosphere at the outset of the incident, the full extent of their carnivalesque spirit is expressed only later when, equipped with the unique vantage point of the living-dead, the corpses are able to see through the materialism and hypocrisies of those in power and, in typical carnival fashion, expose the most corrupt to public denunciation.

Two curious episodes that occur during the confusion in Antares on Friday the thirteenth, in December 1963, are worth noting, in light of both Veríssimo's commentary on Rio Grande do Sul's anachronistic patriarchal system and the historical significance of the incident falling on the same day and month as the promulgation of the Ato Institucional no. 5 in 1968. In chapter 32 of the novel's second part, an old black woman named Acácia, who is described as the "encarnação dum curioso sincretismo religioso" [embodiment of a peculiar religious syncretism], comes to the mayor's office in the early morning to do her usual cleaning (301). Of all the portraits of political figures decorating the office, Acácia recognizes only that of Getúlio Vargas, whom she considers the "Pai dos Pobres" [the Father of the Poor] and adores as if he were a saint. She makes a point, while cleaning, of kneeling before the former president's picture and reciting the Our Father. On this particular morning she asks Getúlio to protect the people of Antares against the "hereges desalmados" [soulless heretics], referring to the strikers who prevented the proper burial of seven corpses (302). As an aside, she asks her presidential saint to intervene on her behalf by ordering her salary to be raised. The inherent inconsistencies of her requests are apparently lost on Acácia.

In the following chapter we learn of the similarly eccentric devotions of another public functionary, Antônio Augusto Mendes, the secretary to the mayor, who, while he is working late into the evening at the mayor's office, has a habit of opening a bottle of cachaça and, with "os ouvidos da memória" [the ear of memory], listening to the political and philosophical discussions emanating from the revered political figures whose portraits hang on the walls (304). The ghosts of Borges de Medeiros, Júlio de Castilhos, Pinheiro Machado, all "chefes com C maiúsculo" [bosses with a capital B] in the eyes of Antônio, debate the relative virtue of various ideological positions, as the secretary listens admiringly in a drunk or sleep-induced trance. Getúlio's portrait merely smiles as the others argue. Jango's [João Goulart's] gaze, symbolically, is turned away from the other figures. It is Júlio de Castilho who has the last word: "A progressão social repousa essencialmente sobre a morte. Os vivos são sempre e cada vez mais governados pelos mortos" [Social progress rests essentially on death. The living are governed more and more by the dead] (306). Castilho's last words are also a succinct summation of the cultlike veneration that people like Acácia and Antônio manifest toward a bygone patriarchal order, one that is predicated on the governance of the living by the dead. Veríssimo seems to suggest, in these two chapters, that the sanctification of

Getúlio Vargas, and other former leaders, not only by the elite but also by the lower and middle classes, has obscured other, more constructive avenues of socioeconomic progress in Brazil.

Before a Chorus of Laughing People

After dealing individually with their own personal matters, the seven corpses return to the Praça República by twelve noon, and wait for their demand for a decent burial to be met. News of the cadaveric demonstration has spread throughout the city and a large crowd begins to form around the square, giving the event a festival-like atmosphere, complete with concession stands and trucks displaying the American flag and advertisements for Coca-Cola and Pepsi. The spectacle also attracts a crowd of bohemian youths who position themselves in a large tree overlooking the square and offer subversive comments during the event that echo Cícero's own accusations of the town leaders. Necessarily present are the many faces of Brazil's patriarchal order, figures of authority who are systematically accused by Cícero of falsehood, hypocrisy, and impropriety. One by one he attacks their arbitrary abuse of power and dubious claims of self-importance. For example, he describes the town patriarch Coronel Tibério Vacariano as a criminal (349); the judge as corrupt and perpetrator of an inefficient legal system; the mayor as a practitioner of two-faced, Jekyll and Hyde–style politics; the professor as a pedant in false dialogue with foreign intellectual trends; the chief of police as a sadist and rapist of the people; and the priest as weak and reactionary. Cícero's sarcasm is particularly potent because he speaks from the point of view of the living-dead:

> Hipócritas!—exclama.—Impostores! Simuladores! Eis o que sois . . . Vista deste coreto, do meu ângulo de defunto, a vida mais que nunca me parece um baile de máscaras.
>
> ["Hypocrites!"—he exclaims. "Imposters! Charlatans! This is what you are. . . . Seen from this perspective, through my dead man's eyes, life more so than ever strikes me as a masked ball."] (341)

It is a ball, however, enjoyed only by the privileged few, as Cícero points out:

> Para vós o importante é que a festa continue, que não se toque na estrutura, não se alterem os estatutos do clube onde os privilegiados se divertem. A canalha que não pode tomar parte na festa e se amontoa lá fora no sereno, envergando a triste fantasia e a trágica máscara da miséria, essa deve permanecer onde está, porque vós os convivas felizes achais que pobres sempre os haverá, como disse Jesus. E por isso pagais a vossa polícia para que ela vos defenda no dia em que a plebe decidir invadir o salão onde vos entregais às vossas danças, libações, amores e outros divertimentos.
>
> [What is important to you is that the party goes on, that no one messes with the structure, that no change is made to the rules of the club where the privileged have such a good time. The scum, who can't join the party and who huddles outside in the open air, wearing only the sad costume of fantasy and the tragic mask of misery, this guy should stay right where he is, because you, the happy guests, believe that the poor will always be among you, as Jesus said. And, thus, you pay your police to defend you on the day that the rabble decides to crash this private party, where you indulge yourselves in dance, drinking, love affairs, and other pleasures.] (344–45)

Cícero's ironic defamation of Antares' most corrupt citizens is met by shouts of approval by the younger generation in the crowd, who punctuate the defunto's speech with taunting insults and whistles. The momentary suspension of hierarchical authority and the reelaboration of social relations that occurs during the defuntos' demonstration in the square is a vivid example of the Bakhtinian marketplace, with its corrosive laughter. In the conclusion of *Rabelais and His World,* Bakhtin asserts that "all the acts of the drama of world history were performed before a chorus of the laughing people." For Bakhtin, "the authentic meaning of the epoch and its events is disclosed in these crowd scenes" (474). To demonstrate his point, Bakhtin concludes with a final quote from Alexander Pushkin's *Boris Godunov* in which Dmitry, the false "pretender" to Russia's throne, describes his worst nightmare: "The people swarmed on the public square / And pointed laughingly at me / And I was filled with shame and fear" (474).

Inherent to Bakhtin's notion of nonofficial, corrosive laughter erupting in the public square is the insinuation that the official voice of the Russian Revolution had lost touch with Russia's folk people. The crowd scene in Antares depicted by Veríssimo is similarly intended, not only to unmask acts of arbitrary authority through folk laughter, but also to underscore "the authentic meaning" of a particular historical period in Brazil, one in which the country's claim to liberty and basic human rights hung in the balance. The drama that unfolded in late 1963 in Brazil was marked, Veríssimo seems to suggest, by the momentary chorus of laughing people, voices that evoked both the promise of change and the imminent threat of a takeover by reactionary forces in Brazilian society.

Though undoubtedly symbolic of a moribund sociopolitical order and decomposing moral values in Brazil, the resurrected defuntos in *Incidente em Antares* concurrently act as carnivalesque harbingers of change and renewal. It is no wonder they are mistaken for carnival revelers. Their subversive presence in the town square verifies that no one speaks with more sincerity or perspicacity about the matters of life and death than the dead themselves. However, the defuntos' return is intended to do more than just teach the citizens of Antares a lesson in morality and social relativity. They also offer themselves as role models of dramatic personal transformation, especially in the cases of Cícero and D. Quitéria, who, in death, are critical of the socioeconomic order that they, in life, represented. They are in this sense emblematic of the kinds of ghosts that inhabit narratives of cultural haunting, as defined by Brogan, for they represent not only debilitating possession by, but also "imaginative liberation" from the past (Brogan, 11).

And initially, during the incident and immediately afterward, change does occur in Antares. Several old enemies reconcile with one another. The public airing of Antares' dirty laundry, including acts of infidelity, has a cathartic effect on the community and even leads to the separation of five or six unhappy couples. Dr. Lázaro, the corrupt physician, confesses to the leftist priest his past crimes and frailties. The judge's wife makes a different sort of confession to her husband when she reveals that she is unsatisfied by their petty bourgeois existence and her husband's complicity with the lies that have built up over time in Antares. When the mayor's wife asks her husband later that evening if there is any truth to Dr. Cícero's charges of city corruption, the mayor responds in a tone that is both condescending and incredulous:

> "Vocês mulheres são muito engraçadas! Donde pensas que me veio o dinheiro para construir esta casa e ter dois carros na garagem? Do teu grande dote? . . . Pronto. Agora já sabes!"
>
> [You women are very funny! Where do you think I got the money to build this house and have two cars in the garage? From your huge dowry? . . . Fine. Now you know!] (390)

More threatening than the hordes of rats and the rumored plague that have befallen the city is the truth which, like an infection, spreads from house to house.

However, when the mayor's wife reminds her husband that the povo heard everything, the mayor's response is particularly foreboding: "Que é o povo? Um monstro com muitas cabeças mas sem miolos. E esse 'bicho' tem memória curta" [What is this thing called the povo? A many-headed monster with no brains and a short memory] (390). Thus begins the official strategy for dealing with the incident's aftermath —to convince both the population of Antares and the outside world that "tudo foi uma ilusão" [everything was just an illusion], a mere promotional stunt to bring tourism to the region (391). Shortly after the gravediggers decide to lift their blockade of the cemetery due to the "recent developments," the defuntos make their way back to their coffins and are promptly buried with little ceremony. The strike ends with the workers receiving most of their demands. What remains to be seen, however, is how the incident will be remembered. In the "battle between anamnesis and amnesia," this ambivalent relationship of the living to the dead (the past) in stories of cultural haunting, amnesia appears to have the upper hand at the conclusion of *Incidente em Antares.* In an effort to raise public morale in Antares, city officials and business leaders discreetly put into motion a secret campaign of collective amnesia called Operação Borracha [Operation Erasure]. According to the organizers, who have already convinced themselves that nothing really happened on Friday the thirteenth in 1963, the strategy has various natural allies, which include common sense, human experience, science, and most of all, time, which like water, they assert, can wash away all unpleasant memories (461). The campaign begins by not permitting the publication of an article written by local journalist Lucas Faia describing the incident in full detail. Subsequently, international newspapers characterize the incident as either a commercially driven hoax, or an example of mass hallucination. Gradually, as the city promotes banquets for the well-to-do and distractions for the povo, the incident begins to fade from the minds of Antares' citizens. The most obstinate are intimidated into forgetting, as in the case of the foreign photographer, precisely "that which he didn't see" (475).

There are some things, however, that the people of Antares are unable to forget, and this is where anamnesis, the inability to forget, goes hand in hand with amnesia. It is the matriarch Quitéria's earlier words that strike at the heart of the matter. Embittered by her family's petty greed following her death she laments: "entre vivos e mortos não há entendimento possível" [between the living and the dead there is no mutual understanding] (356). Herein lies the underlying problem. Veríssimo seems to be saying that before meaningful change can occur, Brazil must first exorcise the ghosts of its past, in other words, those social and political institutions that have outlived their usefulness. The unburied dead in Antares are a metaphor then for those moral doctrines, political structures, and deified figures that continue to haunt the living. By the same token, Veríssimo's political satire is directed most certainly at the Brazilian military dictatorship and, to borrow Antonio Sérgio's expression, its "tyranny of phantoms." Acting much like the military coup of 1964, the Operação Borracha that follows the incident in Antares is intended precisely both to inculcate society with the values of an obsolete era and to erase any evidence of this revolutionary moment from the annals of history and the memory of the people.

Voices of the Dead in Minas Gerais

A different sort of tyranny of phantoms rules over the somber, rather uncarnivalesque pages of *Ópera dos mortos* [The Voices of the Dead] by Autran Dourado. Though he has lived in Rio de Janeiro for much of his life, Dourado has consistently set his novels in Minas Gerais, where he was born in 1926.[5] *Ópera dos mortos* (1967), Dourado's sixth novel, tells the story of a small town in Minas Gerais, sometime in the early part of the twentieth century, in which one family's bitter grudge sets in motion a seemingly endless cycle of resentment, bitterness, and isolation. Each generation is haunted by the legacy and memory of their forebears, in whose name they perpetuate the family's antagonistic relationship with the rest of the community. The arrival of a stranger to this setting momentarily breaks this cycle, yet eventually he too becomes prisoner to the family's all-consuming veneration of the past.

Like *Incidente em Antares,* the narrative of *Ópera dos mortos* unfolds in a fictitious place, a nameless town established by the Honório Cota family in the hills of Minas. The historical and geographical backdrop provided for the reader in Dourado's novel is considerably sparser than the sweeping introduction Veríssimo gives Antares. Instead, the reader is invited, in the opening chapter, to come "see" the family's now abandoned sobrado, the splendor of whose ornamentation has faded with age. Yet the mansion is still an imposing presence at the foot of the Carmo square, alongside the stone church whose style it was intended to imitate. Despite the sobrado's obvious signs of physical (and symbolic) decay, the narrator urges the reader to step back in time and see it as it used to be. Truly seeing, however, is accomplished more through an act of imagination than as a visual experience:

> O senhor atente depois para o velho sobrado com a memória, com o coração—imagine, mais do que com os olhos, os olhos são apenas o conduto, o olhar é que importa. (2)
>
> [Now then, look closely at the old manor, but with your memory, your heart—your mind's eye, not your eyes so much, they're only the access, it's the way you look that counts.] (13)[6]

Similarly, Rosalina, "com aqueles olhos embaciados, aquela neutralidade morna" (3) ["with her glazed eyes, her listless indifference"] (15–16), gazing out at the Carmo square from behind a half-closed curtain, does not "see" the world, she imagines it, or better yet, remembers it. Seeing, we learn in this first chapter of *Ópera dos mortos,* is substituted by memory, or the mind's eye, in the world of the Honório Cota sobrado. Rosalina's myopic perception of the present and future is, therefore, refracted through a mind's eye that is able to focus only on the past. Anticipating the reader's impatience for more concrete details concerning the family and its house, the narrator encourages the reader to view this world through a "baroque" lens, rather than with the eyes of a naturalist, who sees only the here and now. For it is not the eyes that move but the baroque patterns of the sobrado and the Carmo church that are in constant motion, and whose sinuous lines tell the story of this family's secrets.

The first chapter sets into motion a pattern of seeing and not seeing that recurs throughout the novel. The narrator beckons us to come see Rosalina's ghostly image move silently to one of the sobrado's windows, though we know she no longer resides there. Rosalina also gazes out at us, but with unseeing eyes, indifferent to the historical events that occur in the outside world. Seeing and not seeing is also the fate of one of the novel's primary characters, Juca Passarinho, who views the world through one good eye and one eye that is clouded over.

The sobrado is, undoubtedly, a central narrative feature in *Ópera dos mortos,* and the novel's first chapter, much like the beginning of *Dom Casmurro,* initiates the reconstruction of the house through memory. In Machado's novel, Bento relies on his mind's eye to recreate precisely every detail of the house he lived in as he was growing up. Bento's recreated childhood home is, therefore, a physical externalization of his memory. It too tells the story of an individual who is possessed by the past and whose memories are composed as much of imagination as actual recollection. Similarly, the changes that occur to the Honório Cota sobrado over the generations involve constant gestures of atonement toward the family's deceased patriarchal figures. When João Capistrano, Rosalina's father, adds a more lavish second floor onto the sober design of *his* father's original house, he instructs the builder to leave the first floor as is:

> Não quero mudar tudo, disse. Não derrubo obra do meu pai. O que eu quero é juntar o meu com o de meu pai. Eu sou ele agora, no sangue, por dentro. (4)
>
> [I don't want it all changed, he said. I'm not knocking down what my father put up. What I want is to add what I've got to what he had. I am him, now, inside, in the blood.] (16)

Thus, the structure of the sobrado itself, with its heavy ground floor and more refined upper story, represents the fusion of the living with the dead in an "argamassa estranha de gente e casa" (4) ["peculiar bond of people and house"] (16).

Lucas Procópio, João's father and the town's founder, is legendary for his rude manners and the fear he instilled in those who knew him, and his spectral presence lives on in the minds of the townspeople. When João Capistrano's only child is born, a daughter named Rosalina, he prays that as she grows up her feminine grace and beauty will soften the grandfather's brutish features, including "aquelas sobrancelhas cabeludas que ainda estavam na cara de João Capistrano e o faziam voltar sonâmbula ao território do Encantado" (18) ["the bushy eyebrows which lingered on the face of João Capistrano and made him return, like a sleepwalker, to the territory of Haunted Ranch"] (31). The family's conflicting sentiments surrounding Rosalina's birth are contained within this passage, for her arrival brings both a sense of renewal as well as fear—that carried within her are the seeds of a haunting past. Contributing to Rosalina's inauspicious beginnings is João's unspoken disappointment that she is not a boy, and thus unable to carry on the Honório Cota lineage.

Later, when João Capistrano is betrayed, in his bid for election as mayor, by those whom he believed to be his constituents in town, his anger and resentment evoke his father's voice and image, as described here by one of the family's few friends, Quincas Ciríaco:

> Era a mesma voz de Lucas Procópio, viu Quincas Ciríaco. E eu que pensava que esta voz tinha morrido pra sempre! Agora está de nôvo doendo nos meus ouvidos. . . . Os olhos vidrados de João Capistrano na verdade não fitavam ninguém, vinham de um outro mundo, carregados de sombra. Quincas Ciríaco fechou os olhos para não ver aquela bôca, aquelas sobrancelhas cerradas. (24–25)

> [It was Lucas Procópio's voice again, Quincas Ciríaco saw that. And I thought that voice had gone for good! Now it's here again drumming in my ears. . . . João Capistrano's glazed eyes were certainly not fixed on anybody, they had an otherworldly look in them, they were clouded with dark shadows. Quincas Ciríaco closed his eyes so as not to see that mouth, those bushy eyebrows.] (38–39)

The manner in which Rosalina, now a young adult, chooses to support her father is to assume João's bitter silence, his wounded dignity, and undying hatred. Rosalina's emulation of her father's resentment constitutes a continuation of João Capistrano's own reproduction of *his* father's rage. Her stance is therefore the self-fulfilled prophecy of repeated haunting that has marked both her birth and the Honório Cota lineage. It should be stated here that haunting and ghostly apparitions occur in *Ópera dos mortos,* not in the form of "tangible" spirits or resurrected defuntos, as in the case of the novels examined until now, but rather through the obsessive veneration of, and possession by, the Honório Cota family's ancestors. Indeed, the absence of a narrator, character, or circumstance capable of subverting the authoritative nature of this veneration, even momentarily, effectively removes the necessary conditions for the emergence of a carnivalesque element in *Ópera dos mortos.* Of all the Brazilian works of fiction examined thus far, Dourado's novel comes closest, in this sense, to Zamora's definition of an "ancestral impulse" underlying literary ghosts in contemporary Latin American narrative, particularly if we extend the term *ancestral* beyond that of indigenous or historically marginalized narratives and cultural identities.

The death of João Capistrano's wife, Dona Genú, solidifies the impasse between his family and the community. This gulf is widened despite the hope shared by the townspeople, who attend Dona Genú's wake, that the matriarch's death will become an impetus for reconciliation and forgiveness. On the contrary, João Capistrano appears only when it is time to close the coffin and meet his guests with a distant coldness and lowered eyes. The possibility of time acting as a healing agent is negated when João performs the ritual gesture of stopping the hands of the sobrado's old clock at three, the hour of Jesus's crucifixion. Absent, however, in João Capistrano's symbolic gesture of bestowing martyrdom upon his wife, is Jesus's communal sense of compassion and forgiveness.

Just as time is paralyzed by the colonel's gesture, so is the family's estranged relationship to the outside world. From then on time does not pass in the sobrado, it merely repeats itself—hence, the narrator's condensed telling of the family's history in this chapter. A few brief paragraphs later we learn of João Capistrano's demise and the eerie resemblance of his wake to his wife's. Only now, Rosalina's isolation is nearly complete: for much of the wake she does not leave the manor's inner chambers to join the guests who have come to express their condolences and, like the narrator (who frequently positions himself as part of the community), indulge their curiosity by entering the lavish interior of the sobrado and witnessing the enigmatic Rosalina's grief. Nevertheless, the tears that swell in her eyes, when she finally appears before her deceased father at the wake, are produced, at least in part, by the community's own imagination and expectations. Thus, early on, Rosalina's mythical figure is sketched out through the community's collective desire for sanctification of the remaining member of the Honório Cota family. Dressed in mourner's black, but with the flowing grace of a bride, Rosalina repeats her father's gesture by hanging his pocket watch on the wall, its hands stopped on the hour of the patriarch's death. Time is once again paralyzed.

According to Dourado—in a series of essays entitled *Uma poética de romance: Matéria de carpintaria* [The Poetics of the Novel: Materials of Carpentry] (1976), in which he analyzes the creative process of his own fiction—*Ópera dos mortos* is constructed around the development of two essential metaphors: "casa e relógio" [house and clock] (114). The baroque lines of the sobrado, which, though fixed, appear to be moving and multiplying, serve as a metaphor for Rosalina's own pendular movement in the novel: "Quem souber ler o sobrado entenderá Rosalina" [He who knows how to read the mansion will understand Rosalina] (115). The sobrado's stopped clocks establish the novel's underlying illusion of mythical time, measured only by the rhythm of Rosalina's repeated movements in the house. Indeed, Dourado recalls in *Uma poética de romance* that before he began writing *Ópera dos mortos* he envisioned the story's title to be "Relógios de repetição" [Clocks of Repetition] (118).

Perpetual Mourning and the History Lodged Within

In light of the novels examined so far in this study, one might still ask: Where exactly are the revenants in *Ópera dos mortos?* Unlike Amado's *Dona Flor e seus dois maridos* or Érico Veríssimo's *Incidente em Antares,* in which the return of the dead is marked by the tangible, even sensual, recognition of the defunto's presence by the living, the ghosts in *Ópera dos mortos* reside in the very edifice of the sobrado, in the frozen hands of the sobrado's clocks and, perhaps most important, in the mind's eye of Rosalina, who lives possessed by the tormented souls of her ancestors. Some of the ghosts in *Ópera dos mortos* are indeed alive. Rosalina herself, in the sense proposed by Robert Hertz, belongs to the undead. Trapped in a state of perpetual mourning, Rosalina aligns herself with the wandering souls of her deceased ancestors and thus remains estranged from the community in which she lives. Unable, or perhaps unwilling, to exorcise these ghosts and bring closure to her mourning period, Rosalina becomes entrenched in her forefathers' liminal state.

To occupy herself during the long hours of silence in the sobrado, Rosalina makes flowers of pressed fabric and crepe paper, which she has Quiquina, her servant, sell in town. At night she secretly consumes Madeira and listens to the sounds of the house, and what she believes to be the footsteps of her departed family members:

> Mas as coisas naquela casa não eram frias e silenciosas, um pulso batia no seu corpo, ecoava estranhos ruídos, como se de noite acordada tinha sempre uma porta batendo. Agora êle desce a escada, os tacos de sua bota vibravam no corredor. O pai ou vovô Lucas Procópio? Será que Quiquina também ouvia? Mas ela não tinha nenhum mêdo, os fantasmas familiares, queria que êles aparecessem para que sua vida ficasse povoada. A casa vivia de noite, ou de dia naquele ôco de silêncio que ensombrecia como se fôsse de noite, como se ouivesse, como se fôsse um coração batendo a sua pêndula. Coração de quem? Da mãe, do pai, de Lucas Procópio? Nunca a gente sabia. Talvez o coração da casa mesmo. (37)
>
> [But things in that house weren't cold or silent, a pulse was beating in her body, reproducing strange noises, like a door forever banging if she lay awake at night. Now he's coming downstairs, the studs of his boots echoed in the corridor. Her father, or grandpa Lucas Procópio? Did Quiquina hear it too? But she wasn't at all afraid of her family ghosts, she wanted them to come and make her life less empty. The house was alive at night, or in the daytime when that silent emptiness cast shadows

> as if it were night, as if she could hear a heart throbbing in the pendulum clock. Whose heart? Her mother's, her father's, Lucas Procópio's? You couldn't tell. Perhaps the house had a heart.] (53)

In several instances in *Uma poética de romance* Dourado expresses his admiration for Edgar Allan Poe and acknowledges his debt to that North American writer and literary theorist, whom he describes as "[o] mais inseminador e lúcido de todos os criadores-teóricos" [the most creative and lucid of all writer-theorists] (12). The gothic image of the heartbeat emanating from the silence of the sobrado itself is perhaps an allusion to Poe's classic short story "The Tell-Tale Heart." Rosalina's obsession with the heartbeat of the dead, however, stems less from madness and paranoia than it does from the adoration she holds for her ancestors, to the extent that she integrates the dead within herself: "Quem sabe Lucas Procópio não morreu de todo, vivia ainda dentro dela? Ela semente de Lucas Procópio" (105) ["Perhaps Lucas Procópio didn't die completely, was still alive inside her? She was Lucas Procópio's seed"] (131).

Rosalina's existence, her very movements, revolve around her need to maintain her family's mourning rituals—"sempre aqueles vestidos prêtos, o luto permanente" (34) ["she always looked the same, always those black dresses, perpetual mourning"] (50). At night, while she is drinking wine, Rosalina becomes entranced by the gravitational pull of the past, and her memories become even more intertwined with the haunting presence of her forefathers. As the years pass she becomes increasingly estranged from the historical events that occur in the world outside the manor. Indeed, she represents an extreme example, explored so keenly by Kathleen Brogan, of the tragic figure for whom mourning has gone terribly awry, resulting in ghostly possession: "Possession—the dangerous incorporation of the dead—signals a failure of memory to organize history, to render it usable. Flight from history can just as easily lead to possession as a nostalgic return to the past: denied history reasserts itself, much like the return of the repressed" (Brogan, 9). Rosalina's relationship to history is twofold. On the one hand she rejects the flow of history taking place outside the limits of her family's patriarchal edifice. On the other hand she allows herself to remain possessed by a family history that perpetually reasserts itself into the present. On a more intimate level, the return of Rosalina's own repressed past comes in the form of erotic fantasies in which she revisits a forbidden, sensual encounter with her childhood friend Emanuel. Similarly, her repressed sexual energy is often associated, during these nightly trancelike states, with the spirit of her libidinous grandfather Lucas Procópio, whose seed she believes is responsible for the "canto mais escuro da alma, de onde brotava tôda a sua fôrça sombria" (105) ["darkest corner of her soul, where her own force of darkness sprang from"] (131).

The picaresque Juca Passarinho, a seemingly carefree wanderer and weaver of tales, is hired initially by Rosalina to act as her *agregado* [hired hand]; however, it is only a matter of time until Juca becomes an outlet for her repressed sexuality. Nevertheless, her nocturnal encounters with Juca occur in the same entranced state, and serve only to perpetuate and intensify her possession by the past. During their ecstatic lovemaking Juca senses that they converse only with their bodies, "porque a alma e os olhos lhe eram vedados. Dos mortos" (162) ["because her mind and her eyes were denied him. They belonged to the dead"] (199). Several passages in this chapter, entitled "A semente no corpo, na terra" [The Seed in the Body, in the Earth], repeat the idea that while Rosalina's body may have belonged momentarily to Juca Passarinho, her soul belonged eternally to the dead.

Though the chapter's title forewarns the reader of the inevitable result of Rosalina's sexual encounters with her agregado, it does not specify the source of the seed that is taking shape in Rosalina's body. While we know that Juca is the father of her child, the seed is also, and perhaps more importantly, the offspring of her ancestors' ghostly possession of her, that dark force that has been passed down to her through the generations. In other words, this ghostly seed belongs as much to the dead as it does to Juca Passarinho. Rosalina's impregnated body thus becomes the site of multiple symbolic meanings (including divine conception by the Holy Ghost), not the least of which is her family's and, by extension, her community's relationship to the past. Brogan calls attention precisely to this relationship between impregnated bodies and a haunting past: "Possession in haunted American fiction marks a continuity with the past over which one has little control: history lodges within, swollen bodies (a recurring image in this literature) give birth not to the future but to a nightmarish repetition of the past" (9).

Brogan's concept of repressed history transmuting into cultural haunting differs in one important way from Dourado's preoccupation with the unburied dead. The history lodged within Rosalina in *Ópera dos mortos* is not the history of an oppressed people as in, for example, Toni Morrison's *Beloved,* but rather the history of a social order and family ethos driven above all by patrimonial lineage and ancestral worship, and is therefore tragically linked to an idealized past. Moreover, Dourado's portrayal of the landed gentry in Minas Gerais underscores how patrilineal veneration, in turn, shapes issues of land ownership, political power through coronelismo, and the elite's aristocratic sense of entitlement.

Rosalina's increasingly swollen body is hidden away by Quiquina within the privacy of the sobrado like a shameful secret, and Juca Passarinho, the father, is further estranged from his nocturnal lover. Moreover, any possibility of renewal or transition associated with the birth of Rosalina's child is essentially denied by Rosalina's and Quiquina's mutual refusal of the child's existence. Even during Rosalina's labor, Quiquina contemplates, in a kind of stream of consciousness interrupted by her attempts to alleviate the young woman's suffering, how best to dispose of this secret that Rosalina carries within her. Finally, the child appears:

> Ôi, agora a coisa vem vindo. Isto, fôrça! Agarra na cama! Fôrça! Lá vém êle apontando. Só falta um tiquinho, aguenta. Um tiquinho só e pronto. Veio! Amarelo, da côr mesmo do barro tabatinga. (188)
>
> [Phew, now it's coming. That's it, push! Grab hold of the bed! Push! There he comes. Just a wee bit more, keep it up. Just a wee bit and it's done. There it is! Yellow, the colour of potter's clay.] (232)

The image of the newborn, yellow as potter's clay, reverberates with the chapter title's earthy connotations—"Semente no corpo, na terra" —and alerts us to the fate of Rosalina's child. In a "nightmarish repetition of the past," Quiquina instructs Juca Passarinho, on the following night, to carry the newborn wrapped in a bundle out into the cemetery and bury it in the same spot in the earth where, as a child, Quiquina had helped bury the evidence of Dona Genú's attempts at childbirth:

> E lá ia o prêto Damião, seguido da menina Quiquina, levar para o cemitério, sem nenhum outro acompanhamento, a miuçalha perdida, os frutos pêcos do ventre de dona Genú. Que graça podia achar Quiquina naqueles enterros de anjinhos mal nascidos? E o coronel Honório mais dona Genú iam povoando o chão vermelho do cemitério. (18)
>
> [And off would go the Negro Damião, followed by young Quiquina, but with no one else in attendance, carrying another wasted mite to the cemetery, the blighted fruit of Don Genu's womb. What on earth did Quiquina see in the funerals of those scarce-born babes? So Colonel Honório and Dona Genu went on filling the red earth of the graveyard.] (30)

On the way out to the craters where the cemetery is located, spade in hand and guided by the moonlight, a terrified Juca is confronted by the ghosts conceived in Dona Genú's uterus, by the specter of Major Lindolfo, who had raised him, and, after the deed is done, by Quiquina's menacing and ghostlike image: "a imagem de Quiquina crescia, um fantasma na sua frente" (194) ["Quiquina's image grew, like a ghost in front of him"] (239–40).

Rosalina's Ghostly Seed

The planting of dead offspring in the town cemetery by successive generations of the Honório Cota family, like ghostly seed, ensures a continuation of the family's self-induced perpetual mourning and veneration of the past. The family ritual of burying anjinhos becomes the symbolic expression of a social order where change is inconceivable in an endless cycle of unrealized patriarchal aspirations. Maria Lúcia Lepecki, in *Autran Dourado: Uma leitura mítica* [Autran Dourado: A Mythical Reading] (1976), suggests that the dead assume mythical status in Dourado's fiction and, therefore, are able to penetrate the present with regularity. She argues that Dourado's novels are infused with a constant tension between two clearly demarcated spaces—the sacred and the profane: "within the mythical vision proposed by Autran Dourado's fiction, the fusion of the sacred with the profane is prohibited (as is the desacralizing of either realm . . .). On the contrary, both spaces are kept distinctly separate; this however does not impede the frequent passage of certain intermediary figures, those caretakers of certain rituals, between the sacred and the profane" (50). Rosalina is, in this sense, the embodiment of a mythical worldview and her confinement in the family sobrado is characterized by the maintenance of what Lepecki calls "tempo ancestral" [ancestral time] (10). The mythical, ancestral time of the sobrado—what Kathleen Brogan calls "ghost time"—is juxtaposed in *Ópera dos mortos* by the historical, transforming time of the city. Quiquina and Juca Passarinho act as intermediaries between these two spaces, moving from one to the other, without however, as Lepecki points out, allowing others to bridge this gap with them (10). Quiquina, in fact, is as much the sobrado's guardian as she is its intermediary.

Lepecki's assertion that, within a mythical worldview, the dead "continue to live," is particularly relevant to my examination of the unburied dead as a reoccurring motif in contemporary Brazilian fiction: "Throughout the works of Autran Dourado, the dead should not be considered destroyed, obliterated, or in any way expelled from the world of the living, for they *continue to live,* thereby provoking internal conflicts within the protagonists and/or the other characters. There are numerous characters in Dourado's novels that are shaped and influenced by their dead: Rosalina and Quiquina (*Voices of the Dead*), João and Tomé (*Pattern for a Tapestry*), Biela (*A Hidden Life*)" (5–6; emphasis in original). It is precisely the mythical vitality of the *finado* that gives rise to the cult of the dead in Brazil, according to Lepecki: "The world of here and now is thus to some degree incomplete; it is lacking the one who died. Contrarily, within a mythical context, it is also a complete world, for the physical absence of the dead is annulled by its presence as a formative agent and cultish object" (19; emphasis in original). By summoning those who have died and elevating them to mythical status, memory instills the dead with new life. Underlying Lepecki's characterization of the dead as "o vivo por excelência" [the living par excellence] (59) is the understanding that historically within Judeo-Christian cosmology real life begins with one's salvation. Moreover, ancestral cults in Brazil have been further solidified (and diversified) by the arrival of African religious systems, such as Candomblé, in which the dead continue to live on in the form of eguns.

While Lepecki acknowledges that cultic adherence to the past effectively annuls both the present and the future, and therefore the possibility of historical transformation in *Ópera dos mortos,* she does not link this worldview to any particular sociological commentary by the author. In other words, she refrains from ascribing a specific sociopolitical message to *Ópera dos mortos.* While she does propose, in her final chapter, that the author possesses a "profoundly political vision," she does not elaborate on what that vision might consist of. Since the publication of her study Lepecki has indicated her inclination to read *Ópera dos mortos* less as a social commentary against the persistence of archaic institutions and more as an expression of sociocultural and religious identity in Minas Gerais.[7] For her, Rosalina is the "embodiment of a feeling *mineiros* [natives of Minas Gerais] have about themselves, a metaphor for the spirit of *mineiridade.*" Moreover, she adds that mineiros are instilled with a kind of "archeological" sensibility, in the sense that they are predisposed to the gradual excavation and uncovering of their own family, communal, and personal histories. Minas Gerais, according to Lepecki, is a "culture of quotation," where people are brought up hearing the stories of their ancestors and the dead are quoted habitually.

Lepecki points out that, as the surviving scion of the Honório Cota family, Rosalina is the sole guardian of this family's cult of the dead. While she is clearly governed by the dead, it is also true that the life force of her ancestors is largely dependent on Rosalina's preservation of their memory. Within the solitary isolation of the sobrado, however, Rosalina's link with the dead essentially takes the form of a monologue. She has only her mind's eye, and the uninhibiting influence of Madeira, to summon the dead. Though she shares in the sobrado's history, Quiquina's muteness only contributes to the silence that surrounds Rosalina.

Rosalina's best chance of escape from the solitude of her inner world comes to her in the form of Juca Passarinho, who is both a storyteller and a good listener and therefore offers the possibility of dialogue with the outside world. Eventually, Rosalina does relate details of her past to Juca Passarinho, while working on her paper flowers in the drawing room of the manor. Her stories, however, are more the stuff of childhood dreams and never include reflections on her life as a grown woman, when she began to adopt her father's morose silence. Ultimately, the stories told to Juca Passarinho are more spoken monologues than true dialogues, for Rosalina never narrates with an interlocutor in mind:

> Dona Rosalina falava como se não fôsse com êle, como se estivesse ali sòzinha e êle fôsse apenas a mola que acionava o maquinismo das suas lembranças. (91)
>
> [Dona Rosalina talked not so much to him, but as if she were alone and he merely the spring that set in motion the machinery of her memory.] (116)

The wistful child who speaks to Juca during the day stands in stark contrast to the possessed woman who gives her body to him at night. Rosalina's split into two or more personas further prevents her from reconciling the past with the present in a cohesive manner.

Miscarried Patriarchal Legacies

Rosalina's monologic relationship to the dead, combined with the absence of any other surviving relatives, effectively spells the end of the Honório Cota lineage. This raises an important question: in a culture of quotation, who, in this family, will be left to quote the dead? The Honório Cota family's irrevocable decline is symbolized most poignantly by the dead offspring that populate the red earth of the town cemetery. The conspicuous absence of a son, which is the dream of Rosalina's father, João Capistrano, results in a patriarchal crisis that Rosalina's silent isolation only intensifies. The destruction of her illegitimate child (which, since Juca hears a child crying at one point, one presumes was born alive), and its burial in the cemetery, is not only a nightmarish repetition of the past, but also the epilogue to the history of a family destined to plot its own destruction. Rosalina's baby could only be born dead (or nearly dead), because it was conceived by a metaphorically dead person. Even before birth, the child belonged to the dead.

Interpreting *Ópera dos mortos* as the story of miscarried patriarchal legacies that, nevertheless, continue to haunt the living, focuses attention on some of the possible social commentary woven into Dourado's otherwise enigmatic novel. John Gledson's observation that the novel's three principal characters represent the three main segments of rural Brazil's traditional patriarchal structure (Rosalina—the masters; Juca—the agregado class; and Quiquina—slaves and servants) further suggests that the social dilemmas portrayed in *Ópera dos mortos* may also be read on a broader scale and from a sociological perspective (Gledson, 202). The gravest and seemingly most irreconcilable dilemma that emerges in the novel, one might argue, is the lack of communication that exists between the Honório Cota family, the town's elite, and the rest of the community. Published only three years after the 1964 military coup, *Ópera dos mortos* may, on one level, be interpreted then as a commentary on the larger Brazilian "family" (or nation perceived as extended family) and the perpetual cycle of estrangement that has historically characterized the relationship between the elite and the masses in Brazil.

The novel concludes on a highly ambiguous note. The reader is left to wonder about the fate of Rosalina, Quiquina, Juca Passarinho, and Emanuel. Similarly, the town's collective fate is shrouded in mystery in the book's final chapter, "Cantiga de Rosalina" [Rosalina's Song]. What happened to Rosalina's newborn child? Was it born alive? Did Quiquina kill it, as we suspect? Why have the police and Coronel Sigismundo come to the manor? Juca Passarinho was seen slipping out of town a few days before. Where did he go? The townspeople who gather at the house wait eagerly for someone to reveal information about Rosalina's fate. A soldier who has been stationed at the bottom of the staircase imposes order when the nervous crowd begins to meddle with things in the house, including the sobrado's clocks, which they try, symbolically, to wind up. The soldier's function as disciplinarian of the masses (who, in turn, seek to reinstate the progress of time), along with the sudden appearance of the coronel, certainly brings to mind again the 1964 coup, a crackdown the Brazilian military perceived as necessary to restore a sense of order in an increasingly "irresponsible" and unruly populace.

At some unspecified moment during this scene, the sobrado's pendulum clock, the only functioning timepiece in the house, is mysteriously stopped. The repetition of this ritual gesture raises the question, whose death does it mark, the child's or Rosalina's? Though physically alive, Rosalina is already transformed into a wandering spirit. The source of the mysterious nocturnal singing in the cemetery turns out to be Rosalina, who, the town discovers, is leaving the sobrado at night and wandering through the cemetery mesmerized by her song of grief.

Suddenly, just as the crowd is beginning to lose hope of seeing Rosalina, she descends from her room at Emanuel's side and makes her way through the crowd in a kind of nuptial procession:

> De branco, o vestido comprido e rendado, uma rosa branca refolhuda no cabelo, lá vinha ela. Lá vinha Rosalina descendo a escada de braço

> dado com seu Emanuel. Desciam devagar, a passos medidos. . . . A cabeça erguida, o porte empinado, hierático, ela mais parecia uma rainha descendo a escadaria dum palácio, uma noiva boiando no ar a caminho do céu. (200)
>
> [All in white, with a long dress trimmed with lace and a full white rose in her hair, there she came. There came Rosalina, descending the staircase on Mr. Emanuel's arm. They came down slowly, step by step. . . . Head held high, her bearing erect and stately, she was more like a queen descending a palace staircase, a bride floating heavenwards.] (247)

The crowd also detects, for the first time, a smile on Rosalina's face, yet the distant look in her eyes tells them the smile is not intended for them but rather for the spirits of the house that perpetually accompany her movements. Finally, accompanied by Emanuel and the police, Rosalina steps majestically into a waiting car that takes her away. The novel ends as the crowd silently pays its respects to her in a kind of anguished solidarity: "Lá se ia Rosalina para longes terras. Lá se ia Rosalina, nosso espinho, nossa dor" (201) ["There went Rosalina, off to distant lands. There went Rosalina, our thorn, our grief"] (247).[8]

Baroque Endings

How one reads the enigmatic conclusion of *Ópera dos mortos* determines, to a large extent, the degree of sociopolitical commentary proposed by the novel. Clearly Rosalina is being led away by the authorities at the novel's close, but to what extent does the reader believe that she alone is being charged with a crime? Indeed, what crime has she committed exactly? While we presume that Rosalina has, by the story's end, gone insane, it is also true that, by assuming the form of a wandering spirit, she fulfills her ghostly destiny of reuniting with the souls of her dead ancestors.

Ultimately, the open-ended and shadowy nature of Dourado's narrative style permits, I believe, both a social critique of the haunting legacy of Brazil's declining patriarchal system, *as well as* the intimate articulation of a tragic metaphor for mineiridade, with its intrinsic archeological sensibility. In the final chapter the narrator returns to the collective, first-person, plural voice of the townspeople used in the first chapter and, in so doing, brings the novel full circle. As in the first chapter, where the reader is invited to leave behind their naturalist eyes and instead let their mind's eye gaze on the baroque lines of the sobrado, the narrator in the novel's conclusion focuses the reader's eye on the ritualistic, baroque quality of Rosalina's movements. Like the deteriorating sobrado, Rosalina's nuptial elegance is predicated on an illusion—"veja a ilusão do barroco, mesmo em movimento é como um rio parado" (6) ["note the illusion of the baroque, even in motion it's like a still stretch of river"] (19)—however, it is an illusion that is profoundly linked to the community's sense of identity and strikes at its historical core.

It is the intrinsically "open structure" of a baroque aesthetic, according to Dourado, in *Poética de romance,* that allows for multiple possible meanings in his fiction:

> A estrutura aberta do barroco. O autor dispõe de uma maneira os seus episódios mas dá ao leitor a oportunidade de um segundo nível de leitura, em que a disposição fique a seu critério.
>
> [The open structure of the baroque—the author arranges episodes in a certain way, but gives readers the opportunity for a second reading that is determined by their own criteria.] (46)

Like the illusory and often antithetical nature of the baroque sobrado—described in the first chapter as a constant interplay of light and shadow, fullness and empty space, straight lines and curves—the novel's opaque ending permits multiple readings that may, when juxtaposed, appear antithetical. Thus, the paralysis of time and history in the sobrado is also the crystallization of a regional ethos that has managed to survive the passage of time. Similarly, the possession of Rosalina by her ghostly seed and spectral forefathers is also the poetic realization of a mythical worldview, in which nothing is more sacred than the preservation of ancestral ties.

The novel ends on an ominous note, however, as if Rosalina has bequeathed her melancholy to the community. Indeed, the sadness expressed by the collective narrator stems from the realization that, with Rosalina gone, so ends a certain era and way of life. The arrival of a car, perhaps the most poignant symbol of modernity, to take her away punctuates this sense of an irrecoverable past. While Juca Passarinho momentarily raises the possibility of change and the resolution of a possessing past, any real movement toward reconciliation is ultimately squelched. Rosalina tells her story to Juca but never recounts her family's trauma and thus her memories are like the paper flowers with which she whiles away the time, long-lasting but superficial. To borrow Brogan's terminology, dreadful haunting is never given a chance to become historical consciousness. With the disappearance of Juca Passarinho and with Quiquina as mute as ever, the family withers away without the promise of future quotations. In the end, only the townspeople (i.e., the narrator) possess, in their mind's eye, the manor's stories, its dreams, and its nightmares.

In response to a question concerning how the idea for *Ópera dos mortos* was conceived, Dourado underscores the tragic fate of Rosalina and her ghostly ancestors:

> A primeira idéia nasceu de uma frase que de repente brotou no meu espírito: "É preciso enterrar os nossos mortos." Verifiquei posteriormente que era uma reminiscência de Antígona, de Sófocles. Pense-se no livro como tragédia, mais do que como romance, e se terá uma melhor leitura. Os mortos de Rosalina e os mortos de Antígona. Os mortos-vivos.
>
> [The idea first sprang from a phrase that suddenly took hold of me: "It is necessary to bury our dead." I confirmed later that this was a sentiment expressed by Sophocles' Antigone. Think about the book not as romantic novel but as a tragedy and you will have a better reading. Rosalina's dead and Antigone's dead. The living-dead]. (*Poética,* 119)

Like Antigone, who is condemned to death for performing the burial rites for her slain brother Polynices, Rosalina is driven to commemorate her family's unburied dead. Ultimately, however, Rosalina's condemnation is self-inflicted, for she fails to heed Antigone's, and implicitly Dourado's warning that, in the end, "we must bury our dead" in order to give them life.

THE VOICES OF the unburied dead resonate in significantly different, yet profoundly similar ways in the two novels examined in this chapter. While the seven resurrected defuntos in Veríssimo's *Incidente em Antares* embody the carnivalesque voice of public denouncement and accusation, Rosalina's spectral ancestors in Dourado's *Ópera dos mortos* are the private manifestation of both a family's and a community's troubled souls and state of perpetual mourning. Consistent with the elusive nature of spectrality, the revenant may represent either possession by the past, as in *Ópera dos mortos,* or liberation from the past, as occurs, albeit fleetingly, in *Incidente.* The promise of renewal raised by the exhumation of the dead in Veríssimo's novel, and the subsequent carnivalesque inversion of the dominant social order, however, is followed by a flight into collective amnesia and a refusal to assimilate the dead or the past into a new present reality.

Herein lies a salient difference between the two works. Whereas the construction of historical identity in Antares is, in the end, predominantly a function of collective denial and forgetting, narration in *Ópera dos mortos,* particularly in the voice of the collective townspeople, represents an attempt to remember. Yet both novels reveal the highly indeterminate and spectral nature of memory itself, formed by the apparitions and iterations of our mind's eye, and composed of equal parts imagination and recollection.

As in American narratives of cultural haunting, these Brazilian novels tell the story of a society's complex and often troubled relationship with its own past. By evoking the image of the unburied dead, both novels pose a fundamental question: how can a society best integrate the past into the present in a meaningful way? Ultimately, no clear solution to this problem is provided by either Veríssimo or Dourado, though their narratives do indicate, in relatively unequivocal terms, some of the foremost obstacles to change in Brazilian society. On one level, their stories of haunting and mourning gone awry clearly call attention to, and problematize, the troubled transmission of patriarchal legacies in Brazil following the decline of the rural oligarchy and during the country's slow transition into a modern, industrialized nation. On another level, the underlying sense of fatalism that marks the endings of both novels speaks to the authors' inescapable realization, during the late 1960s, that the "tyranny of phantoms" imposed by the military dictatorship, had become no less than a nightmarish repetition of the past. And, together, these uniquely Brazilian stories of cultural haunting elicit the indomitable hold of the unburied dead on Brazilian society's cultural and literary imagination.

Conclusion

THE IRREFUTABLE TRUTH of autobiographical writing is that every memorialist must confront the impossibility of narrating one's own death. Despite the human desire to experience and subsequently recount the ultimate act of transgression, the "undiscovered country" remains a narrative frontier from which there is no return. Posthumous autobiography comes to us from beyond the grave only to the extent that readers breathe new life into a dead author's words and release his or her spirit through their own imaginative readings.

In fiction, however, posthumous memoirs and the narrative summoning of the dead may unfold unhindered by the constraints of empirical reality. Originating beyond the realm of verisimilitude, Brás Cubas's satirical dispatches from the afterworld and Vadinho's spectral displays of malandragem function, on an unconscious level, to satisfy our need to attain the impossible—the narration of our own death. Attaining the impossible, however fleetingly, is also intrinsic to the carnivalesque experience, and therefore it is not surprising that these spirits emanate from a bacchanalian tradition.

I introduced this study by citing Nelson Rodrigues's appeal to return to a time in Brazil when the dead were vested with a saintly aura.

Perhaps to fill this void in his own life and era, Rodrigues pays homage to the dead in his *Memórias,* which he conceives as an "antologia dos meus mortos" [anthology of my dead]. On one level, I have striven to do the same by presenting an anthology of the dead in nineteenth- and twentieth-century Brazilian literature. It is undoubtedly an incomplete collection, as all anthologies are. As such, I hope that readers of this study will assist in filling in the inevitable gaps.

On another, more closely defined level, the focus of this anthology was guided by my interest in a particular variety of the undead. During my journey through the afterworld of Brazilian literature's spectral figures, I have remained especially attuned to the irreverent and subversive voice of Brazil's Menippean shade—the carnivalesque defunto. And I have listened to the sometimes lurid, sometimes playful clamoring of these shades with the conviction that their stories would reveal certain underlying points of tension in Brazilian society. Part Menippus and part malandro, the carnivalesque defunto's literary reincarnations, since the publication of *Memórias Póstumas de Brás Cubas* in 1880, are a testimony to the enduring sententiousness and impact of this figure in Brazilian culture. My research into the topos of the renascent, bacchanalian defunto in modern Brazilian literature has led me to the following five conclusions.

The topos exists as part of a literary tradition that is both perennial and canonical. The image of the deceased and highly ironic narrator in Machado de Assis's pivotal novel *Memórias póstumas de Brás Cubas* has served as a preamble to the emergence of a recurrent motif in twentieth-century Brazilian literature, which I have identified as the carnivalesque defunto. I have called attention to the numerous Brazilian writers who, explicitly or implicitly, refer to Machado de Assis's groundbreaking work in their own incorporation of a deceased character or narrator (chapter 2). The links between *Memórias póstumas* and the novels discussed in chapters 4 and 5, while never expressed ostensibly by the latter authors, are reinforced by virtue of the defunto's prominence in each of these works (even when the carnivalesque element is nominal, as in *Ópera dos mortos*). In other words, both Machado's legacy and the legacy of *Memórias póstumas* are inescapable for twentieth-century Brazilian novelists, such as Jorge Amado, Érico Veríssimo, and Autran Dourado.

The specific dynamics of the topos originate in Brazilian culture. The carnivalesque defunto motif is predominantly not the product of a literary or rhetorical strategy divorced from Brazilian reality but rather stems from preexisting cultural norms and values that have helped shape the historical relationship between the living and the dead in Brazilian society. Furthermore, I argue that both the reader's interpretations and the author's intentions, with respect to the texts, are affected by this relationship. Even Machado de Assis, who was a determined skeptic in spiritual matters, addressed this relationship, through parody, in his characterization of Brás Cubas as a grotesquely distorted spirit guide and wayward soul.

I have outlined the evolution of a "spirit idiom" in Brazilian society in which the dead have routinely, and ritually, been ascribed a prominent place within *this* realm, that is, in close proximity, psychologically, emotionally, and even physically to the living (chapter 1). I also called attention to the historical reasons behind the development of a carnivalesque atmosphere within Brazilian funerary rituals, namely, their association with colonial and nineteenth-century religious feasts and mock funerary processions that, while addressing death, also celebrated both life in this world and the joyful reunion with the divine in the afterworld. Similarly, the dead are bid farewell with the anticipation that they will act as celestial advocates for the living in both everyday matters as well as at the moment of judgment.

Undoubtedly, the relationship between the living and the dead in Brazil today is by no means a facsimile of what it was in colonial times. Moreover, the regional, ethnic, racial, and socioeconomic variations of this relationship endow it with a complexity that denies easy generalizations and oversimplifications. Until a major study is completed, on a national level, regarding contemporary Brazilians' attitudes toward death and the dead, it will remain difficult to verify, definitively, the precise nature of this relationship. Nevertheless, social scientists such as Roberto DaMatta, David Hess, Oscar Calavia Sáez, José de Souza Martins, and Jean Ziegler have shed important light on the continuity of many of this relationship's fundamental features during the twentieth century. It is precisely the enduring vibrancy of these cultural anachronisms within modern times, in conjunction with the indefatigable vitality of carnival as both a national ritual and sign in Brazil, that contributes, in one form or another, to the significance of the carnivalesque defunto in modern Brazilian literature.

The topos performs a specific sociohistorical function in Brazilian literature. Social scientists such as Robert Hertz and Arnold van Gennep have noted how death creates a rupture in the life of a community that necessitates individual and collective self-reflection. In this way the dead demand a reassessment of personal relations and force people to gather and confront unresolved issues. Similarly, in the novels I have analyzed, the defunto serves to expose underlying social fissures in Brazilian history and, by frequently adopting a carnivalesque form, calls attention to the social order or institution responsible for the existing crisis. The defunto figure is, therefore, inextricably linked to concrete and pressing historical circumstances at the time the novels were written. Like the dead in Menippean satire, the carnivalesque defunto subverts and demystifies any and all forms of social, political, and aesthetic authority, including its own. These forms of authority are inevitably interpreted differently in each novel depending on the particular sociohistorical or authorial circumstances at play in their respective time periods.

Brás Cubas, for example, suggests that our lives are like self-edited books and that we submit the definitive version only in death. Yet what is remarkable about his posthumous memoirs is that their content becomes increasingly bitter and gives the impression that its author is aging even in death. In the end, Brás Cubas dies twice, once in life and once again as the defunto autor. The symbolic connotations of Brás Cubas's unsuccessful burials, in life and in death, lie in the novel's un-flattering portrait of both the decline of Brazil's patriarchal past and the superficiality of its republican future. Ultimately, his bad death, like Virgília's miscarriage, is symbolic of the unfulfilled paternalistic dreams and illegitimate liberalism of late-nineteenth-century Brazil's "miscarried" modernity.

Like the wandering soul that his restless narrative style embodies, Brás Cubas belongs neither to the past nor the present. Indeed, his spectral narration constantly shifts in and out of focus and, like a ghost, is never fully present stylistically or ideologically. Moreover, Machado's parody of Spiritist doctrine, through his characterization of Brás Cubas as an inverted, untrustworthy spirit guide (and narrator), underscores his criticism of the Brazilian elite's undiscerning intellectual dependency on Europe. Both this inversion and the volubility of his narrative voice endow Brás Cubas with the ironic, carnivalesque perspective necessary to expose the thin veneer of late-nineteenth-century liberalism in Brazil.

Brás Cubas's (and Brazil's) quintessentially bad death stands in contrast to the relatively good deaths imagined by Jorge Amado in *A morte e a morte de Quincas Berro Dágua* and *Dona Flor e seus dois maridos.* The deceased protagonists of both these works, Quincas and Vadinho, must first, however, pass through a restless liminal phase, before their souls (and their extended communities) may find peace and resolution. This passage is facilitated by the intervention of the living whose "resurrection" of the deceased is carried out through the combined restorative powers of memory and narration. The mischievousness, eroticism, and overall bacchanalian demeanor of both Quincas and Vadinho are similarly experienced collectively, and consequently bring a sense of vitality and renewal to their respective communities, even in the face of death. The continuous metamorphoses of death and rebirth is, of course, central to the carnivalesque spirit.

As Bobby Chamberlain points out, many critics have viewed the publication of *Gabriela, Cravo e Canela* in 1958, as a crucial shift for Jorge Amado. It was at this moment that Amado's novels made the transition from polemical to satirical, proletarian to picaresque (97). The 1960s may also be described as the decade in which the supernatural took center stage in Amado's fiction. Within this literary pantheon of orixás and otherworldly spirits, the carnivalesque defunto emerges as a prominent antihero in Amado's postsocial realism phase. I argue that critics have tended to overstate the affirmation of *individual* freedom in *A morte e a morte de Quincas Berro Dágua,* perhaps in an effort to contrast Amado's earlier and later fiction. Ultimately, Quincas's multiple deaths and spiritual fulfillment unfold through a dialogic process of collective anecdotes and storytelling and as such represent first and foremost the affirmation of communal relations. The assertion of personal relations over impersonal relations, in the face of Brazil's dehumanizing rush to modernize during the 1950s and 60s, links *Quincas Berro Dágua* and *Dona Flor* by a common thread of social criticism.

As in *Quincas Berro Dágua,* the essential struggle in *Dona Flor* is waged around the memory of the dead. Vadinho's spirit must return both because his memory exerts a life-affirming force on Dona Flor and because his supernatural presence strikes a balance with the rational order of things. Unlike the protagonist of *Quincas Berro Dágua,* which is an unflinching affirmation of a personalistic ethos, Vadinho must coexist with the more impersonal modern ethos personified by Teodoro. Written only two years after the 1964 military coup, Amado did not envision *Dona Flor* as a revolutionary statement but rather as a model for mourning and healing during this unstable period.

In Érico Veríssimo's *Incidente em Antares* and Autran Dourado's *Ópera dos mortos,* the defunto motif emerges once again out of a more haunting set of historical circumstances. The unburied corpses in Veríssimo's novel, for example, are a metaphor for those sociopolitical institutions, such as coronelismo, Getulismo, and machismo, that have outlived their usefulness yet continue to haunt the present, much to the detriment of Brazilian society. While the corpses' resurrection and subsequent protest in Antares' central square do, for a brief carnivalesque moment, unmask the sources of hypocrisy and corruption before a chorus of laughing people and suspend the existing hierarchical structure, the moment is short lived. Through a campaign of collectively induced amnesia and anamnesis, Antares soon learns to simultaneously forget its "incident" and remember its veneration of the past. The rather rushed and perfunctory burial given to the corpses at the end of the novel suggests that, like the city's host of patriarchal phantoms, it will not be long before they rise again.

The metaphor of the unburied dead also works in Autran Dourado's *Ópera dos mortos* as a means of articulating the perpetuation of a now dead, but tragically unburied patriarchal structure in Minas Gerais. Even *Ópera dos mortos,* which, of all the novels cultivates the most gothic narrative atmosphere, is not really a gothic novel. Rosalina's family ghosts are just as much the ghosts of the society that upholds her image as the inaccessible matriarch. Dourado's novel is a tale of a haunted community rather than a haunted self and, in this sense, shares certain defining features with both Kathleen Brogan's concept of "cultural haunting" and Lois Parkinson Zamora's notion of an "ancestral impulse" as determinants of the literary ghost. The death and, in effect, nonbirth of Rosalina's illegitimate child, like Virgília's in *Memórias póstumas de Brás Cubas,* may also be interpreted as a symbol of Brazil's miscarried patriarchal legacies. The opaque, baroque ending of *Ópera dos mortos,* however, opens numerous avenues of interpretation, including reading Rosalina's fate as a tragic metaphor for mineiridade. Ultimately, Dourado's novel, though not carnivalesque, shares Veríssimo's concern with how to best integrate the past with the present in a meaningful way.

The topos possesses a metaphorical significance that evokes Brazil's relationship to its own past. Coming to terms with the dead in these works of fiction constitutes a metaphor for reconciling the past with the present, and memory with immediate worldly concerns. Indeed, continuity and discontinuity emerge as two points of the axis around which these works revolve. Roberto Schwarz argues in "As idéias fora do lugar" [Misplaced Ideas] and *Um mestre na periferia do capitalismo* [A Master on the Periphery of Capitalism] that Brazil has chronically suffered from a lack of cultural continuity in which ideas continue to be misplaced. Of course Schwarz is not advocating for an uninterrupted repetition of the past in the name of historical continuity. Rather he is interested in the coherent integration of the past and the present, and foreign and native values within Brazilian society, so that socioeconomic conditions can be established within which real change can occur.

Any death represents a break in continuity—the death of a family member, a political leader, a celebrity, a sociopolitical system. One of the primary purposes of death rituals, anthropologists have suggested, is precisely to restore continuity within a community or society. The varying degrees of observance or disregard and success or failure of these rituals is a reflection of certain underlying modes of continuity and discontinuity. Furthermore, evoking the dead is a potent way of evoking the past and empowering memory. Indeed, death generates the need for memory. As I have proposed, the idea of the dead returning to interact with the living, or to intervene on their behalf, is in response to particular social crises that are being addressed by these novels. Otherworldly interventions can assume positive or negative forms, resulting in either greater resolution to the crisis or lack of resolution, which is symbolized by haunting.

This is why the distinction between a good and a bad death is so crucial within these narratives, as a metaphor for Brazil coming to terms with its own past. As we have seen, the deceased figure (or figures) in each novel moves from a bad death to a good death with varying degrees of success. The degree of resolution achieved by this figure is analogous to the degree of resolution achieved by the wider social group in response to the given crisis. For example, Brás Cubas's bad death(s) negate(s) the possibility of resolution and renewal that his memoirs propose, just as the impending bad death of Brazil's monarchism and system of slavery unfolds without the promise of real structural change. Contrastingly, the resolution achieved by Quincas's and Vadinho's good deaths is emblematic of Brazilian society's potential to embrace modernity without sacrificing its essential humanity. Moreover, Antares' corpses, though buried, represent the perpetual haunting of this society by certain patriarchal institutions whose anachronistic and morbid presence lives on.

The topos is an integral part of a genus of "ghost stories" specific to Brazilian literature. While each of the works I have explored in depth share certain thematic and aesthetic elements with literary traditions outside Brazil, the carnivalesque defunto, in its entirety, is a cultural and literary manifestation particular to Brazilian fiction. This is not to say that one cannot locate bacchanalian figures who return from the dead in other literatures. As we have noted, the Greek Menippean tradition offers numerous examples. The comparative framework I provide in chapter 2 reveals that traces of this figure can be identified in both contemporary Spanish American and Caribbean literature, as well as in ethnic literature of North America. It is, however, the frequency and integrity with which the carnivalesque defunto appears in seminal works of modern Brazilian fiction that solidifies its presence within this country's literary tradition.

With some exceptions, this tradition does not follow the guidelines established by eighteenth- and nineteenth-century English and American gothic fiction, nor does it fit easily into the necrogeographies of buried indigenous narratives and identities stemming from the ancestral impulse of twentieth-century Spanish American literary ghosts. The carnal, bacchanalian, and sensual nature of the carnivalesque defunto, which returns to eat, drink, sleep with, and frequently mock the living, defies both the somber, psychological tones of a strictly gothic aesthetic and the repressed, mythic voice of Spanish American literature's ancestral apparitions. Unlike the gothic mode, the carnivalesque defunto is rarely presented as the projection of one individual's inner psychic turmoil but rather embodies the hopes, fears, values, and dreams of a collective order. Like the American tales of "cultural haunting" studied by Kathleen Brogan, and the Spanish American ancestral apparitions identified by Lois Parkinson Zamora, the "ghosts" I have examined take on meaning in a communal context, as they call attention to the "troubled transmission of culture" at specific moments in Brazilian history (Brogan, 4). Moreover, it is not a coincidence that Brazil's supernatural malandro, the carnivalesque defunto, emerges at times of great sociohistorical transition, when friction between the old and the new order is most apparent. Resurrected in flesh and blood and endowed with corrosive laughter that cannot be ignored, these otherworldly figures speak directly to those who most keenly need to hear their worldly messages.

Notes

Unless otherwise indicated, all translations are my own. A date in parentheses following the title of a work indicates the year it was first published.

Chapter 1: Death Is a Festa

1. David Hess suggests that possessing a "spirit idiom" has become part of "Brazilianness," and that part of Spiritism's wide popularity in Brazil stems from the close relationship of other spirit-medium religions, such as Candomblé, to Brazilian national identity (*Spirits and Scientists,* 210). Spiritism took root in Brazil during the second half of the nineteenth century, following the Portuguese translation of Allan Kardec's *Spirits' Book* (1857). Spiritist movements spread throughout Europe and the United States during this same period. Whereas Spiritism has largely declined in these areas, it continues to flourish in Brazil, which, according to Hess, is "the home of the world's largest Spiritist movement" (201).

2. See, for example, Freyre, *Casa-grande e senzala* (1933); Holanda, *Raízes do Brasil* (1936).

3. For a broader historical discussion of the dead in Iberian culture during the Middle Ages, see Mattoso, *Reino dos mortos.* Legislation was passed in Portugal in the 1830s, with the support of church authorities and the medical establishment, calling for the construction of cemeteries far removed from the church grounds and forbidding the age-old practice of burying the dead in or near the local parish church. For a discussion of the intense popular reaction against this legislation, see Pina-Cabral and Feijó, "Conflicting Attitudes"; Catroga, "Morte romántica."

4. According to Gilberto Freyre, "The custom of burying the dead underneath the house—beneath the chapel, which was an annex of the house—is quite characteristic of the patriarchal spirit of family cohesiveness. The dead thus remained under the same roof as the living, amid the saints and the floral

offerings of the devout. The saints and the dead were, indeed, a part of the family" (*Masters,* xxxvi).

5. David Hess's observation of a uniquely Brazilian "spirit idiom" formed by the confluence of Catholic, African, and indigenous religious elements finds its antecedent in Gilberto Freyre's somewhat generalized affirmation: "Brazilians are, *par excellence,* the people with a belief in the supernatural; in all that surrounds us we feel the touch of strange influences, and every so often our newspapers reveal cases of apparitions, ghosts, enchantments. Whence the success among us of spiritualism in both its higher and its lower forms" (*Masters,* 155; emphasis in original).

6. See Reis, *Morte é uma festa;* Goldey, "Good Death"; Martins, *Morte e os mortos.*

7. Patricia Goldey makes an explicit connection between the notion of a bad death and the appearance of *almas penadas* in Portuguese culture:

> The link between the concept of the "good death" and other parts of the belief system is clearly seen in the case of the "wandering souls," those unfortunates who did not have time to settle their accounts before they died, or whose relatives did not fulfill the customary religious requirements regarding burial. 'Wandering souls' who appear as ghosts (*aventesmas/sombras*) or as tormented souls (*almas penadas*) can be encountered at night either outside the village or around the cemetery (which is usually situated either within the village or very close to it), or they appear in dreams at night to a close relative. The three main reasons given for the appearance of "wandering souls" on earth are that they were left unburied, and so have no resting place, and cannot enter heaven until they have had a Christian burial; or that their kin failed to fulfill the customary ritual; or that they committed some injustice that was not remedied before their death. ("Good Death," 6)

8. Reis, *Death,* 148. In colonial times the majority of Africans and Afro-Brazilians were buried either in slave cemeteries adjacent to the casa-grande's capela, thereby perpetuating their inferior social status posthumously, or, as was more common in urban centers, their bodies were left practically unburied in unmarked locations.

9. Even in Rio de Janeiro, colonial Brazil's capital city as of 1763, burying the dead in local churches effectively continued until 1838, when a municipal law was passed prohibiting the practice. In Portugal, a similar law was passed in 1835, prohibiting burials in churches and instructing local officials to build

cemeteries outside city limits. Popular revolt in Portugal against this policy intensified in 1844 in reaction to the Lei da Saúde Pública, legislation intended to ensure that the 1835 laws were being enforced. In what became known as the Revolta da Maria da Fonte, in March 1844 government soldiers imprisoned several women in the Minho area for performing an illegal burial. Shortly after, a mass of protestors, mostly women, gathered at the jail and released the accused women. Dozens of such incidents occurred. The majority of Portuguese immigrants who settled in Bahia came from the Minho region in Portugal and therefore carried with them their own particular set of values with regard to death and the dead (Reis, *Morte,* 86).

10. In a somewhat similar vein as "Jazigos e Covas Rasas," Freyre did study the tombs of Luso-Brazilian colonials who had moved to Moçamedes in Africa from Brazil in the first half of the nineteenth century. The research for this study, entitled *Em tôrno de alguns túmulos afro-cristãos* (1959) was conducted during Freyre's travels in 1951 and 1952 throughout Portugal's overseas territories. The book reflects Freyre's quest for evidence of both "Luso-tropical" and uniquely Brazilian cultural expressions in the iconographic and funerary tradition of these Afro-Christian gravestones. The gravestones of Christianized Africans combine Catholic iconography, such as the cross or the Madonna figure, with African sculptures or figures. The façade of one gravestone, for example, depicts an Africanized Madonna suckling a child (61).

11. Rio, *Os dias passam . . .* (1912). See also Rio, *Religiões do Rio* (1951).

12. The idea that in Brazilian society there exists an aura around those who regularly speak to the dead brings to mind, for DaMatta, a passage from Érico Veríssimo's book of travel memoirs *A volta do gato preto:*

> Lembro-me das gentes simples de minha terra para as quais a morte e a doença são os assuntos prediletos. . . . De doenças passam para espiritismo. Ciciam histórias de almas do outro mundo. De repente em meio da conversa fazem-se silêncios profundos. Estala uma viga no telhado. Uma das velhas suspira. Na alma de cada uma delas está plantando um cemitério.

> [I remember the simple people from my birthplace for whom death and illness are favorite topics of discussion. . . . From illness the talk would shift to Spiritism. They would whisper stories about otherworldly souls. Suddenly, in the middle of the conversation they would become deeply silent. A beam from the roof would creak. One of the old women would sigh. There is a cemetery planted in the soul of each of these women.] (DaMatta, *Casa,* 120)

Veríssimo's preoccupation with the dead, and particularly the unburied dead, is explored in greater depth in chapter 5 of this study.

13. The absence of a broad, nationwide study regarding Brazilians' attitudes toward death and the dead in recent times, one that takes into consideration the significant cultural and socioeconomic variations involved, has hindered the elaboration of a more precise, verifiable description of these attitudes and belief systems. It is notable that, in their correspondence with me, Roberto da Matta, José de Souza Martins, David Hess, and João José Reis, arguably some of the leading scholars studying this question, either confirmed this lacuna or were unaware of such a study.

14. There was, in fact, ample occasion for deathwatches in Rio de Janeiro while Rodrigues was a boy living in the North Zone. In October 1918, Cariocas started dying in large numbers from the influenza epidemic that spread from Europe to port cities around the world after World War I. In a span of two weeks approximately fifteen thousand people in Rio de Janeiro had died from the disease, about one thousand per day. The epidemic disappeared almost as suddenly as it had appeared, but only after a large percentage of the population was already wearing black. As Ruy Castro points out in his biography of Nelson Rodrigues, Rio de Janeiro responded to the catastrophe with the "carnival of resurrection" of 1919, the most erotic and uninhibited carnival Brazil had ever seen (*Anjo pornográfico,* 25–26). Considering this social climate, it is no wonder that one of Rodrigues's first essays as a boy in school was a story about a case of adultery that had as its primary themes sex and death.

15. According to Calavia Sáez, "Infant tombs are abundant in the Cemetery of Saudade, as is not surprising in a country that has, even today, high infant mortality rates. Whole sections of the cemetery are dedicated to them, and they include some of the most ornate statues and sentimental epitaphs" (*Fantasmas falados,* 41). For a more thorough investigation of the psychological reactions in one northeastern shantytown, provoked by frequent child deaths, see Scheper-Hughes, *Death without Weeping.* With respect to the angelic spirits of deceased infants, she writes: "*Anjinhos* allow Alto mothers to 'let go' of so many of their young children by allowing them to 'hold on' to an idealized image of spirit-children populating the heavens, as close, really, as the stars can seem on a still night" (421).

Chapter 2: Death and the Dead as Literary Motifs in Brazil and Beyond

1. My use of the term *topos* is consistent with the definition proposed in Gerald Prince's *Dictionary of Narratology* (Lincoln: University of Nebraska Press, 1987), 98: "Any of a stable disposition of motifs that frequently appears in (literary) texts. Such *topoï* as those of the wise fool, the aged child, and the *locus amoenus* are very common in Western literature."

2. Sigmund Freud, "The Uncanny," in *Standard Edition of the Complete Psychological Works,* 17:217–52.

3. Although the story is set in eighteenth-century France at the time of Louis XV, one critic has suggested that, given the similarities of the French aristocracy during this period to the nineteenth-century Brazilian elite, the novel warrants the subtitle: "Romance brasileiro" [Brazilian novel] (Azevedo, *Mortalha de Alzira,* xvii).

4. Aluísio Azevedo published "O Impenitente" in his collection of short stories entitled *Demônios* [Demons] (1893).

5. *Noite na taverna* (1878), like the rest of Álvares de Azevedo's work, was published posthumously. The troubled poet died in 1852, at the age of forty-four.

6. The quotation in the heading is from Machado de Assis, *Brás Cubas,* chapter 124.

7. "Delírio" is part of Afonso Schmidt's collection of short stories entitled *Curiango,* published in 1935. Schmidt also wrote poetry and novels and was a member of the Academia Paulista de Letras. His work was compiled into a ten-volume set of *Obras completas* published in 1956 by Editora Brasiliense.

8. "Os olhos que comiam carne" is part of a collection of short stories by Humberto de Campos entitled *O monstro e outros contos* [The Monster and Other Stories] (1935). The first edition of this collection, which does not contain "Os olhos que comiam carne," was published in 1932. Another short story, from the first edition, that deals with the dead in a prominent manner is "A luz dos mortos." Set in the sertão, the story involves a group of soldiers who are tracking a band of outlaws. The story culminates with a battle between the two sides. When the sergeant leading the soldiers is struck by a bullet, one of his men, a humble soldier named Marciano, is compelled to see

that his dying commander receives the last rites, so that his soul will be saved. In the heat of battle, he crawls over to the officer, holds a burning match in his hand, and begins to recite the extreme unction. In the midst of this impromptu absolution of sin for his companion's soul, however, he too is struck in the head by a bullet. Two hours later, when the battle is over, the other soldiers find the two mortos joined together in a mutual gesture of penance: "os soldados encontraram, atrás de uma pedra, dois cadáveres, que serguravam, com os dedos hirtos, os restos do mesmo fósforo" [the soldiers found, behind a rock, the two corpses clutching with their rigid fingers the remains of the match] (59).

9. The story was published in 1895 in the collection *Alma primitiva* [Primitive Soul].

10. The spelling of *defuncto* with a *c* reflects the European variant of Portuguese, still common in Brazil at this time. In his short story "Espectro" Thomaz Lopes also makes use of the ghost motif as a commentary on the suffering caused during the war between Russia and Japan. Lopes, *Histórias,* 76–81.

11. The decomposition of the body is also the focus of a poem published in the *Jornal de Recife* (1903) by Uldarico Cavalcanti, a contemporary of Augusto dos Anjos. Note that the title of Cavalcanti's poem, as well as its opening lines, echo Brás Cubas's morbid dedication—"Ao Verme—que primeiro tripudiar sobre o meu cadáver" [To the worm who first feasts on my flesh]):

> Podes tudo roêr, verme putrido e immundo!
> Esta é a tua missão: devastar a matéria
> Tu primeiro virás, depois virá segundo
> E milhões virão mais tripudiar, no fundo
> Da cova onde atirar-me a peste ou a miséria!
>
> [You can gnaw it all, putrid and filthy worm!
> That is your mission: to devastate the material body
> You will be the first to come, then a second
> And then millions more to feast on me, in the depths of
> This grave where I am inflicted by plague and misery!]
>
> (Augusto dos Anjos, 25)

12. From Manuel Bandeira's *Carnaval* (Rio de Janeiro: Nova Fronteira; Fundação Casa de Rui Barbosa, 1986).

13. In Andrade, *Contos novos* [New Short Stories]. The stories in this collection were written between 1939 and 1944, then published posthumously as a volume in 1947.

14. In Machado, *A morte da porta-estandarte* [The Death of the Standard-Bearer]. This collection of short stories was published first as *Vila feliz* (1944), then revised as *Histórias reunidas* (1959), which in turn was published in 1965 under the title *A morte da porta-estandarte.* Two short stories from the collection, translated into English—"The First Corpse" and "The Death of the Standard-Bearer"—appear in K. David Jackson, *Oxford Anthology of the Brazilian Short Story.* Unless otherwise indicated, the translations in text are from the *Oxford Anthology* (to which the page numbers following the English refer).

15. The translation of the last two sentences in this passage is mine. The translation of "The First Corpse" in the *Oxford Anthology* curiously omits these sentences.

16. See, for example, Albuquerque, "Brazilian Theatre," 117.

17. Rodrigues believed that theater should be endowed with a sacred quality. He writes that, following his brother's murder, it struck him as obscene for an audience to laugh while attending a theatrical performance. It was at that moment that he discovered the essential relationship between theater and death. He imagines the theater to be a kind of church and, as such, a place for solemn observance:

> Liguei as duas coisas—teatro e martírio, teatro e desespêro. . . . Ao sair do vaudeville, eu levava, comigo, tudo um projeto dramático definitivo. Acabava de tocar o mistério profundíssimo do teatro. Eis a verdade súbita que eu descobrira:—a peça para rir, com essa destinação específica, é tão obscena e idiota como o seria uma missa cômica.
>
> [I connected the two—theater and martyrdom, theater and despair. . . . I left vaudeville with a fully defined dramatic vision. I had just realized the profound mystery of theater. And this is the sudden truth that I had discovered: a play created with the primary goal of achieving laughter is as obscene and idiotic as a comic Mass at church.] (*Memórias,* 144–45)

18. "A hora e vez de Augusto Matraga" is included in Rosa's collection of short stories entitled *Sagarana* (1946). For a discussion of Augusto Matraga as a variation on the "kenotic hero," who, akin to Christ, "empties himself" selflessly for the benefit of mankind, see Valente, "Kenotic Hero."

19. *O quarto fechado* was translated as *The Island of the Dead* (1986) by Carmen Chaves McClendon and Betty Jean Craige.

20. For a useful overview of worldwide carnival traditions, see Mauldin, *Carnaval!* A somewhat outdated, but still valuable summary of carnival traditions in Trinidad may be found in Hill, *Trinidad Carnival.* For an in-depth examination of the Death and the Maiden motif in northern Renaissance artists, see Guthke, *Gender of Death.*

21. See, for example, the narrator's description of the changes that ensue in people's lives following the event:

> None of those doused by Uncle Monday that afternoon could remember it afterward, and you could say they all recovered within the hour, none the worse for wear. But the seeds had been planted. And so they found themselves, in the next month or so, for perfectly good everyday reasons (they thought), switching churches or getting saved or writing letters to the editor denouncing Jim Crow or preaching atheism in the town square or taking grocery-store bagboys as lovers or beginning to drink heavily or taking the pledge or buying two-tone Buicks or joining the Klan or the Masons or the Anti-Defamation League or giving all their possessions to colored orphanages or declaring for the fifth congressional seat or burning their hats or crying for two days, all because it's always Monday somewhere. (Hopkinson, *Mojo,* 17–18)

22. See DaMatta, *Carnivals,* 208–9.

23. With regard to these particular authors, specific works containing a strong carnivalesque element or theme include, but are not limited to, João do Rio's crônicas "Zé-Pereira," "Cordões," and "Cinzas" (in Góes, *Brasil, mostra a sua máscara*); Augusto dos Anjos's collection *Eu e outras poesias;* Manuel Bandeira's *Carnaval;* Aníbal Machado's short story "A morte da porta-estandarte"; Lima Barreto's crônicas "Sobre o carnaval" and "O carnaval e a morte" (in Góes, *Brasil*); Roberto Drummond's novel *Sangue de Coca-Cola;* Rubem Fonseca's novel *Vastas emoções e pensamentos imperfeitos;* Moacyr Scliar's short story "Espírito carnavalesco"; Lygia Fagundes Telles's short story "Antes do baile verde"; Silviano Santiago's novel *Stella Manhattan;* João Ubaldo Ribeiro's novel *Viva o povo brasileiro* and crônica "Traumas carnavalescos" (in Góes, *Brasil*); and Sônia Coutinho's novel *Atire em Sofia.* Two anthologies provide further evidence of carnival's profound social and aesthetic resonance within Brazilian literature. The first, *Antologia de carnaval* (1945), organized by Wilson Louzada, includes the prose works of a number

of premodernist authors such as Artur Azevedo, Olavo Bilac, Vieira Fazenda, João Ribeiro, Manuel Antônio de Almeida, Lima Barreto and Luís Edmundo, as well as numerous modernist figures. The second is a recent anthology entitled *Brasil, mostra a sua máscara* (2007) organized by Fred Góes, which brings together short stories, crônicas, poetry, and lyrics with a focus on carnival. Author-songwriters such as Chico Buarque and Vinícius de Moraes appear alongside Machado de Assis and others.

24. DaMatta points to the many variants of the Pedro Malasartes mythical character in Brazilian folklore narratives (with Iberian origins), which Câmara Cascudo and others consider a paradigmatic example of the Brazilian rogue (DaMatta, *Carnivals,* ch. 5).

25. While recognizing the significance of Spanish American literature's development of nonrealistic, often highly ambiguous, narratives, Payne and Fitz suggest that the critical term of ambiguity found different expressions, respectively, in the "new novel" of Brazil and Spanish America: "in the former it relates to language-conscious questions of individual human identity and motivation, while in the latter it tends to relate to problems of 'correct' interpretation, cultural mores, and large-scale sociopolitical conflicts" (5). While this broad distinction might be questioned by some Latin American critics, the relative absence of prominent female voices during the Spanish American Boom of the 1960s, in contrast to the emergence of highly innovative Brazilian female writers as early as the 1940s—with Clarice Lispector's *Perto do coração selvagem* (1944), for example—seems to uphold Payne and Fitz's claim that "the Spanish American writer of the 1960s still shied away from dissolving the security of the male-dominated logocentric system in which binary opposition—especially the male-female opposition in gender representations and character relationships—played such a crucial role" (7).

26. At the same time, Rulfo's vision dialogues with an existentialist approach, one that reminds us of the possibility of being dead in life, or that life is just an illusion.

27. The titles of the aforementioned authors, compiled by Zamora, include "Asturias, *Hombres de maíz* [Men of Maize] (1949); Carpentier, *Los pasos perdidos* [The Lost Steps] (1953); Arguedas, *Los ríos profundos* [Deep Rivers] (1958); Castellanos, *Oficio de tinieblas* [Rite of Shadows] (1962); Cortázar, 'Axolotl' (1964); Fuentes, 'Chac Mool' [a psychological parable] (1974); Fuentes, *Una familia lejana* [Distant Relations] (1981); Valenzuela, 'El lugar

de su quietud' [The Place of Its Quietude] (1975); Galeano, *Memoria del fuego* [Memory of Fire, a trilogy] (1982–86); Vargas Llosa, *El hablador* [The Storyteller] (1987); Allende, 'Walimai,' in *Cuentos de Eva Luna* [The Stories of Eva Luna] (1990). In these works, ancestral apparitions may be given visible form or make themselves heard or felt in other ways: in the disembodied voices in *Pedro Páramo,* the larval salamander in 'Axolotl,' the ancient stone figure in 'Chac Mool.' Or they may be present in the narrative structure of the work itself, in Galeano's trilogy or Vargas Llosa's *The Storyteller*" (Zamora, 123).

28. While this question obviously requires further research, an exploration of African cosmological, narrative, and linguistic influences on the development of Brazilian literature (much in line with Henry Louis Gates's conceptualization of the Signifying Monkey and Eshu as major tropes in African American literature) would be extremely valuable, particularly from a comparative perspective.

29. Despite the novel's somber tones and the rather subdued murmurs of the dead, Danow attributes an inherent carnivalesque spirit to *Pedro Páramo*'s "wanton destruction of established boundaries" between the living and the dead, the past and the present, the self and the other, and even poetry and prose (25–28).

30. It is not clear, however, where Borges and his universalizing vision fits into this essentialist tendency of Spanish American literature, as proposed by Armstrong.

31. The involvement of many Spanish American writers, such as the Chilean Pablo Neruda and the Peruvian César Vallejo, in the Spanish Civil War also contributed greatly to a sense of socialist solidarity among this group of intellectuals (Armstrong, 25).

32. This is not to say that trauma is not a concern of, or expressed by, modern Brazilian fiction (a clearly inaccurate statement), but rather that the form with which that trauma is represented differs from the Spanish American tendency. It is telling, for example, that one of the most unsettling literary depictions of the traumatic *anos duros* of the military dictatorship, Ivan Ângelo's *A festa* [The Celebration] (1976), uses as its backdrop the gathering of wealthy individuals around a birthday celebration.

33. This notion of the ghost as a harbinger of the need to recreate ethnic identity is developed by Kathleen Brogan in *Cultural Haunting,* a study that will be explored at more length in chapter 5.

Chapter 3: The Carnivalesque Defunto in Memórias póstumas de Brás Cubas

1. Spivak's words are in response to her reading of Jacques Derrida's *Specters of Marx:* "I do not applaud Derrida because he has said hello to Marx but because, once again, there is a lesson in reading here. *Specters of Marx* lets me read *Far from Medina* as a ghost dance, a prayer to be haunted, a learning to live at the seam of the past and the present." Spivak, "Ghostwriting," 78.

2. *Revista brasileira* was a biweekly literary and critical periodical edited by Nicolau Midosi that existed from 1879 to 1881. It published the work of Sílvio Romero, José Veríssimo, and Machado de Assis, among other important writers. *Memórias póstumas* began to appear in installments on March 15, 1880.

3. This term is used, for example, by Ivan Teixeira in *Apresentação de Machado de Assis* (93).

4. Translations of passages from *Memórias póstumas de Brás Cubas* are taken from *The Posthumous Memoirs of Brás Cubas,* trans. Gregory Rabassa (New York: Oxford University Press, 1997).

5. For Roberto DaMatta the dead's symbolic force resides in its role as important intermediaries between this world and the spirit world:

> Os mortos, como estamos vendo, são uma peça crítica na dinâmica deste universo social. São entidades tipicamente relacionais e, como tal, comandam atenção e reverência. Por tudo isso, podemos entender por que no Brasil a morte mata, mas os mortos não morrem.
>
> [The dead, as we can see, play a critical role in the dynamic of this social universe. They are emblematic relational entities and, as such, demand attention and reverence. For these reasons, we can see why in Brazil death kills, but the dead don't die.] (*Casa,* 134)

6. This chronicle appeared as part of a series entitled *Bons dias!* published in *Gazeta de notícias* between April 5, 1888, and August 29, 1889. See John Gledson's annotated edition of this series in Machado de Assis, *Bons Dias! Crônicas (1888–1889).*

7. "A Segunda Vida" was published in the collection *Histórias sem data* (1884). See Machado, *Obra completa,* vol. 2, *Conto e teatro.* All bibliographical references to Machado's short stories, in their original Portuguese, are from *Conto e teatro.*

8. This statement is made by the narrator of Machado's fictional crônica "5 de Outubro de 1885" [October 5, 1885], in which he confesses his visit, in the form of a spirit, to the Brazilian Spiritist Federation (*Obra completa,* 3:473). As he takes note of the number of venerable figures in Europe that believe in Kardecism, he begins to doubt his own skepticism regarding the doctrine:

> O orador combateu as religiões do passado, que têm de ser substituídas todas pelo espiritismo, e mostrou que as concepções delas não podem ser mais admitidas, por não permiti-lo a instrução do homem; tal é, por exemplo, a existência do Diabo. Quando ouvi isto, acreditei deveras. Mandei o Diabo ao diabo e aceitei a doutrina nova, como a última definitiva.
>
> [The speaker attacked the religions of the past, that would now be replaced by Spiritism, and demonstrated that their precepts could no longer be accepted because they were an obstacle to man's wisdom; he used the idea that the Devil existed as an example. When I heard this, I became a true believer. I told the Devil to go to hell and accepted the new doctrine as definitive.] (473–74)

Upon returning home, however, the narrator (still in spiritual form) is shocked to find that his body has been, in the meantime, inhabited by none other than the Devil. Applying his new Spiritist doctrine, the narrator rejects such a possibility, to which the Devil merely calls the man's attention to the latest cure-all advertised in the newspapers—iodized turnips! In other words, all religions are a panacea to the evil that, in fact, resides within man himself.

9. Plácido's later disappearance under peculiar circumstances (he is suspected of having gone insane) reiterates Machado's claim that Spiritism gradually leads to dementia.

10. Hutcheon distinguishes between parody and satire in the following manner: "Both satire and parody imply critical distancing and therefore value judgements, but satire generally uses that distance to make a negative statement about that which is satirized—'to distort, to belittle, to wound' (Highet 1962, 69). In modern parody, however, we have found that no such negative judgement is necessarily suggested in the ironic contrasting of texts. Parodic art both deviates from an aesthetic norm and includes that norm within itself as background material. Any real attack would be self-destructive" (Hutcheon, 43–44).

11. When Virgília pays her ex-lover a visit a few days before his demise, Brás Cubas quips, "Anda visitando os defuntos?" (41). Curiously, Gregory

Rabassa translates this question as, "Are you making the rounds visiting dying men?" (*Posthumous,* 14). In an otherwise excellent translation this would seem to be an oversight, for *defunto* implies that death has already occurred. The oversight also speaks to the semantic ambiguity that can arise when moving linguistically between distinct realms of death culture. Virgília perpetuates Brás Cubas's masquerading as the dead when she returns two days later with her son. To Brás Cubas's initial silence she remarks: "Nhonhõ, não repares nesse grande manhoso que aí está; não quer falar para fazer crer que está à morte" (42) ["Nhonhô, don't pay any attention to that big trickster there. He doesn't want to talk so he can make you think he's at death's door"] (15).

12. The symbolic connection between Brás Cubas and Brazil is reinforced early on, in chapters 13 and 14, when the narrator associates the eve of his own manhood with Brazil's declaration of independence, in 1822. He says first in chapter 13: "Vamos de um salto a 1822, data da nossa independência política, e do meu primeiro cativeiro pessoal" (65) ["Let's take a leap to 1822, the date of our political independence and of my first personal captivity"] (32); in the following chapter, entitled "O primeiro beijo" [The First Kiss], a mustache-sprouting seventeen-year-old Brás is captivated by the beautiful Marcela, whom he sees for the first time during independence festivities. The link between Brás Cubas and the nation is clearly suggested in the following passage:

> Vi-a, pela primeira vez, no Rossio Grande, na noite das luminárias, logo que constou a declaração da independência, uma festa de primavera, um amanhecer da alma pública. Éramos dous rapazes, o povo e eu; vínhamos da infância, com todos os arrebatamentos da juventude. (66)
>
> [I saw her for the first time on the Rossio Grande, the night of fireworks celebrating the declaration of independence, a springtime festival, the dawn of the public soul. We were a couple of youths, the people and I. We were coming out of childhood with all the ecstasy of youth.] (34)

By the same token, one cannot help but notice the national allegorical connotations of Marcela's (and Brás Cubas's) premature decrepitude later in the novel.

13. Notwithstanding the problematic nature of these paternalistic links, it stands to reason that an earlier abolition of slavery, and the subsequent nullification of Brazil's dependence on a slavocratic economy, might have prepared slaves for the transition into a modern, industrialized labor force, a shift they were otherwise ill-equipped for in the late nineteenth century.

14. For a detailed analysis of masculinity in Machado's male characters and, specifically "the painful process of constructing a male sense of selfhood" in nineteenth-century Brazil, see Valente, "Machado's Wounded Males." According to Valente, "What has not been properly emphasized, however, is that Machado's depiction of the Brazilian patriarchal family also reveals a keen sensitivity to the harmful psychological consequences that such a traditional, conservative, and strictly regulated society imposes on males, particularly, though by no means exclusively, on white males from the dominant classes. Machado detects a subtle connection between male sensibility and the system that both engenders and is engendered by the destructive and self-destructive behavior in which males often engage" (12).

15. In the short story "Missa do galo" [Midnight Mass] in *Páginas recolhidas* (1899), the character D. Conceição asks the narrator during their conversation while waiting for the midnight Mass, "Não tem medo de almas do outro mundo?" [Are you not afraid of otherworldly souls?] The narrator's response is indicative of the underlying receptiveness to the spirit world in his society: "Quando ouvi os passos estranhei; mas a senhora apareceu logo" [When I heard footsteps I became alarmed; but the madam appeared shortly thereafter] (*Obra completa,* 2:607). A similar indication of such receptivity may be found in the short story "Entre santos" [Between the Saints] in *Várias histórias* (1896), in which an elderly chaplain tells of a bizarre incident he experienced when he was younger. Upon noticing both a mysterious light and voices emanating from the church he was overseeing, the chaplain's first reaction is that these voices belong to the souls of the deceased:

> Como naquele tempo os cadáveres seram sepultados nas igrejas, imaginei que a conversação podia ser de defuntos. Recuei espavorido. . . . A realidade ia dar-me coisa mais assombrosa que um diálogo de mortos.

> [Since in those days the cadavers were buried in the churches, I thought the conversation might be between the dead. I recoiled in fear. . . . What I saw was more haunting than any dialogue of the dead.] (*Obra completa,* 2:484)

In fact, the chaplain enters to discover four saints—S. José, S. Miguel, S. Francisco, and S. João—sitting on their altars conversing casually. This satirical short story captures fundamental elements of Brazilian society's "spirit idiom," that is, the belief in a constant dialogue between this world and the spirit world, made up of both the saints and the dead.

16. Translations of passages from *Dom Casmurro* are taken from *Dom Casmurro,* trans. John Gledson (New York: Oxford University Press, 1997).

17. For a detailed discussion of the numerous instances in which Bento expresses intimate feelings for Escobar, see Valente, "Machado's Wounded Males."

18. Translations of passages from *Esaú e Jacó* are taken from *Esau and Jacob,* trans. Elizabeth Lowe (New York: Oxford University Press, 2000).

19. Translations of passages from *Memorial de Aires* are taken from *Counselor Ayres' Memorial,* trans. Helen Caldwell (Berkeley: University of California Press, 1972).

Chapter 4: Jorge Amado

1. The editions cited in this study are Jorge Amado, *A morte e a morte de Quincas Berro Dágua* (Rio de Janeiro: Editora Record, 1998); *Dona Flor e seus dois maridos* (São Paulo: Martins, 1966). The translations referred to in this study are *The Two Deaths of Quincas Wateryell,* trans. Barbara Shelby (New York: Knopf, 1965) and *Dona Flor and Her Two Husbands,* trans. Harriet de Onís (New York: Knopf, 1969).

2. See esp. Metcalf and Huntington, *Celebrations of Death.* According to the authors, Hertz's essential proposition is: "Close attention to the combined symbolic and sociological contexts of the corpse yields profound insights regarding the meaning of death and life" (37).

3. For a symbolic reading of Quincas's transformation, see Affonso Romano de Sant'Anna, "De como e porque Jorge Amado em 'A Morte e a Morte de Quincas Berro D'água' é um autor carnavalizador, mesmo sem nunca ter-se preocupado com isto."

4. Robert Stam's defense of carnival's present-day relevance and "progressive" potential is largely a response to Umberto Eco's discussion of carnival in *Carnival!* by Eco, V. V. Ivanov, and Monica Rector, edited by Thomas Sebeok (New York: Norton, 1984). According to Stam, Eco reduces carnival to a "purely textual entity" by equating it with the "comic," and in so doing, reflects a perspective that is "ultimately elitist, Eurocentric, and undialectical" (Stam, 91).

5. Bastide's article is contained in a collection of essays dedicated to Jorge Amado's work entitled *Jorge Amado: Povo e Terra, 40 anos de literatura* (1972).

6. For the literary manifestation of the supernatural as therapeutic agent in recent Brazilian fiction, see Nelson H. Vieira, "*Bruxaria* [Witchcraft] and *Espiritismo* [Spiritism]: Popular Culture and Popular Religion in Contemporary Brazilian Fiction." Vieira affirms, for example, that this manifestation occurs in Dalton Trevisan's work: "With his latest foray into the cultural mindset and modes of characters who convey a sense of the diverse cultural behaviors as well as the widespread hardships and problems of Brazil's popular classes, the Brazilian short story writer *par excellence,* Dalton Trevisan, stages a world of people in need of drastic therapeutic measures. Ergo, the inevitable appeal of popular religions for the popular classes, a socio-spiritual phenomenon recreated and restaged by Trevisan and other contemporary Brazilian writers" (175).

Chapter 5: Voices of the Unburied Dead

1. The interviews with Érico Veríssimo contained in *A liberdade de escrever: Entrevistas sobre literatura e política* were conducted between 1963 and 1975. They provide the reader with Veríssimo's impressions concerning both the development of his own literary work and the dramatic sociopolitical and economic changes that occurred during the period of the military dictatorship in Brazil.

2. Though the structure of "Hora do sétimo anjo" was essentially complete, Verrísimo eventually shelved the project in order to write *Incidente em Antares.* Veríssimo later expresses his intent, in a 1975 interview, to complete the second and third volumes of his memoirs, *Solo de clarineta,* before returning to his unfinished novel. By this time, the novel's provisional title had changed to "O dia do sétimo anjo" (*Liberdade,* 157).

3. See, for example, Chaves, *Érico Veríssimo,* 115; Furlan, *Estética e crítica,* 122; Maria Fonseca, "Levante dos mortos."

4. The first volume of Veríssimo's memoirs was published during the author's lifetime, in 1973. Veríssimo was unable to complete the second and third volumes of *Solo de clarineta* before his death, in 1975, at which time those chapters that he had completed for the second volume were published posthumously. The third volume was intended to comprise a combination of self-

reflections and observations on both real and fictitious people Veríssimo had known through his lifetime.

5. Earlier works by Dourado include his first novel *Teia* [Web] (1947), *Sombra e exílio* [Shadow and Exile] (1950), *A barca dos homens* [The Ship of Men] (1961), and *Uma vida em segredo* [A Hidden Life] (1964). Following *Ópera dos mortos,* Dourado would publish *O risco do bordado* [Pattern for a Tapestry] (1970), *Os sinos da agonia* [Bells of Agony] (1974), *A serviço del rei* [At His Majesty's Service] (1984), *Um artista aprendiz* [An Artist Apprentice] (1989), and *Monte da Alegria* [Mount Happiness] (1990), among other works.

6. Translations of passages from *Ópera dos Mortos* are taken from *The Voices of the Dead,* trans. John M. Parker (New York: Taplinger, 1981).

7. Maria Lúcia Lepecki, interview by author in Providence, Rhode Island, April 20, 2001. All quotes by Lepecki in this paragraph are taken from this interview.

8. As Luiz F. Valente has pointed out to me, Dourado may be responding in this final scene of *Ópera dos mortos* to Guimarães Rosa's short story "Soroco, sua mãe, sua filha," particularly, the final image of the populace joining in song to bid a collective farewell to the woman who is leaving by train, evidently to an insane asylum. The title of Dourado's chapter, "Cantiga de Rosalina," with its reference to Rosalina's eerie song, lends weight to this idea.

Glossary

adivinha—fortune-teller; from the Portuguese word *adivinhar,* to predict, to foretell.

agregado—a landless tenant or add-on member to a household who, though not related biologically to the family, maintains a relationship of favors and services with its members.

anjinho—a deceased infant whose postmortem transformation into a "little angel" was routinely observed as a celebratory occasion in colonial and imperial Brazil. This custom continues today in poor communities of the northeast and other parts of Brazil.

auto—a single-act play of medieval origin, with content that ranged from religious to profane. The form emerged in Brazil with the sixteenth-century autos of the Jesuit priest José de Anchieta. Twentieth-century manifestations of the form were used by Brazilian playwright Ariano Suassuna and poet João Cabral de Melo Neto, who combined elements of the auto with folklore from the Brazilian northeast.

búzio—small conch shell used in divination practices of Candomblé and other Afro-Brazilian religious systems.

caboclo—mestizo; used in Brazil to designate an individual of mixed European and Brazilian Indian descent.

cafezinho—a small cup of coffee, generally sweetened and without milk, served in Brazil at almost all social occasions. It is a common beverage at wakes.

calavera—the Spanish word for skull; the calavera is a ubiquitous motif in Mexico's Day of the Dead celebrations, particularly in the form of candy skulls.

cangaceiro—an outlaw who roamed through the backlands of the Brazilian northeast with fellow criminals, particularly during the 1920s and 1930s.

Certain cangaceiros, such as Lampião, gained notoriety as either Robin Hood figures or cold-blooded bandits.

capela—chapel; the capela increasingly became the site of wakes in Brazilian society during the first half of the twentieth century, replacing the home as the traditionally preferred location for this mortuary gathering.

carpideira—paid mourner, keener.

cartomante—fortune-teller.

casa-grande—literally, the "large house" or manor of a plantation in colonial and imperial Brazil.

coronel—a local boss or landowner exercising political and economic power in rural areas.

cova rasa—an unmarked grave, generally used for the poorest segment of Brazilian society.

craque—someone endowed with superior talents, as in a star soccer player.

crônica—a very popular Brazilian literary genre, consisting of a short composition that often blurs the lines between newspaper column, essay, and fiction.

curandeiro—healer.

Danse Macabre—the Dance of Death; a late medieval allegory and artistic motif exhibiting dancing skeletons, intended to remind the living of their mortality and the vanities of earthly life.

defunto—deceased or dead person; unlike the English equivalent, the term can imply either the body (corpse) or the spirit (deceased or beloved), or both.

douen—in Caribbean folk tradition, the soul of a child that has died.

Egun—the spirits of the dead, either anonymous or ancestral, within the belief system of Candomblé in Brazil, as well as other religions of African origins in the Americas.

Espiritismo—Spiritism; doctrine of spiritual healing and guidance through mediumship, or communication with the dead, founded in the nineteenth century by the French educator Allan Kardec.

Exu—an important orixá within Yoruba-based syncretic religious traditions, such as Candomblé and Santería, who has many roles, including that of messenger between humans and the divine, god of crossroads and fertility, and trickster.

feiticeiro—conjurer, shaman, or other wielder of occult powers involving communication with the spirit world.

finado—dead person; used with some frequency, in Brazilian society, in place of the name of the deceased.

gaúcho—a native of the state of Rio Grande do Sul in southern Brazil.

irmandade—brotherhood; devotional association of Catholic laity. In Brazil brotherhoods were formed on the basis of diverse factors such as race, occupation, wealth, and status. One of the most important functions of brotherhoods was the fulfillment of mortuary rituals for their members.

jagunço—a gunman or assassin hired by rural landowners; also a backlands ruffian.

jazigo—a grave, vault, or burial monument.

jeito—literally the "way," by which, within Brazilian society, one manipulates, influences, or circumvents otherwise rigid rules or circumstances, often through a personalized approach or intervention. Also *jetinho.*

jumbie bird—or simply *jumbie*—in Caribbean lore, a spirit or entity that returns from the dead.

luto—state of mourning; also mourning dress, typically black.

mãe-de-santo—literally "mother of saints"; female priest in Candomblé, and other syncretic Afro-Brazilian religions, who acts as liaison to the orixás and keeper of sacred knowledge.

malandro—Brazilian society's street-wise and guileful rogue, who oscillates between the world of order (work, family) and disorder (vagrancy, popular culture, crime). The ethos of the malandro is called *malandragem.*

mas—abbreviation of "masquerade"; a group of revelers or musical band in Trinidad and Tobago's carnival tradition.

mineiro—a native of the state of Minas Gerais in southeastern Brazil.

moribundo—a dying person; to be on the verge of death.

ojojo—a dish from northeastern Brazil consisting of porridge with yam, corn, and snails.

orixá—(also spelled *orisha*), a supernatural being within the Yoruba-based pantheon of deities. Closely tied to the forces of nature, the orixás in Candomblé are also generally associated with specific Catholic saints.

peixada—Brazilian fish stew.

pernambucano—a native of the state of Pernambuco in northeastern Brazil.

Pomba-gira—a spiritual entity, more commonly invoked by practitioners of Umbanda, who personifies female sexuality, desire and promiscuity, and is often associated, in the female form, with the orixá Exu.

preto velho—a spiritual entity, invoked by Umbanda practitioners, characterized as an old black slave smoking a pipe and embodying the virtues of benevolence, wisdom, and humility.

psychography—the practice of "automatic writing," the channeling of spirit messages through involuntary writing.

retirante—a migrant from the drought-stricken regions of northeastern Brazil.

saudade—an expression or feeling of extreme longing or nostalgia for times past or estranged loved ones. The term is often considered innate to Portuguese and, to a lesser degree, Brazilian identity.

Sebastianismo—the messianic belief in the return of Portugal's King Sebastian, who was said to have disappeared in the sixteenth-century battle of Alcácer-Quibir, but who would someday return, bringing with him the promise of salvation to Portugal. This belief also took root in the Brazilian northeast, for example, during the Canudos rebellion.

senzala—the slave quarters on a plantation in colonial and imperial Brazil.

Sertão—the semi-arid "backlands" region in the interior of the Brazilian northeast that suffers from periodic, extreme draught conditions, forcing its inhabitants (*sertanejos*) to seek relief in coastal cities and other regions of the country.

sobrado—mansions in an urban setting, traditionally owned by rural plantation owners.

terreiro—the sacred space of worship, either within a simple building or outside, for practitioners of Candomblé and Umbanda.

velório—a wake, deathwatch.

vidente—a clairvoyant, prophet.

Bibliography

Albuquerque, Severino João. "The Brazilian Theatre up to 1900." In *The Cambridge History of Latin American Literature,* 3 vols., edited by Roberto González Echevarría, 3:105–25. Cambridge: Cambridge University Press, 1996.

Amado, Jorge. *Capitães da areia: Romance.* Rio de Janeiro: José Olympio, 1937.

———. *Conversations avec Alice Raillard* Paris: Gallimard, 1990.

———. *Dona Flor and Her Two Husbands: A Moral and Amorous Tale.* Translated by Harriet de Onís. New York: Knopf, 1969.

———. *Dona Flor e seus dois maridos: História moral e de amor: Romance.* São Paulo: Martins, 1966.

———. *Gabriela, cravo e canela: Crônica de uma cidade do interior: Romance.* São Paulo: Martins, 1958.

———. *Jubiabá: Romance.* Rio de Janeiro: José Olympio, 1935.

———. *A morte e a morte de Quincas Berro Dágua.* Rio de Janeiro: Editora Record, 1998.

———. *The Two Deaths of Quincas Wateryell.* Translated by Barbara Shelby. New York: Knopf, 1965.

———. *Os velhos marinheiros: Duas histórias do cais da Bahia.* São Paulo: Martins, 1967.

Amorim, Enrique. *La desembocadura.* Montevideo: Centro Editor de América Latina, 1968.

Andrade, Mário de. *Contos novos.* São Paulo: Martins, 1978.

———. *Macunaíma: O herói sem nenhum caráter.* São Paulo: Martins, 1981.

Andrade, Oswald de. *Serafim Ponte Grande.* São Paulo: Editora Globo, 1990.

Andrade, Rodrigo M. F. de. *Velórios: Contos.* Rio de Janeiro: José Olympio, 1974.

Ângelo, Ivan. *A festa.* São Paulo: Summus, 1978.

Anjos, Augusto dos. *Augusto dos Anjos: Poesia e prosa.* Edited by Zenir Campos Reis. São Paulo: Editora Ática, 1977.

Armstrong, Piers. *Third World Literary Fortunes: Brazilian Culture and Its International Reception.* Lewisburg, PA: Bucknell University Press, 1999.

Arreola, Juan José. "El Condenado." In *Confabulario.* 3rd ed. Mexico City: Joaquín Mortiz, 1973.

Asturias, Miguel Angel. *Mulata.* Translated by Gregory Rabassa. New York: Delacorte Press, 1967.

Azeredo, Carlos Magalhães de. *Alma primitiva.* Rio de Janeiro: Cunha e Irmãos Editores, 1895.

Azevedo, Aluísio. *O cortiço.* São Paulo: Martins, 1970.

———. *Demônios.* Rio de Janeiro: F. Briguiet, 1937.

———. *A mortalha de Alzira.* São Paulo: Martins, 1961.

———. *O mulato.* São Paulo: Martins, 1970.

Azevedo, Manuel António Álvares de. *Macário, Noite na taverna, e Poemas malditos.* Edited by Hildon Rocha. Rio de Janeiro: Francisco Alves, 1983.

Bakhtin, Mikhail. *Problems of Dostoevsky's Poetics.* Translated by Caryl Emerson. Minneapolis: University of Minnesota Press, 1984.

———. *Rabelais and His World.* Translated by Hélène Iswolsky. Bloomington: Indiana University Press, 1984.

———. *Speech Genres and Other Late Essays.* Translated by Vern W. McGee. Edited by Caryl Emerson and Michael Holquist. Austin: University of Texas Press, 1986.

Bandeira, Manuel. *Carnaval.* Rio de Janeiro: Nova Fronteira; Fundação Casa de Rui Barbosa, 1986.

Barreto, Lima. *Histórias e sonhos: Contos.* Rio de Janeiro: Schettino, 1920.

———. *Vida e morte de M. J. Gonzaga de Sá.* Rio de Janeiro: Livraria Garnier, 1990.

Bastide, Roger. *The African Religions of Brazil: Toward a Sociology of the Interpretation of Civilizations.* Translated by Helen Sebba. Baltimore: Johns Hopkins University Press, 1978.

———. "Sobre o romancista Jorge Amado." In *Jorge Amado: Povo e Terra.*

Bombal, María Luisa. *La amortajada: Novela.* 3rd ed. Santiago: Nascimento, 1962.

Borges, Jorge Luis. *Collected Fictions.* Translated by Andrew Hurley. New York: Penguin, 1998.

Brodber, Erna. *Louisiana: A Novel.* Jackson: University Press of Mississippi, 1997.

Brogan, Kathleen. *Cultural Haunting: Ghosts and Ethnicity in Recent American Literature.* Charlottesville: University Press of Virginia, 1998.

Buse, Peter, and Andrew Stott, eds. *Ghosts: Deconstruction, Psychoanalysis, History.* New York: St. Martin's, 1999.

Cabral de Melo Neto, João. *Morte e vida severina e outros poemas em voz alta.* Rio de Janeiro: José Olympio, 1989.

Calavia Sáez, Oscar. *Fantasmas falados: Mitos e mortos no campo religioso brasileiro.* Campinas: Editora da UNICAMP, 1996.

Caldwell, Helen. *Machado de Assis: The Brazilian Master and His novels.* Berkeley: University of California Press, 1970.

Campos, Humberto de. *O Monstro e outros contos.* Rio de Janeiro: Livraria Editora Marisa, 1932.

———. *O Monstro e outros contos.* Rio de Janeiro: José Olímpio, 1935.

Candido, Antonio. "Dialectic of Malandroism." In *On Literature and Society,* translated and edited by Howard S. Becker, 79–103. Princeton: Princeton University Press, 1995.

Cascudo, Luis da Câmara. "Anubis, ou o culto do morto." In *Anubis e outres eusaics: Mitologia e folclore.* Rio de Janeiro: Edições o Cruzeiro, 1951, 11–30.

———. *Dicionário do folclore brasileiro.* Belo Horizonte: Editora Itatiaia, 1988.

Castro, Ruy. *O anjo pornográfico: A vida de Nelson Rodrigues.* São Paulo: Companhia das Letras, 1992.

Catroga, Fernando. "Morte romántica e religiosidade cívica." In *História de Portugal,* edited by José Mattoso, 8 vols., 5:595–607. Lisbon: Editorial Estampa, 1993.

Cerqueira, Dorine. *A ironia e a ironia trágica em* A morte de Quincas Berro Dágua. Rio de Janeiro: Razão Cultural, 1997.

Chagas, Wilson. *Mundo velho sem porteira: Ensaio sobre a obra de Érico Veríssimo.* Porto Alegre: Editora Movimento, 1985.

Chamberlain, Bobby J. *Jorge Amado.* Boston: Twayne Publishers, 1990.

Chaves, Flávio Loureiro. *Érico Veríssimo: Realismo e sociedade.* Porto Alegre: Mercado Aberto, 1981.

Cisneros, Sandra. *Woman Hollering Creek and Other Stories.* New York: Random House, 1991.

Coelho Neto, Henrique Maximiano. *Contos da vida e da morte.* Porto: Livraria Chardron, 1927.

———. *Turbilhão.* Rio de Janeiro: Edições o Cruzeiro, 1964.

Coleman, James W. *Faithful Vision: Treatments of the Sacred, Spiritual, and Supernatural in Twentieth-Century African American Fiction.* Baton Rouge: Louisiana State University Press, 2006.

Coutinho, Sônia. *Atire em Sofia.* Rio de Janeiro: Rocco, 1989.

Cunha, Euclides da. *Os sertões: Campanha de Canudos.* Edited by Leopoldo M. Bernucci. São Paulo: Ateliê Editorial, 2001.

Cypress, Sandra Messinger. "The Dead Narrator in Modern Latin American Prose Fiction: A Study in Point of View." PhD diss., University of Illinois, 1968.

DaMatta, Roberto. *Carnivals, Rogues, and Heroes: An Interpretation of the Brazilian Dilemma.* Notre Dame: University of Notre Dame Press, 1991.

———. *A casa e a rua: Espaço, cidadania, mulher e morte no Brasil.* São Paulo: Editora Brasiliense, 1985.

———. *O que faz o brasil, Brasil?* Rio de Janeiro: Rocco, 2001.

Danow, David K. *The Spirit of Carnival: Magical Realism and the Grotesque.* Lexington: University Press of Kentucky, 1995.

Debret, Jean Baptiste. *Viagem pitoresca e histórica ao Brasil.* 3rd. ed. 3 vols. São Paulo: Martins, 1954.

Derrida, Jacques. *Specters of Marx: The State of the Debt, the Work of Mourning, and the New International.* Translated by Peggy Kamuf. New York: Routledge, 1994.

Dixon, Paul B. *Retired Dreams: Dom Casmurro, Myth and Modernity.* West Lafayette, IN: Purdue University Press, 1989.

Dourado, Autran. *Um artista aprendiz.* Rio de Janeiro: José Olympio, 1989.

———. *A barca dos homens.* Rio de Janeiro: Editora do Autor, 1961.

———. *Monte da Alegria.* Rio de Janeiro: F. Alves, 1990.

———. *Ópera dos mortos.* Rio de Janeiro: Editora Civilização Brasileira, 1967.

———. *Uma poética de romance: Matéria de carpintaria.* São Paulo: Difel/Difusão Editorial, 1976.

———. *O risco do bordado.* Rio de Janeiro: Editora Expressão e Cultura, 1970.

———. *A serviço del Rei.* Rio de Janeiro: Editora Record, 1984.

———. *Os sinos da agonia.* Rio de Janeiro: Expressão e Cultura, 1974.

———. *Sombra e exílio: Romance.* Belo Horizonte: Edições João Calazans, 1950.

——. *Teia: Novela.* Belo Horizonte: Edições Edifício, 1947.

——. *Uma vida em segredo.* Rio de Janeiro: Editora Civilização Brasileira, 1964.

——. *The Voices of the Dead: A Novel.* Translation of *Ópera dos mortos* by John M. Parker. New York: Taplinger, 1981.

Drummond, Roberto. *Sangue de Coca-Cola.* Rio de Janeiro: Editora Nova Fronteira, 1985.

Due, Tananarive. *Joplin's Ghost.* New York: Washington Square Press, 2006.

Erdrich, Louise. *Tracks: A Novel.* New York: Harper and Row, 1989.

Faoro, Raymundo. *Machado de Assis: A pirâmide e o trapézio.* Rio de Janeiro: Editora Globo, 1988.

Fausto, Boris. *A Concise History of Brazil.* Translated by Arthur Brakel. Cambridge: Cambridge University Press, 1999.

Feijó, Rui, Herminio Martins, and João de Pina-Cabral, eds. *Death in Portugal: Studies in Portuguese Anthropology and Modern History.* Oxford: JASO, 1983.

Ferreira-Pinto, Cristina. "The Fantastic, the Gothic, and the Grotesque in Contemporary Brazilian Women's Novels." *Chasqui: Revista de literatura latinoamericana* 25.2 (1996): 71–80.

Finucane, Ronald C. *Appearances of the Dead: A Cultural History of Ghosts.* Buffalo: Prometheus Books, 1984.

Fitz, Earl. "Structural Ambiguity in Jorge Amado's *A morte e a morte de Quincas Berro Dágua.*" *Hispania* 67.2 (May 1984): 221–28.

Fonseca, Maria Nazareth Soares. "O levante dos mortos: Um episódio fantástico." *Cadernos de lingüística e teoria da literatura* 6 (December 1981): 57–68.

Fonseca, Rubem. *Vastas emoções e pensamentos imperfeitos.* São Paulo: Companhia das Letras, 1988.

Freud, Sigmund. "The Uncanny." In *The Standard Edition of the Complete Psychological Works of Sigmund Freud,* 24 vols., 17:217–52. London: Hogarth Press, 1953–74.

Freyre, Gilberto. *Casa-grande e senzala: Formação da família sob o regime da economia patriarcal.* Rio de Janeiro: Editora Record, 1992.

——. *Em tôrno de alguns túmulos afro-cristãos.* Vitoria: Livraria Progresso, 1959.

———. *The Mansions and the Shanties: The Making of Modern Brazil.* Translated by Harriet de Onís. Berkeley: University of California Press, 1986.

———. *The Masters and the Slaves: A Study in the Development of Brazilian Civilization.* Translated by Samuel Putnam. Berkeley: University of California Press, 1986.

———. *Sobrados e mucambos: Decadência do patriarcado rural e desenvolvimento do urbano.* 5th ed. 2 vols. Rio de Janeiro: José Olympio, 1977.

Furlan, Oswaldo Antônio. *Estética e crítica social em* Incidente em Antares. Florianópolis: Universidade Federal de Santa Catarina, 1977.

García, Cristina. *Dreaming in Cuban.* New York: Knopf, 1992.

García Márquez, Gabriel. *Cien años de soledad.* Barcelona: Plaza and Janes, 1980.

———. *El otoño del patriarca.* Barcelona: Plaza and Janes, 1975.

Garro, Elena. *Los recuerdos del porvenir.* Mexico City: Joaquín Mortiz, 1963.

Gates, Henry Louis, Jr. *The Signifying Monkey: A Theory of Afro-American Literary Criticism.* New York: Oxford University Press, 1988.

Gledson, John. "Brazilian Prose from 1940 to 1980." In *The Cambridge History of Latin American Literature,* 3 vols., edited by Roberto González Echevarría, 3:189–206. Cambridge: Cambridge University Press, 1996.

Góes, Fred, ed. *Brasil, mostra a sua máscara.* Rio de Janeiro: Língua Geral, 2007.

Goldey, Patricia. "The Good Death: Personal Salvation and Community Identity." In Feijó, Martins, and Pina-Cabral, *Death in Portugal,* 1–16.

Goyen, William. *The Collected Stories of William Goyen.* New York: Doubleday, 1975.

Guthke, Karl S. *The Gender of Death: A Cultural History in Art and Literature.* Cambridge: Cambridge University Press, 1999.

Harris, Wilson. *The Carnival Trilogy.* London: Faber and Faber, 1993.

Hertz, Robert. *Death and the Right Hand.* Translated by Rodney and Claudia Needham. Glencoe, IL: Free Press, 1960.

Hess, David J. *Samba in the Night: Spiritism in Brazil.* New York: Columbia University Press, 1994.

———. *Spirits and Scientists: Ideology, Spiritism, and Brazilian Culture.* University Park: Pennsylvania State University Press, 1991.

Hess, David J., and Roberto A. DaMatta, eds. *The Brazilian Puzzle: Culture on the Borderlands of the Western World.* New York: Columbia University Press, 1995.

Hill, Errol. *The Trinidad Carnival: Mandate for a National Theatre.* Austin: University of Texas Press, 1972.

Holanda, Sérgio Buarque de. *Raízes do Brasil.* Rio de Janeiro: José Olympio, 1993.

Hollanda, Chico Buarque de. *Ópera do Malandro.* Lisbon: Edições O Jornal, 1987.

Homer. *The Odyssey of Homer.* Translated by Richard Lattimore. New York: Harper Perennial, 1991.

Hopkinson, Nalo. *Midnight Robber.* New York: Warner Books, 2000.

———, ed. *Mojo: Conjure Stories.* New York: Warner Books, 2003.

Hutcheon, Linda. *A Theory of Parody: The Teachings of Twentieth-Century Art Forms.* London: Methuen, 1985.

Jackson, K. David, ed. *Oxford Anthology of the Brazilian Short Story.* Oxford: Oxford University Press, 2006.

Jackson, Rosemary. *Fantasy: The Literature of Subversion.* London: Methuen, 1981.

Jorge Amado: Povo e Terra, 40 anos de literatura. São Paulo: Martins, 1972.

Kardec, Allan. *The Spirits' Book.* Rio de Janeiro: Federação Espírita Brasileira, 1996.

Kennedy, William. *Ironweed: A Novel.* New York: Penguin, 1984.

Kingston, Maxine Hong. *The Woman Warrior: Memoirs of a Girlhood among Ghosts.* New York: Random House, 1989.

Lepecki, Maria Lúcia. *Autran Dourado, uma leitura mítica.* São Paulo: Edições Quíron, 1976.

Lewis, Matthew. *The Monk.* Edited by Howard Anderson. Oxford: Oxford University Press, 1998.

Lima e Silva, Márcia Ivana de. *A gênese de* Incidente em Antares. Porto Alegre: EDIPUCRS, 2000.

Lomnitz, Claudio. *Death and the Idea of Mexico.* Brooklyn, NY: Zone Books, 2005.

Lopes, Thomaz. *Histórias da vida e da morte.* Rio de Janeiro: H. Garnier, 1907.

Louzada, Wilson, ed. *Antologia de Carnaval.* Rio de Janeiro: O Cruzeiro, 1945.

Lovelace, Earl. *The Dragon Can't Dance: A Novel.* New York: Persea Books, 1998.

Lucian of Samosata. *Selected Satires of Lucian.* Edited and translated by Lionel Casson. New York: Norton, 1968.

Luft, Lya. *The Island of the Dead.* Translated by Carmen Chaves McClendon and Betty Jean Craige. Athens: University of Georgia Press, 1986.

———. *As parceiras.* Rio de Janeiro: Editora Guanabara, 1986.

———. *O quarto fechado.* São Paulo: Editora Siciliano, 1991.

Macedo, Joaquim Manuel de. *O fantasma branco.* Vol. 1 of *Teatro completo.* Rio de Janeiro: Serviço Nacional de Teatro, 1979.

Machado, Aníbal M. *A morte da porta-estandarte e outras histórias.* Rio de Janeiro: José Olympio, 1971.

Machado, Ubiratan. *Os intelectuais e o espiritismo: De Castro Alves a Machado de Assis.* Rio de Janeiro: Edições Antares, 1983.

Machado de Assis, Joaquim Maria. *Bons dias! Crônicas, 1888–1889.* Edited by John Gledson. São Paulo: Editora Hucitec, 1990.

———. *Conto e teatro.* Vol. 2 of *Obra completa,* edited by Afrânio Coutinho. Rio de Janeiro: José Aguilar, 1962.

———. *Counselor Ayres' Memorial.* Translated by Helen Caldwell. Berkeley: University of California Press, 1972.

———. *Crônicas de Lélio.* Edited by Raymundo Magalhães Júnior. Rio de Janeiro: Civilização Brasileira, 1958.

———. *The Devil's Church and Other Stories.* Translated by Jack Schmitt and Lorie Ishimatsu. Austin: University of Texas Press, 1977.

———. *Diálogos e reflexões de um relojoeiro.* Rio de Janeiro: Edições de Ouro, 1966.

———. *Dom Casmurro.* São Paulo: Ática, 1989.

———. *Dom Casmurro: A Novel.* Translated by John Gledson. New York: Oxford University Press, 1997.

———. *Esau and Jacob.* Translated by Elizabeth Lowe. Oxford: Oxford University Press, 2000.

———. *Esaú e Jacó.* Belo Horizonte: Autêntica, 1998.

———. *Memorial de Aires.* Rio de Janeiro: Edições de Ouro, 1966.

———. *Memórias póstumas de Brás Cubas.* Belo Horizonte: Autêntica, 1999.

———. *Obra completa.* Org. Afrânio Coutinho. 3 vols. Rio de Janeiro: José Aguilar, 1962.

———. *The Posthumous Memoirs of Brás Cubas: A Novel.* Translated by Gregory Rabassa. New York: Oxford University Press, 1997.

———. *Ressurreição.* São Paulo: Ática, 1993.

Maia Neto, José Raimundo. *Machado de Assis, the Brazilian Pyrrhonian.* West Lafayette, IN: Purdue University Press, 1994.

Martins, José de Souza, ed. *A morte e os mortos na sociedade brasileira.* São Paulo: Editora Hucitec, 1983.

Maso, Carole. *Ghost Dance.* Hopewell, NJ: Ecco Press, 1995.

Mattoso, José, ed. *História de Portugal.* 8 vols. Lisbon: Editorial Estampa, 1993–94.

———. *O reino dos mortos na idade média peninsular.* Lisbon: Edições João Sá da Costa, 1995.

Mauldin, Barbara, ed. *Carnaval!* Seattle: University of Washington Press, 2004.

Menezes, Adolfo Bezerra de. *A Loucura sob novo prisma.* Rio de Janeiro: Federação Espírita Brasileira, 1939.

Metcalf, Peter, and Richard Huntington. *Celebrations of Death: The Anthropology of Mortuary Ritual.* Cambridge: Cambridge University Press, 1991.

Monteiro, Jerônimo, ed. *O conto fantástico.* Rio de Janeiro: Editora Civilização Brasileira, 1959.

Morrison, Toni. *Beloved: A Novel.* New York: Plume, 1987.

Naylor, Gloria. *Mama Day.* New York: Ticknor and Fields, 1988.

Payne, Judith A., and Earl E. Fitz. *Ambiguity and Gender in the New Novel of Brazil and Spanish America: A Comparative Assessment.* Iowa City: University of Iowa Press, 1993.

Paz, Octavio. *The Labyrinth of Solitude: Life and Thought in Mexico.* Translated by Lysander Kemp. London: Penguin, 1967.

Peregrino Júnior, João. *Doença e constituição de Machado de Assis.* Rio de Janeiro: José Olympio, 1976.

Pereira, Lúcia Miguel. *Machado de Assis: Estudo crítico e biográfico.* Belo Horizonte: Editora Itatiaia, 1988.

Pina-Cabral, João de, and Rui Feijó. "Conflicting Attitudes to Death in Modern Portugal: The Question of Cemeteries." In Feijó, Martins, and Pina-Cabral, *Death in Portugal,* 17–43.

Piñon, Nélida. *A república dos sonhos.* Rio de Janeiro: Livraria Francisco Alves, 1984.

Power, Susan. *The Grass Dancer.* New York: Putnam's, 1994.

Prieto, Jenaro. *Un muerto de mal criterio.* Santiago: Editorial del Pacífico, 1960.

Prince, Gerald. *A Dictionary of Narratology*. Lincoln: University of Nebraska Press, 1987.

Quinlan, Susan Canty. *The Female Voice in Contemporary Brazilian Narrative*. New York: Peter Lang, 1991.

Quiroga, Horacio. "El Espectro." In *Cuentos de amor, de locura, y de muerte: Anaconda, El desierto, Más allá*. Mexico City: Promexa, 1979.

———. "Más Allá." *Más Allá y otros cuentos*. Montevideo: Claudio García, 1945.

Radcliffe, Ann. *The Mysteries of Udolpho*. Edited by Bonamy Dobrée. Oxford: Oxford University Press, 1998.

Ramos, Graciliano. *Insônia*. São Paulo: Editora Record, 1977.

———. *São Bernardo*. Rio de Janeiro: Editora Record, 1988.

———. *Vidas secas*. Rio de Janeiro: Editora Record, 1989.

Ramos Meza, Ernesto. *La muerte de Pamilo*. Mexico City: Ediciones Tlacuilo, 1964.

Reed, Ishmael. *Mumbo Jumbo*. Garden City, NY: Doubleday, 1972.

Rego, Enylton José de Sá. *O calundu e a panacéia: Machado de Assis, a sátira menipéia e a tradição luciânica*. Rio de Janeiro: Forense Universitária, 1989.

———. "Warning: Deadly Humor at Work." Pref. to Machado de Assis, *Posthumous Memoirs*, xi–xix.

Rêgo, José Lins do. *Menino de engenho: Romance*. Rio de Janeiro: José Olympio, 1977.

Reis, João José. "O cotidiano da morte no Brasil oitocentista." In *História da Vida Privada no Brasil*, edited by Fernando A. Novais and Luiz Felipe de Alencastro. São Paulo: Companhia das Letras, 1997.

———. *Death Is a Festival: Funeral Rites and Rebellion in Nineteenth-Century Brazil*. Translated by H. Sabrina Gledhill. Chapel Hill: University of North Carolina Press, 2003.

———. *A morte é uma festa: Ritos fúnebres e revolta popular no Brasil do século XIX*. São Paulo: Companhia das Letras, 1991.

Ribeiro, João Ubaldo. *Viva o povo brasileiro: Romance*. Rio de Janeiro: Editora Nova Fronteira, 1984.

Rio, João do [João Paulo Coelho Barreto]. *Os dias passam . . .* Porto: Lelo, 1912.

———. *As religiões no Rio*. Rio de Janeiro: Organização Simões, 1951.

Roa Bastos, Augusto. *I, the Supreme*. Translated by Helen Lane. New York: Knopf, 1986.

Rodrigues, Nelson. *À sombra das chuteiras imortais: Crônicas de futebol.* São Paulo: Companhia das Letras, 1993.

———. *Memórias.* Rio de Janeiro: Edições Correio da Manhã, 1967.

———. *Teatro completo de Nelson Rodrigues.* 4 vols. Rio de Janeiro: Editora Nova Fronteira, 1981–89.

Romero, José Rúbén. *Anticipación a la muerte.* Mexico City: Antígua Librería Robredo, 1944.

Romero, Sílvio. *Machado de Assis.* Rio de Janeiro: José Olympio, 1936.

Rosa, João Guimarães. *Primeiras estórias.* Rio de Janeiro: José Olympio, 1969.

———. *Sagarana.* Rio de Janeiro: José Olympio, 1976.

Rulfo, Juan. *Pedro Páramo.* Translated by Margaret Sayers Peden. New York: Grove Press, 1994.

Sant'Anna, Affonso Romano de. "De como e porque Jorge Amado em 'A Morte e a Morte de Quincas Berro D'água' é um autor carnavalizador, mesmo sem nunca ter-se preocupado com isto." *Tempo brasileiro* 74 (July–September 1983): 45–65.

Santiago, Silviano. *The Space In-between: Essays on Latin American Culture.* Durham, NC: Duke University Press, 2001.

———. *Stella Manhattan.* Translated by George Yúdice. Durham, NC: Duke University Press, 1994.

Santos, Itazil Benício dos. *Jorge Amado: Retrato incompleto.* Rio de Janeiro: Editora Record, 1993.

Scheper-Hughes, Nancy. *Death without Weeping: The Violence of Everyday Life in Brazil.* Berkeley: University of California Press, 1992.

Schmidt, Afonso. *Curiango.* Rio de Janeiro: José Olympio, 1935.

Schwarz, Roberto. "As idéias fora do lugar." *Estudos CEBRAP* 3 (1973).

———. *A Master on the Periphery of Capitalism: Machado de Assis.* Translated by John Gledson. Durham, NC: Duke University Press, 2001.

———. *Um mestre na periferia do capitalismo: Machado de Assis.* São Paulo: Livraria Duas Cidades, 1990.

———. *Misplaced Ideas: Essays on Brazilian Culture.* Edited by John Gledson. London: Verso, 1992.

Scliar, Moacyr. "Espírito Carnavalesco." In *O imaginário cotidiano.* São Paulo: Global Editora, 2001.

Scott, Dennis. "An Echo in the Bone." In *Plays for Today*, edited by Errol Hill. Essex: Longman, 1985.

Shakespeare, William. *The Riverside Shakespeare*. Boston: Houghton Mifflin, 1974.

Shelley, Mary W. *Frankenstein, or The Modern Prometheus*. Cambridge: Cambridge University Press, 1998.

Silko, Leslie Marmon. *Almanac of the Dead: A Novel*. New York: Simon and Schuster, 1991.

———. *Ceremony*. New York: Penguin, 1986.

Skidmore, Thomas. *Brazil: Five Centuries of Change*. New York: Oxford University Press, 1999.

Southerland, Ellease. *Let the Lion Eat Straw*. New York: Scribner, 1979.

Souza, Márcio. *Galvez, Imperador do Acre*. Rio de Janeiro: Marco Zero, 1983.

Spivak, Gayatri. "Ghostwriting." *Diacritics* 25.2 (1995): 65–84.

Stam, Robert. *Subversive Pleasures: Bakhtin, Cultural Criticism, and Film*. Baltimore: John Hopkins University Press, 1989.

Sterne, Laurence. *The Life and Opinions of Tristram Shandy, Gentleman*. New York: Random House, 1950.

Stevens, David. *The Gothic Tradition*. Cambridge: Cambridge University Press, 2000.

Stevenson, Robert Louis. *The Strange Case of Dr. Jekyll and Mr. Hyde*. Lincoln: University of Nebraska Press, 1990.

Stoker, Bram. *Dracula*. New York: Oxford University Press, 1996.

Suassuna, Ariano. *Auto da compadecida*. Rio de Janeiro: AGIR, 1964.

Suro, Joaquín Rodríguez. *Érico Veríssimo: História e literatura*. Porto Alegre: D. C. Luzzatto Editores, 1985.

Tan, Amy. *The Hundred Secret Senses*. New York: Putnam's, 1995.

Teixeira, Ivan. *Apresentação de Machado de Assis*. São Paulo: Livraria Matins Fontes, 1987.

Telles, Lygia Fagundes. *Antes do Baile Verde*. Rio de Janeiro: Edições Bloch, 1970.

———. *Ciranda de pedra*. Rio de Janeiro: Editora Nova Fronteira, 1984.

———. *As horas nuas*. Rio de Janeiro: Editora Nova Fronteira, 1989.

Trevisan, Dalton. *Cemitério de elefantes: Contos*. Rio de Janeiro: Editora Civilização Brasileira, 1977.

———. *Novelas nada exemplares.* Rio de Janeiro: Editora Civilização Brasileira, 1970.

Valente, Luiz F. "Machado's Wounded Males." *Hispania* 84.1 (March 2001): 11–19.

———. "Parody and Carnivalization in the Novels of Márcio Souza." *Hispania* 70.4 (December 1987): 787–93.

———. "Variations on the Kenotic Hero: Tolstoy's Ivan Ilych and Guimarães Rosa's Augusto Matraga." *Symposium* 45.2 (Summer 1991): 126–38.

Vasconcelos, José. "El Fusilado." *Obras completas,* 2:609–15. Mexico City: Libreros Mexicanos Unidos, 1957–61.

Vasconcelos, Montgomery José de. *A poética carnavalizada de Augusto dos Anjos.* São Paulo: ANNABLUME, 1996.

Veríssimo, Érico. *Caminhos cruzados.* Porto Alegre: Editora Globo, 1934.

———. *Fantoches.* Porto Alegre: Editora Globo, 1972.

———. *Incidente em Antares.* Porto Alegre: Editora Globo, 1977.

———. *A liberdade de escrever: Entrevistas sobre literatura e política.* Porto Alegre: Editora da Universidade, 1997.

———. *Um lugar ao sol: Romance.* Porto Alegre: Editora Globo, 1936.

———. *México: História duma viagem.* Porto Alegre: Editora Globo, 1957.

———. *O prisioneiro: Romance.* Porto Alegre: Editora Globo, 1967.

———. *Saga: Romance.* Porto Alegre: Editora Globo, 1940.

———. *O senhor embaixador: Romance.* Porto Alegre: Editora Globo, 1964.

———. *Solo de clarineta: Memórias.* 2 vols. Porto Alegre: Editora Globo, 1975–76.

———. *A volta do gato preto.* Porto Alegre: Editora Globo, 1946.

Vessels, Gary M. "Érico Veríssimo, o fantástico, e a tradição menipéia." *Letras de hoje* 28.3 (September 1993): 145–51.

Vieira, Nelson H. "*Bruxaria* [Witchcraft] and *Espiritismo* [Spiritism]: Popular Culture and Popular Religion in Contemporary Brazilian Fiction." *Studies in Latin American Popular Culture* 15 (1996): 175–88.

Walpole, Horace. *The Castle of Otranto: A Gothic Story.* Edited by W. S. Lewis. Oxford: Oxford University Press, 1996.

Wilde, Oscar. *The Picture of Dorian Gray.* Oxford: Oxford University Press, 1999.

Wilson, August. *The Piano Lesson.* New York: Plume, 1990.

Zamora, Lois Parkinson. *The Usable Past: The Imagination of History in Recent Fiction of the Americas.* Cambridge: Cambridge University Press, 1997.

Ziegler, Jean. *Os vivos e a morte: Uma "sociologia da morte" no Ocidente e na diáspora africana no Brasil, e seus mecanismos culturais.* Translated by Aurea Weissenberg. Rio de Janeiro: Zahar Editores, 1977.

Index

The letter *n* following a page number refers to a note on that page.
The number of the note follows the *n*.